Class of '31

A German-Jewish Émigré's Journey across Defeated Germany

The Holocaust:
History and Literature, Ethics and Philosophy

Series Editor:
Michael Berenbaum (American Jewish University)

Class of '31

A German-Jewish Émigré's Journey across Defeated Germany

WALTER JESSEL

Edited with an introduction by
BRIAN E. CRIM

Boston
2017

Library of Congress Cataloging-in-Publication Data

Names: Jessel, Walter, 1913-2008, author. | Crim, Brian E., editor. | Neufeld, Michael J., 1951- writer of added material.

Title: Class of '31 : a German-Jewish âemigrâe's journey across defeated Germany / by Walter Jessel; edited with an introduction by Brian E. Crim; foreword by Michael J. Neufeld.

Other titles: Class of thirty-one

Description: Brighton, MA : Academic Studies Press, 2017. | Series: The Holocaust: history and literature, ethics and philosophy | Includes bibliographical references and index.

Identifiers: LCCN 2017043748 (print) | LCCN 2017044621 (ebook) | ISBN 9781618116512 (e-book) | ISBN 9781618116529 (hardback) | ISBN 9781618116505 (paperback)

Subjects: LCSH: Jessel, Walter, 1913-2008. | Germany—History— 1933-1945. | Germany—Social conditions—1933-1945. | Frankfurt am Main (Germany)—Biography. | National socialism—Moral and ethical aspects. | World War, 1939-1945--Germany. | Jews—Germany— Frankfurt am Main—History—1933-1945. | Jews—Persecutions— Germany—Frankfurt am Main. | BISAC: BIOGRAPHY & AUTOBIOGRAPHY / Military. | HISTORY / Holocaust.

Classification: LCC DD256.5 (ebook) | LCC DD256.5 .J47 2017 (print) | DDC 943.086—dc23

LC record available at https://lccn.loc.gov/2017043748

©Academic Studies Press, 2017
ISBN 978-1-61811-652-9 (hardback)
ISBN 978-1-61811-651-2 (electronic)
ISBN 978-1-61811-650-5 (paperback)

Book design by Kryon Publishing Services (P) Ltd.
www.kryonpublishing.com

Published by Academic Studies Press
28 Montfern Avenue
Brighton, MA 02135, USA
press@academicstudiespress.com
www.academicstudiespress.com

Table of Contents

Foreword

I first encountered Walter Jessel in the late 1980s, while following up investigative journalism into the Nazi records of Wernher von Braun and his team of rocket engineers. Jessel's June 1945 assessments of their characters and political attitudes, which are found in their Army security records in the US National Archives, were acerbic, penetrating and highly quotable. He noted the blinkered, Nazi-influenced views of many his interrogees, who offered themselves as "the true saviors of Western Civilization from Asia's hordes. Which does not prevent them from playing with the idea of selling out to Asia's hordes if such recognition is not soon extended."

Jessel, having been young and clear-eyed enough to leave Nazi Germany in 1933, went to Palestine and then the US. Like many German and Austrian Jewish male refugees in his age group, he became a US Army intelligence officer in World War II because he was a native speaker of German. After serving in front-line intelligence roles, he was at the US military occupation headquarters in ruined Frankfurt am Main, his hometown. There he sought out members of his small high-school class of 1931, leading to the memoir that follows. More detail on his life and the origins of his heretofore-unpublished book is given in Brian Crim's Introduction. All I can do is to endorse Jessel's work. His stories of the varying fates of his classmates—who ranged from Nazi enthusiasts to a Communist resistance figure who died as a concentration-camp prisoner—are consistently fascinating. These profiles demonstrate the same penetrating evaluation of character seen in Jessel's assessments of the rocket engineers.

Class of '31 is very much a document of its time, late 1945 into mid-1946. Jessel found most of his non-Jewish classmates were more-or-less-willing collaborators with the Nazis, but unable to see how they were responsible for Hitler's seizure of power or the crimes of the regime. It made him pessimistic about the future possibilities for a German democracy. Noteworthy is how he much expected a continuing cooperation with the Soviets in Germany—a liberal position. He certainly felt differently only a few years later, as he continued his intelligence career in the newly created Central Intelligence Agency (CIA).

More than anything else, the book paints a vivid picture of what western Germany was like during the first year of American occupation: ruined cities contrasted with a nearly intact countryside, while most of the population struggled for basic necessities, but refused to accept responsibility for anything that happened to them. West German democracy turned out better than Jessel expected, but his observations explain much about why that society took two decades or longer to come to grips with the Third Reich's crimes. I am sure you will find it engaging reading.

Michael J. Neufeld
National Air and Space Museum
Smithsonian Institution
Washington, DC

Introduction

In early 1945, intelligence and technical teams assigned to Anglo-American forces descended upon the disintegrating Third Reich determined to locate and secure Germany's "wonder weapons" before they wreaked more havoc. Hitler's infamous March 1945 Nero decree pledging a horrific scorched-earth strategy was no empty threat, especially after months of indiscriminate V-1 and V-2 attacks on London and the Netherlands during the war's endgame. Neutralizing the missile sites, equipment, and personnel responsible for unleashing a last barrage of nihilistic destruction was a priority for Allied armies racing towards Berlin. The most coveted prize were the rocket scientists and engineers responsible for building the V-2 ballistic missile, especially the wunderkind Wernher von Braun. As the Red Army approached the Peenemünde missile complex on the Baltic coast, the SS evacuated the most valuable personnel and material into the interior of the country. Fearing the SS would rather liquidate him and his elite team of scientists and technicians than allow them to fall into enemy hands, von Braun and his inner circle disappeared into the Bavarian countryside and patiently awaited contact with American troops. It was the beginning of a long and fruitful relationship. More than the freighters full of equipment and caches of documents recovered from caves and hastily abandoned warehouses, the "German brains" who designed and built the V-2 rocket along with dozens of other weapons in various stages of development proved invaluable to America's emerging military-industrial complex.

The rocket team's journey from captivity in Germany to their brilliant "second act" with the US Army and eventually NASA began with a series of debriefings with the Army Counter-Intelligence Corps (CIC) in a ski chalet near Garmisch-Partenkirchen in Upper Bavaria. One of the interrogators assigned to the rocket team was thirty-two-year-old Second Lieutenant Walter Jessel. Jessel had explicit instructions from Supreme Headquarters Allied

Expeditionary Force (SHAEF) to sort out, in Jessel's words, "Nazi hangers-on and enforcers from technical staff in order to bring the latter to the US."[1] Jessel and his fellow officers faced a difficult task distinguishing between esteemed scientists responsible for revolutionary military technology and those who were either expendable or so tainted by the regime's criminality as to preclude contractual employment of any kind. As candid as Jessel's military screening report reads, his diary entries from that week in June are even more frank: "The team consists of rocket enthusiasts, engineering college graduates, professors, all unrepentant Nazis aware of their bargaining power with the Americans." Jessel noted that German army personnel attached to the team understood "that their chances of going to the US are smaller than those of technicians. To improve these chances, they sing."[2]

Walter Jessel was no ordinary American intelligence officer. Born in Frankfurt, Germany in 1913, Jessel understood more about his interrogation subjects than their language. The product of a wealthy assimilated Jewish family, Jessel watched his native land sink into Nazi tyranny as friends and business associates either aligned themselves with the new regime or accepted it without question. Now donning an American uniform, Jessel spent the final days of the war vetting everyone from prominent Nazis to craven opportunists desperate to avoid the consequences of the previous twelve years. Jessel acquired an understanding of the culture of wartime science inside Nazi Germany, particularly the overriding ambition and amoral technocratic outlook of the rocket team living in the isolated enclave of Pennemünde. After several days of interviews and surveillance, Jessel arrived at this damning assessment of his subjects:

> They were enthusiastic technicians with the mission according to Goebbels of saving Germany. As a team, they were granted all the financial support, materials and personnel they required, within the means of the German war machine. Continuance of the work depended on continued conduct of the war. At a time when the generals were dissatisfied with the party rule to the extent of attempting to overthrow it, Peenemünde was out of touch and sympathy with such developments—not for love of the party necessarily but because their work and the war were one.[3]

---

1 Walter Jessel, *A Travelogue through a Twentieth-Century Life: A Memoir* (1996), 140.
2 Jessel, *A Travelogue*, 140.
3 Appendix A—HQ Third US Army Intelligence Center, Interrogation Center: Special Screening Report, June 12, 1945, RG 260, FIAT, Box 8, National Archives and Records Administration.

While most American observers fawned over the rocket team, easily seduced by the charismatic von Braun and excited by his promises, Jessel exercised the cautious skepticism one might expect from an intelligence professional. As an educated German forced to flee his own country at the hands of men like those he interrogated, Jessel's perspective deserved more attention than it ultimately received.

Jessel's evaluations of his interrogation subjects were so comprehensive and insightful that historian Michael Neufeld quoted them at length in his definitive study, *The Rocket and the Reich: Peenemünde and the Coming of the Ballistic Missile Era* (1996). During the course of researching my book on Project Paperclip, the intelligence operation responsible for bringing the rocket team to the US, I read Neufeld carefully and decided to retrieve every report Jessel wrote during his stint as an interrogator with the CIC. As a former intelligence analyst and consumer of intelligence products, both historic and contemporary, I consider Jessel's reports unusually honest and forthright assessments obscured by thousands of repetitive and mostly indistinguishable documents. Jessel's reports belied personality, experience, and even caustic humor. I was determined to learn more about the man behind the intelligence and soon discovered an obituary for Walter Jessel, dated April 2008. I acquired an e-mail address for his eldest son, Alfred, and requested any personal papers or memoirs which might aid my research. I was not disappointed. Not only did Jessel keep a diary from his time in the military, adding even more detail to his meticulous screening reports, he wrote a remarkable separate memoir recounting a four-month long investigation into the fate of his former classmates from Frankfurt. The more I read about Jessel's life before and after his one week interrogation of rocket scientists, the more convinced I became that *Class of '31* deserved the audience Jessel hoped for when he completed the manuscript in 1946.

Walter Jessel's Twentieth-Century Life

In June 1945, just days after interrogating the rocket team, Jessel drove two German counter-espionage officers to a farm and exhumed the order of battle for the Soviet Union's intelligence services. "It was promptly couriered to Washington," Jessel wrote, "where government analysts pronounced it the single most complete and understandable report on that—by then—high priority intelligence target." The operation resulted in his promotion to first lieutenant and his distinguished postwar intelligence career. When Jessel recounted the story to his son Alfred almost fifty years later, Alfred responded, "Pa, you've got to write your memoirs."[4] For the next year Jessel poured through his private archives, organized them, and produced *A Travelogue through a Twentieth-Century Life*. He dedicated the work to his grandchildren and donated a copy to Harvard University. Fortunately for me, Jessel's very personal memoir derives from detailed diary entries and a wealth of personal documents from every phase of his life on three continents. A journalist for many years, Jessel writes beautifully and is as thorough and reflective in the autobiography as he was in his intelligence reporting. Walter Jessel's extraordinary personal journey spanned Germany's two world wars and America's Cold War. He may have been more fortunate than most German Jews ensnared in the Third Reich, a fact he freely admits, but Jessel never lost sight of the regime's cruelty or the extent to which his fellow countrymen collaborated.

Walter Jessel was only five years old when World War I ended, plunging Germany into prolonged economic despair and humiliating national decline. The Jessel family avoided this misery thanks to the ingenuity of Jessel's "workaholic inventor-businessman" father.[5] Julius Jessel formed a profitable electronics and radio company at a time when every German household was in the market for the invention. Julius Jessel's sales catalog listed his "expert understanding, solid business principles and intensive work" as the reasons why he became a "leader in the radio wholesale business in Germany [and earned] an outstanding reputation."[6] Walter Jessel similarly credits his father's success to financing boarding schools for his sister, exotic vacations, and, most important, the family's escape from Nazi Germany. Julius Jessel employed thirty people in his company and amassed a net worth of approximately three million dollars. When the Nazis came to power and instituted the policy of "Aryanization," which amounted to the systematic dismantling and theft of Jewish wealth in Germany, the Jessel family lost approximately ninety percent of its wealth.

Both Julius Jessel and Walter's mother, Bertha Kaufherr, were raised in Orthodox Jewish environments, but they rejected their upbringing and embraced German liberalism and strove for total assimilation for themselves and their children. Three of Bertha's brothers served honorably in the Imperial German Army during World War I, each earning an Iron Cross. Walter recalled

4 Jessel, *A Travelogue*, 1.
5 Jessel, *A Travelogue*, 6.
6 Jessel, *A Travelogue*, 9–10.

bitterly that after his uncle Max fell ill and died in 1941, "the Nazis shipped his widow to the gas chambers."[7] One of the more insidious myths propagated by the Nazis throughout their years in the shadows of Weimar politics was the so-called "stab in the back" legend claiming that German Jews either shirked military service, profited from the war, or fomented communist revolution at home and abroad. In truth, approximately 100,000 Jews served in the military, 80,000 of whom saw front service; 35,000 were decorated; 23,000 promoted; 2,000 became officers; and 12,000 died in action.[8] The Kaufherrs were more typical than the Nazis cared to admit. Walter Jessel recalled several examples of friends and family continuing to embrace their "Deutschum" (Germanness) in the face of state-sponsored racial animus. In describing his parents' "German" worldview, Jessel specified certain core values: "Anti-imperialist, anti-nationalist, anti-revanchist, pro-Weimar, pro-League of Nations, religion-blind, pro-democratic social progress (mother more than father), and avid readers of the liberal *Frankfurter Zeitung*."[9] The Jessel family watched helplessly as the Nazis eradicated each of these values and institutions in a few short years.

When it came time to send Walter to school, his parents could have sent him to the Jewish school or the more humanistic gymnasium in Frankfurt, the Musterschule. They chose the latter. Of the twenty-two boys in the class of 1931, eight were Jews. "If there was an underlying anti-Semitism," Walter recalled, "the ... faculty kept it easily in check. Looking back at this environment, I was growing up to be a secure, sub-patriotic, social-democratic German and budding European."[10] Jessel cited his favorite teacher, Paul Olbrich, for instilling respect for Weimar institutions and helping organize one of Jessel's formative experiences in his life—a four-week boy scout camp with French school children designed "as an experiment in practical rapprochement."[11] Jessel fell in love with languages and continued to foster the cosmopolitan perspective he received at home. In 1929, two Eastern European Jewish immigrants joined his class and exposed, according to Jessel, the deep cultural divide between the "assimilated Frankfurt Jewish families" and the immigrants carrying all the visible markers of Jewish difference. "To them," Jessel wrote, "we were

---

7 Jessel, *A Travelogue*, 14.
8 Brian E. Crim, *Antisemitism in the German Military Community and the Jewish Response, 1914–1938* (Lanham, MD: Lexington Books, 2014), 13.
9 Jessel, *A Travelogue*, 21.
10 Jessel, *A Travelogue*, 23.
11 Jessel, *A Travelogue*, 24.

anti-Semites like the rest of Germans."[12] The newcomers' presence represented the world Jessel's parents rejected, but soon Jewishness of any kind would become a liability. Twenty students graduated from the Musterschule in 1931 with an Abitur, the rough equivalent of a high school degree combined with junior college. With the Third Reich just around the corner, Jessel noted that there were no class reunions: "Our interests, our personal relations, our ideals and soon our allegiances became centrifugal."[13] Aside from a chance meeting with a former teacher in New York City in 1939, Jessel did not see anyone associated with the Musterschule again until the fall of 1945.

As Germany's situation deteriorated, the Jessel family experienced increased anti-Semitism from unexpected quarters. "The culture of envy flourished among the unemployed," Jessel wrote.[14] Julius Jessel began illegally transferring money to Switzerland and later to France and Walter, at age seventeen, began a flirtation with Zionism. Walter joined the Kadimah, a boy scout troop, and consumed the works of Émile Zola and Theodor Herzl. He was never "unduly enthusiastic," he recalled. "I couldn't quite see embracing a new narrow nationalism to escape a regressive old one." One day when his scout troop encountered a Hitler Youth group in the Taunus mountains, the Nazi boys began singing their trademark song, "Wenns Judenblut vom Messer spritzt, dann gehts nochmal so gut" ("When Jewish blood squirts off the knife, all goes twice as well").[15] Jessel understood, more so than his father, that his future might lie outside Germany: "I sensed war coming—civil war at least ... and saw no sense in joining my father's business."[16] Historian Marion Kaplan determined that women and children were often the first to experience and internalize the suffocating hatred of Nazi laws and culture.[17] In Walter Jessel's case, thanks to his quick mind and liberal education at the Musterschule, he recognized that "the handwriting was on the wall" several years before Hitler's election. Jessel thought his mother "had a clear perception of likely events, but my father looked to his advisers and relatives than at that wall."[18] Eighteen years old and idealistic in 1931, Jessel enrolled in French courses at

---

12 Jessel, *A Travelogue*, 25.
13 Jessel, *A Travelogue*, 26.
14 Jessel, *A Travelogue*, 25.
15 Jessel, *A Travelogue*, 25. Jessel's translation.
16 Jessel, *A Travelogue*, 26.
17 Marion A. Kaplan, *Between Dignity and Despair: Jewish Life in Nazi Germany* (Oxford: Oxford University Press, 1999).
18 Jessel, *A Travelogue*, 9.

the Interpreters Institute in Mannheim Business College in hopes of working for the League of Nations. His father arranged for an apprenticeship at Ideal Blaupunkt Werke, another electronics firm in Berlin. Jessel capitalized on his fluency and represented the company in Paris for three months in 1931–32, but the events of 1933 shattered Jessel's privileged existence and scattered his family across the globe.

With the League of Nations out of reach, Jessel took a job with his father and watched in horror as Hitler assumed power in 1933. "I felt scared and apprehensive," he wrote, "not only as a Jew, but aware of the consequences for Europe—that the continent would be torn apart by war."[19] Assured by his "Aryan" business partners and employees that the Nazis were only targeting "recent Jewish immigrants from the east" rather than a successful businessman "with a long German history," Julius Jessel "was carried along by his conviction that the Germans needed him so badly that, as a vitally essential Jew, he could continue his normal life."[20] Nonetheless, Julius prepared for the worst and opened an account with $4,000 in Strasbourg, France, and Walter acquired an identity card for commercial travelers, allowing him greater freedom of movement than most Jews. Meanwhile, Walter watched former friends in the company turn against him, one even arriving to work wearing his "SS officer's black deathhead uniform."[21] As bitter and angry as Jessel was, he remembers his former friend warning him in all seriousness to "get out, leave Germany. He probably could have had me picked up by the Gestapo ... but he did not."[22] A few months later, Walter emigrated to Palestine, but his parents and sister remained in Germany, enduring many more difficult years in the Third Reich. Walter recounts his family's most frightening experience in the fall of 1936, when the regime rounded up Jewish men for forced labor and escalated the pace of imprisoning "enemies of the Reich" in the growing complex of concentration camps:

> Expecting the Gestapo, Mama went to bed with a butcher knife by her side determined "to take one of them with me." Next day, according to my sister, two Gestapo men appeared at the front door a noon, arrested my father and took him to the police station. Lisa [Walter's sister] and my mother remained "dumfounded and numb, well aware that we would never see Papa again."[23]

---

19 Jessel, *A Travelogue*, 28.
20 Jessel, *A Travelogue*, 10.
21 Jessel, *A Travelogue*, 28.
22 Jessel, *A Travelogue*, 28.
23 Jessel, *A Travelogue*, 11.

Fortunately, Julius came back a few hours later. Walter theorizes that one of his father's powerful friends interceded, but financial records indicate Julius' freedom was purchased at the cost of his remaining wealth.

When the time came for Walter Jessel to contemplate emigration, he and his father never seriously considered America even though several family members already resided in Chicago and San Francisco. Walter and Julius shared a legitimate fear that "with so many German Jews seeking refuge there Nazi-exported antisemitism might infect that society as well."[24] The Nazis made Palestine an appealing option by allowing emigrants to take a certain amount of money with them, a policy designed to undermine British rule in Palestine and inflame the Arab population. Walter put a plan into action. First, he purchased a Mercedes convertible. Second, he retrieved his father's money from France and Switzerland. Third, he signed on as contributing reporter covering the Middle East for the *Neue Züricher Zeitung*, and, finally, he drove to Trieste and caught a boat to Palestine. Walter was the first to admit how lucky he was in comparison to his fellow German Jews, but at age nineteen he held his family's fate in his hands. Walter's ability to get his family out of Germany depended on his gainful employment. Furthermore, the longer they stayed in Germany the fewer options were available to them, even with financial resources.

Jessel was one of thousands of "Zekes," German immigrants who lived alongside Jewish natives of Palestine, immigrants from Eastern Europe, and Zionists from all over the world. "Zekes were accepted as bona fide Jews," Jessel wrote, "but most were thought to lack the deep, single-minded conviction required by Zionism."[25] Jessel fell into this category, but he clearly enjoyed his four years living in Palestine, although his first attempt at finding work ended in failure. Partnering with another "Zeke" he knew from Frankfurt, Jessel tried selling electrical equipment in Jerusalem without any knowledge of the market or the fact that electrical outlets differed from one continent to the other. The business folded quickly, but Jessel received a tip from a British army officer and joined *The Palestine Post*'s international, multilingual staff. While working at the small publication, Jessel learned the advertising business, did some reporting, and generally made himself useful in Jerusalem and Tel Aviv. In June 1936, Jessel discarded his German passport and became a citizen of Palestine, which meant he was free to travel anywhere in the Middle East as a British subject. Shortly after this benchmark, the Arabs began a three-year revolt in Palestine

---

24 Jessel, *A Travelogue*, 29.
25 Jessel, *A Travelogue*, 35.

protesting the dramatic increase in Jewish immigration. The revolt drew Jessel further into Palestinian politics than he cared for. The Jewish paramilitary force known as the Haganah came calling, and Jessel balked after witnessing their violent tactics: "To me it promptly brought to mind what the Nazis were doing to their political enemies of all races and faiths. I simply wasn't enough of a Zionist to accept inhumane treatment of other human beings; it hit an exposed nerve."[26] The manner by which Jessel recounts this period in the memoir suggests he wanted succeeding generations in his family to know that he never strayed from the liberal and cosmopolitan values inherited from his family and progressive teachers at the Musterschule.

By 1938, Walter believed his family's future in Germany was coming to an end and decided America was the best option for all concerned. Jessel applied for and received an immigration visa to the US on the German quota. His parents booked him passage on the SS Europa leaving Bremerhaven on February 18, 1938, allowing him one last glimpse of Germany before his return as an American soldier seven years later. Protected by his British passport, Jessel traveled freely, observing the odd mixture of oppression and misplaced optimism taking hold of Germany, even among some Jews. Honoring a request from his father, Walter agreed to help a prominent Jewish businessman take a message to his son in America. As they drove together on the Autobahn, the man raved about Hitler's public works project. "Isn't this a wonderful road?" he exclaimed. "I can now drive to Berlin in seven hours. Hitler has done some remarkable things for Germany. Business is good. People have money to spend. If only they'd drop that anti-Jewish nonsense. I'm as good as a German as any of his followers."[27] Walter included this story in Class of '31, noting that the businessman died in Buchenwald in 1939 and the rest of the family fled to New York. Jessel believed the message he carried helped this rescue. Around this time, Jessel's family too faced danger, and time was running out for emigration. Jessel's family was still in Frankfurt during Kristallnacht (November 9–10, 1938) and one of his uncles, Theo, committed suicide rather than enter the concentration camps. In an incredibly risky act, Walter's parents hid an "Aryan" anti-Nazi writer named Gottfried Kapp in their home and escaped a visit by the Gestapo unscathed. Kapp was eventually caught and killed himself during interrogation on November 21, 1938. Urged by his wife and children, Julius

---

26 Jessel, A Travelogue, 39.
27 Jessel, A Travelogue, 46.

Jessel finally relented and left Germany for England in March 1939. Bit by bit, the Third Reich had fleeced Julius Jessel, leaving him the total of 400 Reichsmarks when he arrived in America in April 1940. Walter rarely saw his father after emigrating in 1933, but his mother wrote he spent his last years "in despondency."[28] He never recovered financially and struggled to adjust to life in America. After a series of heart ailments, Julius Jessel died in March 1949.

Walter did not have a job waiting for him in America, but, as luck would have it, he befriended some influential friends of Henry Luce, the owner of the TIME–LIFE media empire, on the voyage to New York. Walter regaled them with his life story and passed along glowing letters of reference from *The Palestine Post*. After just a few months of odd jobs in New York, including giving speeches promoting tourism to Palestine, *TIME* magazine hired Jessel to scour international news, translate, and occasionally summarize news from Europe. The junior position paid just enough to sponsor his family's immigration to America. Jessel eventually worked for Luce-owned publications in Connecticut, both as a photographer and reporter, capitalizing on his impressive foreign language abilities and experience with *The Palestine Post*. Jessel was mostly appreciative and positive about his first years in America, but he quickly determined the limits of acceptance from his conversations with recent immigrants and American Jews. Walter's old friend from Germany, Helmut Kurz, now an American citizen, admonished Walter over dinner. "Walter," he said, "you must know your place in society. You must not court a Christian girl. If you refugees don't respect our code, anti-Semitism in America will become as virulent as in Germany."[29] According to Jessel's memoir, he rarely experienced anti-Semitism in America, but was constantly aware of his status as a minority.

Jessel enjoyed working for the *Hartford Courant*, but with Europe at war and his adoptive country edging closer and closer to joining the fight, Jessel believed his background and skills had to count for something. A few months before America entered the war Jessel offered his services to an editor he knew to be a reserve officer in military intelligence:

> He sent me to see Thomas Dodd, (later Congressman and Senator Dodd, and Christopher Dodd's father), who ran the Hartford office of the FBI at the time. After a little conversation, Dodd asked me to mingle with the crowd at a downtown bar which was a hangout of the

---

28 Jessel, *A Travelogue*, 12.
29 Jessel, *A Travelogue*, 64.

German-American Bund, and report back to him. The Bund was Hitler's mouthpiece in the US and suspected of espionage. I flunked.

Undeterred by his initial foray into the world of intelligence gathering, Jessel was eager to enlist just days after Pearl Harbor. Unfortunately, Jessel was still classified as an "enemy alien" and had to wait another two years before the draft board declared him eligible. Jessel remembers being put off by the parade of National Guard troops marching through Hartford on December 8, 1941. "Sorry, but it reminded me of one my earliest childhood memories: the parade of the defeated German Army down the main street in Frankfurt," Jessel wrote. He was also worried that the men so eager to fight were "appallingly far from a match for Hitler's robots."[30]

Increasingly frustrated with watching and reporting about the war instead of fighting it, Jessel enhanced his already impressive fluency in languages by applying to the American Council of Learned Societies for a full fellowship in Egyptian Colloquial Arabic. He was accepted and spent two months at Columbia University, but never got the chance to use Arabic during the war. Jessel wrote the Connecticut Navy recruiting station that he was wasting time as a reporter, lamenting that "I can't quite resign myself to popping flashbulbs at women's clubs for the rest of this war."[31] The draft board conducted a loyalty investigation and finally inducted the thirty-year-old Walter Jessel into the US Army on May 20, 1943. Four months later, Jessel became an American citizen. The army sent Jessel to the University of Mississippi to instruct GIs in advanced German, specifically military jargon, and moved him around to different units where he sat idle for months. Jessel felt aimless and unappreciated by the expansive military bureaucracy. His diary entry from April 1, 1944, read simply, "End of a completely wasted year."[32]

Jessel's fortunes changed when he received orders to attend the Military Intelligence Training Center at Camp Ritchie near Hagerstown, Maryland. Jessel was one of 2,200 recent German Jewish refugees assigned to the facility because of their knowledge of European languages and German culture. The Army realized the "Ritchie Boys" were natural interrogators, counter-intelligence assets, and intuitive psychological warfare specialists and entrusted them with extremely sensitive and dangerous missions.[33] Jessel's commander at

---

30 Jessel, *A Travelogue*, 88.
31 Jessel, *A Travelogue*, 89.
32 Jessel, *A Travelogue*, 111.
33 See the award-winning documentary *The Ritchie Boys* (2004) directed by Christian Bauer for a profile of some prominent German Jewish refugees serving in the US Army.

Camp Ritchie, General Banfill, told him laughingly at a dinner in Germany after the war, "I always knew there was something we could do with them kikes."[34] Jessel took the comment in stride. Upon completing the course in September 1944, Jessel was given a temporary appointment as a second lieutenant for the duration of the war.

Jessel finally landed in France in November 1944, in time to participate in the final drive into his native Germany. Jessel specialized in interrogating captured German intelligence officers and participated in surveilling POWs. His diary from February 12, 1945, offers an intriguing window into the mindset of some "typical" German soldiers:

> "People in the Rhineland say the cities were being destroyed because of the persecution of Jews." ... Overheard at bugged office quarters: A Captain PW [POW]: "They are said to have exterminated 3 million Jews." Medical officer: "I heard 4 million." Captain: "I can't believe it."[35]

Jessel received his final wartime assignment on April 7, 1945, joining Patton's Third Army as an intelligence officer. Jessel witnessed his hometown of Frankfurt in ruins, but neither he nor his family felt any regret. "Now those who wanted Hitler can thank the Führer for everything," wrote Jessel's mother, "There would have been no need to destroy the cities if those beasts hadn't wanted to keep their heads a little longer."[36]

Jessel's job only intensified with the German collapse as he and other "Ritchie Boys" began screening and interrogating "the overflowing POW compounds" in Bavaria.[37] Jessel was so overwhelmed by the sheer number of detainees he ordered the rank-and-file POWs to type their own personal histories.[38] Embittered by his countrymen's expedience and historical amnesia, Jessel wrote his mother on Victory in Europe Day (V-E Day) that "the Nazis are gone, so much so that nobody knows anyone who ever was a Nazi. Only cowards are left, but that was to be expected."[39] Jessel's CIC unit landed some of the

---

34 Jessel, *A Travelogue*, 215.
35 Jessel, *A Travelogue*, 121. Jessel's entries echo the remarkable transcripts published in Sönke Neitzel and Harald Welzer's *Soldaten: On Fighting, Killing, and Dying, The Secret WWII Transcripts of German POWS* (New York: Alfred A. Knopf, 2012).
36 Jessel, *A Travelogue*, 130.
37 Jessel, *A Travelogue*, 135.
38 Jessel, *A Travelogue*, 135.
39 Jessel, *A Travelogue*, 134.

more infamous Nazis in the regime, including SS General Ernst Kaltenbrunner, chief of the Reich Security Main Office (RHSA); Julius Streicher, the savagely anti-Semitic publisher of *Der Stürmer*; Ernst Bohle, head of the Nazi party office responsible for using Germans citizens abroad to influence foreign policy and Undersecretary of State in the German Foreign Office; Professor Karl Haushofer, the academic inspiring Hitler's "Teutonic version of geopolitics"; and members of the Abwehr's (Germany's intelligence organization) document forgery unit.[40] It was during this marathon of interrogations, most of which contributed to the International Military Tribunal proceedings in Nuremberg, that Jessel spent a week in June 1945 with Wernher von Braun's rocket team. A few days later Jessel embarked on the mission to unearth the Soviet intelligence order of battle, which resulted in his promotion to First Lieutenant on June 16, 1945 and a golden ticket to join the intelligence outfit of his choosing.

Invited by a friend, Jessel transferred to the Economic Branch of the Field Intelligence Agency, Technical (FIAT) for the remainder of 1945. FIAT cataloged, evaluated, and disseminated German scientific and technical information to interested parties throughout the government and private industry. The position brought Jessel home to Frankfurt where he began the process of tracking down his classmates and wrote the bulk of *Class of '31*. Jessel enjoyed the down time and light workload, but his objective was joining the Strategic Services Unit (SSU), the surviving remnant of the Office of Strategic Services (OSS) and core of the future Central Intelligence Agency. Cashing in on his fame as the officer who discovered the Soviet intelligence cache, Jessel transferred to the SSU in February 1946 and remained with the CIA until 1963. Once more, Jessel's background and natural skepticism came in handy as legions of former Axis notables came out of the woodwork to ingratiate themselves with Americans hungry for intelligence on the expansive Soviet target. "Rivalries between intelligence services left us wide open to intelligence swindlers in a lucrative market," Jessel wrote, "a subject on which I specialized in CIA."[41]

Shortly after joining the SSU, Jessel met the love of his life, Cynthia Jacobsen, who worked in the highly secretive X-2 department (counter-intelligence). Their courtship extended throughout 1946 and 1947, although Walter joked he was never permitted to know what she did on a day to day basis. The two were married in Heidelberg in the summer of 1947 and remained in Germany and Austria until 1949. The couple returned to the US and Jessel

---

40 Jessel, *A Travelogue*, 136–40.
41 Jessel, *A Travelogue*, 216.

continued his career with the CIA, performing a variety of roles that included managing information systems. Jessel discovered a passion for information technology and even enrolled in Harvard Business School at the CIA's expense. Jessel partnered with IBM on a CIA project and eventually decided to "look over the wall" at the private sector, joining IBM full time in September 1963.[42] The Jessels moved to Wilton, Connecticut, and eventually Boulder, Colorado, where Walter retired in March 1979. A lifelong nature lover and activist, Walter spent the next thirty years working on numerous environmental causes. Walter Jessel died in April 2008 at age 95.[43] Cynthia Jessel died in December 2014 at age 91.[44] They were married for sixty-one years.

CLASS OF '31

Walter Jessel was the consummate professional, but the reality of living amid the rubble of his hometown and learning the fate of not just German Jews, but European Jewry altogether, weighed on him heavily. Jessel spent months in 1945 interrogating the people responsible and grew to loathe the weak-willed Germans almost as much as the genuine Nazis. He related his perspective in the introduction to *Class of '31*: "Frankfurt's ruins were the logical outward consequence of the mental and moral decay of its people—a decay, which, as a boy, I had witnessed in its early stages, and which had impelled me to leave."[45] Jessel's parents cautioned him against judging the family's former friends and neighbors too harshly, including those who distanced themselves from the Jessels for being Jews. Jessel's father wrote Walter that their neighbor Held was in fact "a decent person" and urged Jessel to remember Held was only human "so that *we* don't commit an injustice."[46] Soon after settling in Frankfurt for the FIAT posting, Jessel discovered that his aunt, his father's sister who refused to leave Germany, died in a death camp in Poland. Thinking his father could not handle the truth in his ailing state, Jessel told him she died in a Jewish old-age home, most likely Theresienstadt, and perpetuated the lie until he returned to America in 1949.

---

42 Jessel, *A Travelogue*, 77.
43 "Walter Jessel spent his life fighting for change," *Daily Camera*, April 15, 2008, accessed March 19, 2017, http://www.dailycamera.com/ci_13140551.
44 "Cynthia Jessel, 1923-2014," *Daily Camera*, December 15, 2014, accessed March 19, 2017, http://www.legacy.com/obituaries/dailycamera/obituary.aspx?pid=173460769.
45 Jessel, *Class of '31*, p. 3.
46 Jessel, *A Travelogue*, 155. Emphasis in the original.

FIAT disbanded in November 1945, approximately four months before Jessel joined the SSU. Jessel decided to use this interval to find his surviving classmates or their families and address the question haunting him since his emigration—"Would the people of other nations, if they were placed in the same position as the German during the Hitler regime, behave in the same manner?"[47] Jessel credits his interview subject Ilse Rossert, the wife of the only classmate to openly oppose the regime, with a related question crucial to the book: "What was it for 12 long years that kept the German people from sweeping the Nazi government from the face of the earth?"[48]

Jessel left his family the original manuscript for *Class of '31* and included a few chapters in his 1996 memoir, but he changed some of the names in the 1996 version, leading me to believe he was protecting the identities of his interview subjects in case *Class of '31* was published soon after the war. Jessel probably feared repercussions for his interviewees, either from OMGUS (Office of the Military Government, United States) authorities or embittered ex-Nazis, depending on the sentiments expressed. After decades of leaving *Class of '31* on the shelf, Jessel had a visceral response revisiting the memoir in the 1990s: "Re-reading this … after half a century moves me deeply and immerses me again in the horrors of 1944 and 1945 and the events leading up to these years—to the point of not sleeping too well. I suggest to the reader that it is not bedtime reading, but this is the way it was."[49] Jessel further explained to his family the reason for not including his Jewish classmates in the original manuscript, noting that "the eight who emigrated, myself included, knew the enemy; in Germany we would have faced slavery and death." Jessel wrote that "our fates cannot be compared with those of the classmates we left behind— who were equally young, educated and adaptable."[50] He implied that if the Jewish members of the class of 1931 could leave Germany and prosper, so too could the non-Jews, but they chose to remain. Interestingly, Jessel revealed that most of his Jewish classmates also became US soldiers.

Jessel essentially organized his diary entries into the narrative structure of *Class of '31*, introducing each classmate or their surviving family with the character sketch written by "Dr. Erding," the alias for Jessel's mentor at the Musterschule, Paul Olbrich. Readers will undoubtedly be shocked by how personal and often hyper-critical Olbrich's sketches appear, considering the modern American

---

47 Jessel, *Class of '31*, 164.
48 Jessel, *Class of '31*, 165.
49 Jessel, *A Travelogue*, 194.
50 Jessel, *A Travelogue*, 205.

educational system. Can you imagine your high school teacher offering opinions about physical disabilities, religious upbringing, and relationships with domineering parents as part of the official record? This organizing tool is quite effective for Jessel. After establishing the classmate's perceived personality, the reader determines whether the individual confounded expectations or behaved in unexpected ways during the Third Reich. The results are often surprising.

Jessel provided an accounting of his months writing *Class of '31* in his 1996 memoir, noting that he "had not expected to trace as many as eleven out of the twelve who had remained in Germany. I had found six alive, three dead, and two missing."[51] One can envision Walter Jessel the interrogator sitting down with each subject and leading his classmates through the fascinating details of their lives over the last twelve years through pointed questions and patient listening. Whether conversing with the German colonel sitting in Erding's (Olbrich's) office who lamented "the biological extinction of my people,"[52] or enduring the unrepentant nationalist drivel of his old friend Harro Wegener, Jessel let his subjects tell their story without interruption and curt moral judgement. The result is this stunning historical document originating from the immediate aftermath of defeated Germany. Jessel described the shortages facing ordinary Germans, their humiliation, bravado, and almost universal deflection of guilt or responsibility. He made it a point to press subjects about Auschwitz and their knowledge of concentration camps, but most responded reflexively with a variation of "Was konnten wir den tun?" (What could we do?). The classmate Jessel admired the most was Paul Rossert, whose real name was Arnulf Krauth, "the only member of my class of 1931 to rebel against the Nazis at the risk of his and his wife's lives."[53] Krauth died in Nazi custody on May 2, 1945, just days before the war ended. Jessel concluded his manuscript admitting that his class was "not a complete cross-section of Germans on whose motives of action or inaction a sound judgement may be based."[54] However, I think readers will agree Jessel provides invaluable insight into ordinary Germans living in the shadow of the Third Reich. "They were victims of two things," Jessel wrote, "the secondary effect of the Nazi terror, and their readiness to be cowed by it."[55]

Class of '31 was not meant to stay in a desk drawer. Jessel shared chapters with his parents in 1946 since they too knew many of the families involved.

---

51 Jessel, *A Travelogue*, 205.
52 Jessel, *Class of '31*, 8.
53 Jessel, *A Travelogue*, 194.
54 Jessel, *Class of '31*, ##.
55 Jessel, *Class of '31*, ##.

Jessel's mother wrote, "I like your simple, unadorned style" and thought the visit with Olbrich was extremely moving: "One really feels that if you hadn't shown up that day, they would have ended their lives." She agreed that Krauth's "fate is sickening and excellently described." Like any loving mother, Bertha Jessel was encouraging: "I think your book will be published. It well describes the conditions in Germany and the thinking among the Germans. . . . But don't be too disappointed if it isn't published."[56] Walter shopped the manuscript around New York in the spring of 1946 with the help of some friends in the newspaper business. He received mostly positive reviews and a few nibbles, but nothing concrete. Jessel's colleague from the *Hartford Courant* wrote him in May 1946 that the chief editor at Harpers rejected *Class of '31* because of a "paper shortage" and a "dwindling interest in Germany."[57] Others wanted Jessel to include a "love interest."[58] Jessel chose not to pursue publication again, content to leave *Class of '31* with his children along with *A Travelogue through a Twentieth-Century Life*. I am grateful to Michael Neufeld for bringing Walter Jessel to my attention, Jessel's family for granting me access to his writings, and Michael Berenbaum and David Michelson at Academic Studies Press for agreeing to publish this extraordinary memoir.

---

56 Jessel, *A Travelogue*, 206.
57 Jessel, *A Travelogue*, 207.
58 Jessel, *A Travelogue*, 209.

Class of '31

Germany, March 1946

Contents

Walter Jessel included this Table of Contents in his original 1946 manuscript. Chapters correspond to dates in the manuscript, although the page numbers differ. The chapter titles are quotes from Germans he encounters or interviews during his travels.

October 1, 1945

The 600-room I.G. Farben building in Frankfurt is probably the most imposing single unbombed structure in Germany today. It was completed in 1930. When it was under construction,—a day and night rush job,—my father who emphatically liked his nightly rest, threatened to sue the Farben company for disturbance of the peace. We lived two blocks away.

It would have taken a better than average star gazer to foresee then that fifteen years later the same building would become the headquarters of the US Forces in the European Theater, and that I, as an officer in the Army of the United States, would have a desk in one of its efficiency-inspiring managerial offices.

I had left my native city and Germany soon after graduating from school in 1931, and it had not been my desire to return. However, now that personal history had run full circle, I could not turn my back on the town as though I had never known it. I would be a stranger to most of its people, an enemy to some, a long-lost friend to others. To me, Frankfurt's ruins were the logical outward consequence of the mental and moral decay of its people,—a decay which, as a boy, I had witnessed in its early stages, and which had impelled me to leave.

I received a letter from a friend, a German author who now lives and works in the United States. He wrote:

"I have always drawn the line between the German people and its Government. Aren't we making the people pay for something in which they participated only under duress? Tell me what your impressions are. Tell me whether you don't after all agree with my rigid thesis: that all peoples, once they are placed in the same position as the Germans then were, would behave in the same way."

That was a challenge. It equaled the challenge of the opposite extreme: that all Germans are guilty, and that their country must now be emasculated economically to prevent it from ever committing aggression again.

My author friend had arrived at this thesis through his memories of the plain pre-Nazi German people, and his sympathy for them. His extreme opponents were under the impression of two German wars of aggression and their horrors. The controversy was one for history to decide. Meanwhile, would not the hopes, motives, and fates of a few Germans who had lived through the Nazi regime, suggest the stuff of which the answer will be made?

I first returned to Frankfurt in April, 1945, some three weeks after Patton had swept through. It was a lovely spring day. The fruit trees were in blossom along the highway from Mainz. As the jeep approached the city, its familiar silhouette appeared unchanged. Then we drove in.

Frankfurt was a heap of rubble, smelling of decomposition. The sidewalks downtown overflowed with bricks, broken stones, dirt, on which grass and weeds were beginning to sprout. There was just enough room for traffic to wind its way through.

In the midst of the heavy military traffic, taking the implements of war further east to the last act, the people of Frankfurt were walking about. A bent old woman carried a heavy bundle of belongings on her back. A well-dressed man picked up the cigarette butt a solider in the jeep before me had flung away. A woman in a fur coat stood on top of a heap of rubble, where her house had perhaps once been, pulling out what looked like a stove pipe. Another was carrying a bucket of water, filled at the fire plug, to her cellar, from which a stove pipe protruded at street level. Others walked along, eyes to the ground, or gazing at the ruin as though it would be too much for their energies ever to clean up. Only in a side street, people of all ages were removing a tank barrier of lumber and rock which had barred the way to no one.

I thought of H.G. Wells' movie "Of Things to Come." They had come. These people were de-civilized cave-dwellers. I took my jeep past the houses in which my family had once lived—all burnt and ruined. The opera house, dedicated in 10-foot letters across its front "to the Beautiful, the True, and the Good",—an empty stone shell. Instinctively I looked up at a corner of the Opernplatz, where a large clock in the tower of a business building had told me innumerable times that I was again late for school—no building, no tower, above the second floor. The Old City with its historic, timbered houses and winding lanes,—as flat as parts of the City of London. On the Römerberg, where medieval emperors were crowned, a large basin had been built as a reservoir for fire-fighting. Of the ancient Römer building, only the front wall was standing; it looked dangerously close to collapse. The Cathedral tower was still there, but the rest of the structure was burnt out. Goethe's birth place, at the fringe of the Old City,—a mass of rubble with a sign neatly stuck where once there was an entrance: "Historical Monument—Off Limits to All Military Personnel." The Paulskirche, where German liberals signed a democratic Constitution in 1848,—an empty shell, with the cross limply hanging over the edge of the spire.

The Nazis had blown all bridges across the river in their retreat. One span of an old footbridge, supported in its center by a pier, hung with one end in the water, pointing the other into the air at a crazy angle. A bridge downstream, quickly repaired by engineers, carried our military traffic. The people of Frankfurt stood in long lines along the banks to gain access to a barge which was slowly shuttling back and forth. They were back to the same means with which they crossed their river many centuries ago.

I drove through the rubbled streets, where four times a day for 13 years I had helped wear down the pavement on my way to school. The building was half caved in, lifeless. I wondered then what those past 14 years had done to my class-mates. They were ready to cast their first votes when the time for personal decision came a few years after we left school. What had they done with these 14 years?

My curiosity had little to do with sentimental school-day reminiscences. I have none. But their lives in the past 14 years would be revealing. To fight for the Nazis, to submit to them, to protest against their acts, to fight them from within, to leave the country, were some of the possible reactions to Nazidom Germans could have. Would not the fate of these boys symbolize the course of many? Should it not reflect the exhaustion of material and intellectual powers in war? Would it point a way, teach a lesson, for the future, ours as well as theirs?

In March 1931, our class of 20 graduated from the Friedrich Ebert Realgymnasium, the equivalent of a US high school minus girls, plus junior college and much foreign language work. We were 18 years old. Before the assembled student body, our diplomas were handed out by the "Chef", Oberstudiendirektor Werner Schulze, Weschu for short. He was a ball of fire of about 45, who took the school stairs two steps at a time, and breezed through the corridors at 30 mph. Teachers and students respected him for his determination in getting anything the school needed. He was never seen without a cigar.

Weschu gave us an earnest valedictory about our responsibilities, the struggles and pleasures of the wide world outside. The fate of the Fatherland, he said, its rights and prestige in a modern peaceful world, lay in the hands of our generation. Then we sang: "Deutschland, Deutschland über alles" without much enthusiasm, and scattered to the four winds. Four months later, Germany hit the bottom of its depression.

There never was a reunion, nor any attempt, as far as I know, by anyone of us to remain in contact with one another. Our interests, our personal relations, our ideals, and soon our allegiances, were centrifugal.

During September, 1945, I was relieved of my assignment in Bavaria, and was transferred to a not too arduous headquarters job in Frankfurt. By now I could hope that some of the men I wanted to find and talk to, would have returned from Prisoner of War Camps, or wherever else they might have been scattered in the last spasms of Hitler Germany. The first thing to do was to find Weschu, our former Headmaster.

October 6, 1945

Back in the twenties at the Friedrich-Ebert-Schule, we had an art teacher whose name I have now forgotten because he was known to us only as "Mussolini". He seemed to do his best to live up to his nickname. He was a bull-necked, bull-headed, bull-voiced man, with jutting lips a la Duce, and free and easy manners. If he didn't like a boy's composition, he'd pick it up and tear it to shreds. I had few conflicts with him, because my two-dimensional doodlings never aroused his interest, and because I cut his class whenever I could. "Mussolini" was a Socialist with a particular dislike for bankers, and he insisted that everybody know about it. "Blunt-head," he'd call one of us by his nom de plume "you're going to become a banker like your ole man? I tell you— you and your capitalist clique are going to be the ruin of Germany. Besides, you can't draw. What are you going to be,—a Fascist banker, or a capitalist banker?"

"Just a capitalist banker, sir," "Blunthead" replied.

One fine summer day in 1939, I ran across "Mussolini" in Central Park, New York. He was surrounded by a dozen poorly dressed youngsters, on the average 10 years old, all with pad and pencil. They were sprawled on the grass and on rocks, facing the 59th Street skyline which they were sketching. "Mussolini" was walking among them. When from a slight distance I saw him pick up one boy's sketch and tear it to pieces, I had no further doubt about his identity. I walked up behind his broad back as he was giving heavy-accented advice to his students: "Don't sketch vot you see, sketch vot it makes you sink about." I knew that line well.

He turned around and recognized me:

"Want to join the class? You could learn a lot. This is where true art is born."

Neglecting his art class, he then told me that he had left Germany the year before. "No chance to fight 'em. Had to get the hell out. They would have strung me up. Besides, American children have much more talent. Especially these here from the lower east side and the Bronx. Irish, Jews, Negroes,—wonderful."

He pulled some of his students' work, sketches and water colors, out of his brief case. I said that his instruction had failed 10 years ago, and I still knew nothing about art. But what news did he have about Weschu?

"He quit in 1937. Good man. Capitalist, but reasonable. Catholic, but broad-minded. Couldn't stand the Nazi rot anymore and got himself pensioned at half pay. Went to work for a publisher. Just proof-reading and that kind of thing. Won't write a line. What are you doing in Central Park? Just going home? Where do you live? I'll call you up. Got to get back to work."

That was the only news I had of Weschu since 1931.

By October, 1945, Frankfurt's municipal services had recovered to some extent. There was, for instance, telephone service for essential users. The obvious thing to do to find Weschu, was to call up the Frankfurt School Department.

I dialed the town hall, and asked for the department.

"Schulze, school department."

"Are you Oberstudiendirektor Werner Schulze, formerly headmaster of the Ebert Schule?"

"I am."

I gave my name and the class with which I graduated.

"I must see you," Weschu said. "Come right over here. You're an American, aren't you? Are you in the American army? Do you have anything to do with education in Military Government? My office is down here near the railway station", and he gave me the address.

I tried to answer as much I could without getting out of breath—no, I had nothing to do with education, not even with Military Government.

"What are you in the school department?" I asked.

"The boss," he said.

I told him I'd be right over.

A hand-scripted sign near the entrance pointed to the entrance pointed to the "Frankfurter Schulamt." The building was quite modern, of red brick, with large windows and a flat roof. Only half of it was still standing—the other consisted of rubble, and the ripped interiors of former offices. On the second floor a bashed-in desk hung with one end over a twisted steel girder, and the toilet on the third looked as though it was in working order.

Weschu had his office on the second floor. He sat behind his desk in his overcoat, talking over the telephone. A visitor was facing him. The desk lamp was burning—the large glass-less window was boarded up. Some light came through a gaping hole in the ceiling. Large chunks of plaster were missing from the walls.

Weschu had hardly changed. His hair was a little grayer, and his clothes seemed too large. He winked at me with a familiar young twinkle, as he finished his telephone conversation. He had been called out of the room. After a brief, mumbled introduction to his visitor, he raced across the room and out, his overcoat flying.

I had not understood the man's name, but I needed no special introduction to his profession. He wore the high soldier's boots of the German Army, and a disheveled suit of civilian clothes. His hair was close-cropped as in the cartoons of German officers, and his face bore some Slavic traits. As I entered, I had the feeling that he was shrinking and stiffening at the same time, if that's physically possible. He sat in an easy chair which permitted him no military bearing.

I asked him whether his home was in Frankfurt.

"No," he said, "I'm an East Prussian. Just got out from the Russian zone."

I asked him why he had left it. He gave me a bitter laugh in reply:

"Why I left it? I'll tell you why I left it. Until two months ago I was a colonel in the army. Then, after 38 years of service, I was discharged from one of your prisoner of war camps, and made my way home—illegally, of course. I have no more home. First the Russians took it, then they gave it to the Poles. I finally found my people in Zwickau in Saxony. They are living in indescribable misery. I got out and came here to see whether an honest man can still make a living in Germany."

Then he let himself go about rape, starvation, confiscation of property,— conditions he claimed he had witnessed in the Russian zone of occupation. It was a personal story—what would his mother-in-law of 70 now live on? Her state pension was blocked. How about his wife whom the Russians had pressed into a labor gang to clear up the rubble in Zwickau? How about the property- and shelterless family of his commanding general who was taken prisoner by the Russians? Then he began to deplore the fate of his defeated country:

"The Poles and Czechs have driven 10 million Germans out of Eastern Germany. They are now crammed into Russian occupied Germany. This winter they'll starve,—the children at least. This is the biological extinction of my people. It is a terrible injustice."

He had left himself go, and my refusal to accept the "biological extinction" and "injustice" part of his speech struck him hard. I said that the facts of the case were plain a Europe which had lost its economic substance through Germany's war, a Germany which no longer could live on the fat of other lands, and a victorious world which insisted on rehabilitating the victims before the aggressors.

The German ex-colonel said nothing in contradiction. He was sitting in his chair, stiff, red-faced, staring at me in a not too friendly manner. I realized that he was regretting having entered into the discussion at all, and having lost some of his self-control. Evidently, the past turbulent months of wandering through Russian and Polish-held territory, and the fate of his family, had left their mark on his composure. His position now was not rosy. I wondered what he wanted from Schulze.

He tried what he probably considered a more reasonable approach:

"I spent several years in France after our victory in the west," he said quite calmly. "We didn't let the French starve. As a matter of fact, they had hardly exploited the potentialities of their soil. We introduced modern methods and took a lot of French soil under the plough."

"And a lot of Frenchmen".

"I don't understand what you mean. The French had imported almost all their food from North Africa. Without us they would have starved."

I still could not agree with him. Obviously, the French would have gladly continued to import "almost all" their food from North Africa, had the Germans left them alone in the first place.

It struck me from this, as from many other talks with German professional soldiers, that the idea of the criminality of aggressive war was entirely foreign to their minds. The German professionals of war consider themselves upright men of unimpeachable character who obey the rules of land warfare to the T, and kill only those who are in the way of their military mission. They draw a sharp line between themselves and the bad Nazis who kill and rob because they are criminals. They regard themselves free from all responsibility. They only did their duty in first building up the Wehrmacht, then fighting the war when it was declared by their political superiors, then sticking out to the very bitter end. There always were wars, there always will be, and there is no reason why the technicians of war, the officers, should be in any way blamed. They had always condemned the political regime. But when the fatherland called upon them to do their patriotic duty, to fight and to die, they could not haggle about politics.

Weschu returned to the room and was a worried witness to the last part of the discussion. The visitor realized that his point of view was not sympathetically received, jumped from his chair, bowed militarily from the waist, and said he would wait outside.

The German ex-colonel closed the door behind him, and Weschu half-sat on his desk before me.

"Don't take this too seriously," he said "He is one of the many applicants for teaching jobs whom I have to send away every day. He thinks it's about all he can do now. With his education, he could probably teach math and physics all right. Of course, it's out of the question, even though he never was a party member. Did he lose his temper?"

"I wouldn't say that. But considering the customary self-control of the professional German officer, he became quite lively."

"It's understandable," Weschu said. "Some tragic things happened to him. His wife and three children were caught between the American and German lines last April. His children were killed, and his wife slightly injured. It was the crowning tragedy in the collapse of his whole world, and he is now desperate. Nothing he may do in the future would surprise me."

"What makes him think he could teach under American occupation rule?"

"It's not so difficult to see. I said he is an educated man. He believes that German youth after 12 years of education to crime and prejudice must be reeducated to be worthy of the good name of Germany, to have character and backbone in adversity, and to reestablish German prestige. That was the basis of his appeal to me as a German to let him teach. When I turn him down, as I shall have to, he will consider me a traitor."

The colonel's story had delayed the exchange of some personal news. I complimented Weschu on his young and energetic looks—unchanged in 14 years.

"I still take two steps at a time," he said laughingly.

Then he settled himself behind his desk again. He was smoking a vile brand of stogy, and when I produced some havanas of PX origin, he beamed:

"Trouble is I'll finish these by tomorrow. Can you get more?—A little cool in here isn't it? I have to keep my overcoat on even now. I don't think we'll get anything repaired or heated this winter. This super-air-conditioning through the ceiling is a little too much. I'll have some trouble working in here when it gets really cold."

"Well," he continued, "so you're back in Frankfurt. You're not the only former student of mine who has come back in American uniform. What did I say when you graduated? Usually something to the effect that the young generation would leave its mark on the fatherland. I'll confess that I didn't quite mean it that way. But you were right, absolutely right."

He paused, and leaned forward:

"I had a British infantry rifle at my home all those years. With 250 rounds of ammunition. But I ask you, could I have made a revolution all by myself?"

I granted him that some resistance would have been helpful.

"Where did you keep your rifle?" I asked.

"In my attic at home in Kronberg. I had it pretty well hidden. But, fortunately, they never searched my home. You did not know I had moved out there, did you?"

"No, I hadn't."

"I moved in 1939," he said. "A few months before the war started. I knew it would be an air war, and it was perfectly clear that ultimately Frankfurt would become a target. So I got out of there."

Kronberg, Weschu's new home, is a small resort town in the rolling, wooded Taunus Mountains north of Frankfurt. He had picked himself a nice spot in which to sit out a war. In this way, he said, he saved all of his belongings, his library, and his standard of living.

"What did you do all those years, after you had yourself pensioned?"

"To tell you briefly,—I worked for a publisher here in Frankfurt who printed a few rather good books besides his quota of Nazi literature. I edited and proofread the good ones. That left me a lot of time, so I wrote some stories. As the Nazis would have disliked them, they had to remain hidden in the attic with my rifle until the end of the 1000-year Reich. Now I'll see about publication. What else? Yes—I did some skiing on the hills and trails behind my house. Also I grew apples."

To emphasize this last-named achievement, he pulled out a small bag of apples from his desk, and pointed out which one to take. It was the most delicious apple I had ever eaten, and I told him so with enthusiasm.

"You see," he said, "there are useful occupations even during a war."

I inquired after his family.

"My wife is all right, thank you," he said. "She is a little more nervous, perhaps, than 15 years ago. My son is still a prisoner of war in one your camps. But we've heard from him and we are not worried. Unfortunately, he knows English. The camp authorities are using him as an interpreter and won't release him."

Then with a gesture toward the boarded window, he asked:

"And how do you like your native city?"

"Slightly dented," I said.

"You know," Weschu replied, "The bombardment of Frankfurt on March 22, 1944, was the most magnificent spectacle I have ever seen. We watched it from our porch. The searchlights roaming the skies, the roar of the planes, the thuds of the bombs, then the fires—it would have baffled Dante's powers of description. We were terribly conscious of the agony and death below,— you'll realize that,—but whenever a searchlight caught one of your planes, we prayed for your boys up there. Only, if you forgive me for saying so, I wish you had hit more industries and fewer residential quarters. The Old City especially—it's a sad loss."

His wish, I said, was probably shared by our air strategists who aimed at the destruction of war potential to bring about victory as soon as possible. But Weschu needed no lecture on how this type of warfare started or on its shortcomings:

"Sometimes when a night passed quietly," he said, "and no planes came over, I sat up listening and wondered what delayed them. I'm not saying this to you now to make a good impression,—believe me I'm not. My wife will tell you it's true. We knew that only military defeat would rid us of this tyranny. We also knew that the sooner it came, the less the total destruction of our country. At the same time, I'll tell you frankly that I have just about as much contempt for your allied statesman who concluded naval treaties, commercial agreements, and non-aggression pacts with Hitler, as for the late Adolf himself."

He sat back, and puffed on his cigar.

"Anyhow," he continued in a low voice, "now we're faced with the ruins and we have to rebuild them. My job is the schools. Those that aren't a heap of rubble were either requisitioned by your troops, or taken over by the city administration for office space. Then, at short notice, we received orders directly from General Eisenhower, through the Military Government, to reopen the schools by October 1st. We opened on October 1st, and I see by the papers that all children under 14 are now going to school. Well,—not quite. We have 16,000 who should go, and so far we accommodated 9,000. Military Government promised that the troops would evacuate 10 school buildings. Actually, only one was turned over to us in time. The City promised us eight more buildings. They gave us four. So we hold school in shifts. Two in the morning, two in the afternoon. That'll keep the children in school for two or three hours every day, enough time, at least, for the teacher to assign home work."

But these were not all of Weschu's difficulties. Military Government had so far not been able to allocate building materials to him to put the schools in shape. They had asked for his requirements—how many thousands of bricks, tons of cement, square meters of roofing paper and glass,—he would need.

"They love statistics," he said. "Every day I have to submit another one. On these requirements: I had to turn in the information practically overnight. Would have taken the building department weeks to calculate. I made the best guess I could,—I hope they never try to check it. I'm afraid I won't get my building materials as quickly as they had their statistics."

Weschu added that no coal had been delivered yet, and that none was in sight for the winter. He wondered how long the schools would remain open. By November or December, it would be impossible to keep the children sitting still and studying.

"When the ink in their desks freezes over, we'll have to send them home again. Their mothers are out in the woods now, collecting all the fuel they can to keep at least the kitchen warm. If that fails, they'll have to spend the winter in bed."

I asked him what provisions had been made to put the 15-18 year olds to school.

"They're the real problem," he replied. "We have neither the space nor the teachers to put them to school. By next spring we hope to be ready. There is little work for that age-group in the city. If there was, I doubt whether they would take it. They roam the streets. They realize that they can make a good living on the black market. Next comes stealing to keep the black market supplied. Unchecked delinquency is apt to be the rule rather than the exception for that whole group. It's a very black picture, as I see it. Probably you Americans don't care whether or not these people remain uneducated, but you can't be indifferent to the growth of a political and moral cancer of this kind. It's too contagious."

He looked at his watch.

"Excuse me," he said hastily, "I don't want to let that colonel wait outside any longer. I'll be right back." He flew off.

Just then the phone rang. I picked it up and answered for Weschu. It was a Military Government Officer who tried to get something across in broken German. Switching languages, I said that Schulze had just left the room. Could I give him a message?

"Yes," said the telephone. "Please tell him we need a table on the number of teachers available, if all those who joined party before May 1, 1937, are eliminated. We'd like to have that information by morning."

When Weschu came back into the room, I told him about the call.

"Well," he said, "this time I'm prepared."

He pulled a folder from his desk with sheets of paper covered with neat columns of figures.

"This is the teacher situation", he said. "In the country schools, I'll have to fire 90% of all teachers, because they were party members before May 1, 1937. In Frankfurt it's 50%. That's because in the small villages teachers are among the few people of some education and influence. The party put the pressure on them first. They may not have been unwilling victims, on the whole,—I don't know. But I don't believe in your methods of throwing people out of their jobs by categories without an individual investigation. I don't think that's according to your principles either. You see, I am the one who has to do the firing. And that's awfully tough in cases where it's not justified, as the individual record stands. I assure you, where real Nazis are concerned, no matter how they cringe and whine today, I don't need to be spurred on."

The difficulty was, I reminded him, that Military Government needed some definite yardstick by which to proceed. Otherwise the door would be wide open for personal politics and bribery.

Weschu agreed, but he thought that German officials and commissions, appointed and trusted by Military Government, should be given sufficient leeway to judge cases on their own merits. Then, Military Government should hold the German officials responsible for selections, instead of proceeding by rigid categories.

"Look," Weschu said, "the other day I had a man in this room who wanted his job back as teacher. He had just come back from a prisoner of war cage. I said, fine, glad to have you back,—were you a member of the party before 1937? He said, yes, I was. I'm sorry, I said, in that case you can't have your job back. He became red in the face and told me this: '10 years ago, when I left the university and wanted a teaching job, I stood in a room just like this, and there was an official behind a desk, just like you behind this one. I told him I wanted a teaching job. He said that's fine, teachers are needed,—was I a member of the party? I said no, I wasn't. Sorry, he said, in that case you can't teach at our schools. So I paid my 3 ½ marks a month, joined the damn party, and did my job without paying any attention to them otherwise. And now? The same business in reverse.' There was nothing I could do."

Weschu cited the cases of two of his closest friends, teachers with whose anti-Nazi convictions he was familiar. All through the war, he had freely exchanged his views with them, and maintained their faith in Nazi defeat. They had become party members for the sake of convenience, and it was now Weschu's duty to fire them. He considered the decisive date—May 1, 1937—arbitrary. By that time, some early party members had turned against Nazi ideas and policies. They would now be barred. On the other hand, teachers who joined the party after that date, even as late as the forties, should have known from the record with what a bunch of gangsters they were identifying themselves. He could employ them.

Weschu pointed his cigar at me authoritatively:

"Categories and generalizations are always unjust. The worst blunder I know of under the present rules, is the one about the VDA."

This was a complicated case. The VDA—Verein für das Deutschtum im Ausland—was until Nazi time a cultural organization which supported German-language schools for Germans abroad. Contributions were from pupils in German schools, usually by teachers who volunteered for this unrewarding job. Later, the Nazis made the VDA a vehicle of their Fifth Column work, while officially maintaining its cultural cover. Now, all the teachers who at any time, pre-Nazi or Nazi, collected money for the VDA, no matter what their Nazi or anti-Nazi record was otherwise, had to be fired. Weschu was quite upset about this particular instance of what he called "arbitrary categories". It was unnecessarily depleting the number of reliable teachers, he thought.

I asked him what was being done to fill the gap created by denazification.

"We're starting an abbreviated teacher training program to get fresh blood into our schools by next fall. But I don't think we should take it for granted that all those we pick for the course will turn out to be pure-blooded democratic missionaries."

Then he picked up a sheaf from his desk:

"See these? Applications from former party members to be readmitted to their jobs. I have to turn them down. And I need them badly—them or anybody else who's had the training. We don't have enough personnel to staff even the elementary school program we have started. I'd like to know this—what is the greater risk? To have even some questionable characters teaching,—and we could keep them under control all right,—or to let the children get their education in the streets of Frankfurt? If the people who write your denazification laws have thought that problem out, and think they know the answer—all right. Then let's de-Nazify. Personally, I find it's a hell of a responsibility. Perhaps this,"—and he lifted the teacher statistics folder from the desk—"will carry some weight."

Weschu lit another cigar, and ran his finger through the sheaf of applications:

"Another thing. How much thought have your denazification law makers given to this: You're throwing party members out of the teaching profession and out of leading positions everywhere. Excellent. Unfortunately, most of them have some intellectual standing—negative if you will—otherwise they would not have been in those positions. Aren't you creating the nucleus of leadership for a fanatic, unreasonable opposition to any sound, moderate development in Germany? How long will you be with us to keep that kind of movement in check? Probably just long enough for it to mature and blossom, and then we'll have to deal with it alone again. Perhaps your people have thought it out. I don't know. I hope they have. I still think it's a great responsibility."

I asked Weschu whether he wanted no elimination of Nazis at all.

"I certainly do," he answered. "As long as we're less categoric, more reasonable, and above all just about it."

He laughed.

"I didn't mean to tell you all of my worries in one day", he said. "You'll forgive me. I had a rough time keeping my mouth shut under the Nazis— that's why I resigned. It's doubly difficult when you talk to representatives of a democratic nation. I put these ideas I talked to you about into a memorandum for Military Government. I hope it will receive some consideration."

I broached my curiosity about the fate of my class-mates to him. There was very little he knew about them.

"I wish we still had our school records. We had pretty good files. The records of your class, for instance, had every man's autobiography. Don't know whether you remember, but it was one of the requirements for graduation. You also had to outline your plans and ambitions for the future. Then there was a character sketch of every one of you, written by the teacher who knew you best."

This would have been wonderful material, indeed, with which to start the hunt for my class-mates. I asked Weschu what had happened to the records.

"When the air raids started, the school thought they would be safer at the so-called fire-proof city archives. I'm afraid the archives suffered badly in the raid of March 22, 1944. Anyhow, our records are gone."

"Who wrote our character sketches?"

"For your class, I believe, Dr. Erding did." Weschu replied.

Dr. phil Harold Erding had taught us languages. I had no trouble remembering him. He was an outstanding philologist, with an international reputation in his field. Weschu told me that early this year Dr. Erding had suffered a stroke, and that he might not be in very good health now. I would find him in Grünberg, some 60 miles north of Frankfurt. Two years ago, when the Ebert school building in Frankfurt was first hit, remnants of the student body, and a few teachers, evacuated to this small town to continue working as well as possible. Erding, who had been completely bombed out in Frankfurt, was among them.

"You know how great an interest Erding always took in your class especially," Weschu continued. "I wouldn't be surprised if he remembered every one of you in detail."

I told Weschu that I had intended to find Erding, and that I would soon go out to Grünberg. Meanwhile, weren't there any records left at the school itself?

"There might be," he said. "I'll find out for you. Come back in a couple of days."

When I closed his door behind me, there was a line of five men waiting for him. Three of them were still partly in German army uniform. Probably applicants for teaching jobs. Equally probably party members.

When I returned to Weschu's office two days later, the room was filled with noise and dust. Someone was hammering away at the ceiling from above. Weschu had screened himself and his desk from the flying dirt with sheets of the local German-edited newspaper, the Frankfurter Rundschau. "Best purpose this sheet ever served," he said.

Then, with a motion to the ceiling:

"Had to sacrifice some of your invaluable cigars to get this hole closed in the ceiling. You don't get workers these days by just giving them money."

Economists will soon write scientific treatises on the underlying reasons for the substitution of smoke as a currency for money. It's a fascinating subject.

Weschu triumphantly waved a large black book at me.

"The search at the school was worthwhile," he said. "Here is a list of all the students at the Ebert Schule for the year 1930/1931."

In neat, Gothic handwriting, the list contained the names of students, the date and place of their birth, their parents' names, professions and addresses. I looked over the names of the class of 1931. No more than half of them sounded familiar. I doubted that I would remember anything about these men until I saw them again.

However, it was a good start. The addresses were 15 years old, and if Frankfurt averages were applied, only half of the houses would still be standing. But neighbors, police precincts, the post office, might be counted upon to provide first leads.

Of the twenty men in our class, eight had left Germany. Twelve would have to be traced. Weschu recommended a young man of 18, who would probably be eager to help me in this time-consuming endeavor. His name was Hans Obrecht. Weschu had found him to be intelligent and energetic on some equally complicated errands that had to be done for the school department. I would find him in a cellar on Jahn-Strasse.

Night had fallen by the time I made my way through the main streets of the city to find Obrecht. Street cars were bulging with people returning to their homes. Rubble was still heaped along the side-walks, but a narrow path had been cleared along the buildings. In the ruins of some of them, shops were open for business. Crude brick walls with a square yard or so of window had taken the place of the great display fronts. For sale were post cards and pictures of Frankfurt as it once was, crude wooden handicraft, costume jewelry, ersatz leather bags, hats. Prices, especially of what could pass as "art", were high. Landscape paintings, dilletantish rot even to the untrained observer, were marked in the hundreds of marks. Bait for people who were ready to invest their otherwise unemployable funds in lasting values.

In a house where nothing but walls seemed to be standing, a fourth-floor window was lit. At the corner a prostitute was talking to two soldiers who had been drinking. A multitude of hand-painted signs at the entrance of a building advertised businessmen who had found some useable office space, with an intact staircase leading to it. A photographer, a radio repair shop, a tailor (bring your own cloth), a fountain pen repairer, shared the more or less damaged premises inside.

I passed the Eschersheimer Tor, an ancient thick-walled tower which once formed part of Frankfurt's defenses when it was still a walled city. The structure was undamaged, although the area around it was almost completely destroyed. The tower is round—perhaps the blast of bombs was deflected by its shape. That would explain the large number of chimneys left standing in industrial areas which had felt the full weight of strategic bombing.

Where corner buildings had been destroyed entirely, street signs were neatly embedded at eye level into the piles of stone and brick. The address at which I was to find Obrecht belonged to such a corner heap of rubble. There was not even a wall left standing. One of the stone pillars which had formed the entrance was still erect. It bore the house number in neat white figures on a blue enamel sign. The wrought-iron gate was hanging limply from one hinge.

Light was coming out of a basement window one foot high at street level. A large white arrow and the letters L.S.R.—Luftschutzraum, air raid shelter—pointed around the entrance pillar to a narrow stair case leading down. When I knocked at the door, a dark-haired, red-checkered youngster opened. He was Hans Obrecht, the young man Weschu had recommended.

I told him what I had come for, and he asked me inside. We went past a heavy iron door into a corridor. Its thick, concrete walls separated four small, door-less cubicles. Obrecht took me into one of these. It had a small table, two chairs, and a German army cot as furniture.

We sat down, and I offered him a cigarette. "No, thanks, I don't smoke," he said.

"Take it for one for your friends," I urged.

"No, thanks, really, I have no use for them," he answered. "We are lucky to have this place. We used to live upstairs before the bombing. The landlord had evacuated his family into the country. When the war was over, he first wanted to throw us out and move in himself, but then, fortunately for us, he changed his mind."

Obrecht had returned from captivity as a US prisoner of war only two months ago. The German Labor Service had sent him to Czechoslovakia to dig "fortresses" in the fall of 1944. He had caught a cold which developed into pneumonia. Due to inferior German medical treatment, he said, he had lost one lung and was now totally disabled.

"Now the Americans have stopped all payments, and we don't know what to live on. Mother is ill, and my two sisters are too young to go out and work. My father died five years ago."

I told Obrecht that the stoppage of payments was undoubtedly only a temporary measure. Also, according to what Director Schulze had said about him, he was clever enough to make a living for the time being. Then he eagerly listened to the details of the tracing work I wanted him to do. He was familiar with the directories, police precinct stations, and postal redirection offices, where information on the movements of my class-mates in the past 14 years might be found. He had his bicycle, he said, and he would be able to get results pretty soon.

"You know, I've come to despise the Germans", he suddenly said.

"You have?"

"Yes. They aren't happy unless they can slit each others' throats."

"Or, failing that, someone else's."

"I suppose so. But look, now they're trying to say they're Bavarians, or Hessians, or Swabians. You Americans are always Americans, and the British always British. Why not we Germans?"

"Why not the Europeans," I asked.

"B — but—I never thought of that."

It was difficult to pry into the reason for his sudden patriotic outburst. He had sufficient native intelligence to form his ideas independently, and he insisted that they hadn't been suggested by Goebbels. I asked him about the political and racial views he was taught at school.

"Oh, that nonsense," he said. "I don't think there were more than five in our class who believed it. We did our homework so we'd get passing marks. Just to get by. I liked the teacher who instructed us in the racial sciences. He kept me after class once. I thought it was a penalty for making noises during his lecture. But he wanted to talk to me. He told me not to believe a word of what he was teaching in class. Then he gave me a little typewritten pamphlet. I had to read it that night, and return it to him next morning. It was very short. There were two things in it. One was a speech by one of your presidents—I still remember his name: Lincoln, isn't it? The other was something from the French revolution. The rights of man. But he was the only teacher like that I ever had."

In spite of his idealistic teachers, however, a few simple questions showed that Obrecht's political ignorance was abysmal. He thought that Japan had fought Russia since 1941, as well as the western powers. He was certain that the United States had declared war on Germany first—and he had never been able to understand why. The facts were a great surprise to him. The Communists, he thought, were bad. About their positive aims, he hadn't the foggiest idea. Was it true that America was so full of gangsters that you couldn't cross the street without being mowed down by a tommy gun? And wasn't Roosevelt a dictator just like Hitler? That's what an American soldier once told him. The devastation of Russia by the German armies was news to Obrecht. He thought the Germans had done efficient industrial development work in Russia's western provinces. That the liberated countries of Europe were as badly off for food and coal as Germany, came as another surprise to him. After their victory, he felt, they were lands of milk and honey.

I asked him whether he and his school chums had believed their teachers and Hitler youth leaders, that Germany would win ultimate victory.

He laughed. "Believe them? We didn't believe anything. How could we believe we were winning the war, and then the sky was full of planes coming from America, and my house was blown to dust and rubble? We weren't that dumb. After Stalingrad, it was over. The only thing that counted was not to be killed before the end."

"Did you listen to the foreign radio stations?"

"Only sometimes," he said. "Everybody said they were lying, so we didn't believe them either. And now people say you can't believe a word that's in the new papers. I don't read them. Would be a waste of time. I don't believe anything unless I see it."

"And what is it you see and believe?"

Obrecht leaned on the table and bent forward, whispering:

"I see that my youngest sister, who is eight, comes back with a piece of sausage she stole from under the butcher's counter. And we're too hungry to send her back with it and give her a whacking. And I see my other sister, who is now fourteen, being stopped in the streets by your soldiers. She thinks that's wonderful, and now she paints her lips. I do beat her up. Then I had my friends. They think I'm crazy. That's because I don't join them begging or stealing cigarettes from the Amis. They say that for a hundred cigarettes I could support my family for two months. I also see my mother on her sick bed here. I'd like her to have a good doctor, and a little comfort. I'd like to get us out of this hole. I know there are a lot of people without a roof over their heads, but I still want to be a little better off than a ground hog. Everybody says the American troops throw away all the food they don't eat, and forbid us to take it. And when I tried to go to the Military Government to find out about my disability pension, I couldn't talk to anyone. They were all busy, and the German interpreter threw me out. That's what I see. It's enough."

I wanted to give him some American magazines to read—I had a copy of both TIME and Newsweek in my pocket. Unfortunately, he knew no English. That issue of TIME carried a blistering report on our Military Government in Germany, and I translated a few paragraphs to him.

He sat there with his mouth open.

"They can print that?" he gasped. "Won't they be put in jail?"

I had to translate the story for him word for word, while he followed the printed lines. "That's incredible," he said.

That, I told him, was the reason why he could believe the new papers, at least the ones published wholly by Americans. I had a few mental reservations as I made the statement, but Obrecht's reeducation, a long and difficult job, had to begin somewhere.

After instructing him on how he could send notes to me on the results of his detective work, I left the air raid shelter for the luxurious mess hall behind the I.G. Farben headquarters building, where, as a friend once put it, "never did so many get so much for so little."

I picked a dismal day to drive to Grünberg for a visit with Dr. Erding. It was foggy part of the way, and the roads were slippery. A slight fall drizzle just moistened the pavement, and mixed with the dust into a jelly-like substance. It was the one road condition which makes even our GI drivers slow down.

I had seen Dr. Erding once since 1931. We met in Switzerland in 1936. He went there occasionally "on a breather from the prison air of Germany." He had given me a solemn warning then:

"Tell everybody you know, that all we are educating German youth for today, is war. The youngsters have stopped studying peace-time subjects. Afternoons and Sundays they spend crawling on their bellies through the woods, playing war games. When they come to class without their homework, they bring an excuse from their Hitler Jugend Führer that they've been engaged in physical exercise. Intellectually, they are consciously being made stupid. The Führer principle has replaced individual thought and decision. There is no hope for this youth. There will be war."

When I suggested to him then that he leave Germany, he refused to consider the thought. His place was with his students, he said, to do at least in individual cases as much as he could to offset official de-education. Later, I heard, he refused a philology chair at an American college. His reasons probably had not changed.

Erding was the man who had made the Weimar Republic come to life for us. Probably due to his influence, I never had a clear perspective about its actual weakness as long as I was at school. His language instruction was not confined to grammar and syntax—it included the philosophy and government of the countries whose languages we were studying. Erding had traveled widely. His scholarship was balanced by his human insight. When he told us (in French) about the French rentier who had settled at 45 in moderate comfort in a small town to enjoy time, he spoke with envy, not with Teutonic contempt. When he discussed the history of the French revolution (also in French), he pointed with pride to the fact that Germany too had a liberal tradition, largely generated by French thought, and he traced the influence of French, English and American constitutional ideas on the framers of the Weimar Constitution of 1919.

As a student and admirer of English parliamentary practice and tradition, he lectured to us (in English) on some of the flaws of the Weimar Constitution.

He felt that its attempt to be entirely just to all sides was its primary drawback. Proportionate representation gave all parties, large and small, sincere and crackpot, an equal chance before the electorate, and none a working majority for the job of governing. Coalitions meant compromise in party platforms, until few program elements were left. They meant that the minority did not really abide by the will of the majority, but maintained a power, often decisive, out of all proportion to the will of the electorate. Dr. Erding preferred a two-party system. As the supreme example of fair play in a democracy, he taught us the term 'His Majesty's loyal opposition.'

Political lethargy, especially of those opposed to the radicalism at both ends of the political scale, was another of Dr. Erding's objections. He believed that every citizen had not only the right, but an obligation to vote. Abstention from the ballot-box, he suggested, should be punished by a fine.

But these were only points of criticism, not condemnation, to our language professor. He thought they would be worked out in time. After all, German democracy was yet young. He probably saw in us, our whole generation, the people who would make it a living organism, after ridding ourselves of the nationalist heritage which culminated in the World War. He did his best to encourage exchange trips to France and England to bring us into direct contact with the people whose languages and ways he taught us.

The outstanding personal tragedy in Dr. Erding's life was that he had no children. His and his wife's affections were diverted to his students, not all of whom were intelligent enough to appreciate his qualities. His home with its huge library was always open to us. There, he dropped the teacher's authority, and became a good friend.

Dr. Erding, of course, was not the only type of educator we were exposed to. We were taught modern history by a man who ranted endlessly about the "lie of Germany's war guilt", and the "Dictate of Versailles". Our geography teacher made Professor Haushofer's "Zeitschrift für Geopolitik" required reading. Both held the Weimar Republic which was paying them, in open contempt, although they had sworn to defend its Constitution. When the more determined democrats among us protested to Dr. Erding that this was an anomalous state of affairs, he praised the Weimar Republic for its tolerance in permitting the opposition absolutely free expression. He was convinced that this generosity would finally work to the benefit of the Republic. Truth and progress would win the minds of all Germans over reaction and hatred all the faster, if no one was given an excuse for protesting suppression of free speech.

Of our students, I don't remember in detail who believed what. Probably individual boys permitted themselves to be influenced by the teacher who came closest in point of view to what they heard at home.

I thought about Erding who had stayed with the hated Nazis because he thought he could rescue a few of the minds they were intent on poisoning. Even three years before the war broke out, he had told me that his battle was lost. Yet, he stayed on his post. In a way I was afraid to see him again.

When I reached Grünberg, I asked for Dr. Erding's address at the Bürgermeister's office. He was living in the house of a local shop keeper. A boy outside said he knew exactly where it was. He climbed into the front seat of the jeep beside me, and rode through that town past the local population, like a general reviewing his troops. As soon as we reached our destination, he ran off. It was shortly after noon.

A woman downstairs directed me to Dr. Erding's second floor room. I went up the narrow staircase and knocked. Erding opened the door and stared at me. Then he stammered my name, almost fell in his chair a few paces away and buried his head in his hands. I don't exactly recall what I did next— I think I stood beside him and patted his shoulders. There was no point in saying anything.

He had aged terribly. He was in his fifties, and looked 70. Apparently, he had been dozing in his chair when I knocked. He was in shirt sleeves and slippers. A book lay open on the table—the Bible. Then there was a typewriter, a disorderly mess of papers, and more books. This was a bedroom. Every inch of floor space was used for some piece of furniture, probably rescued from his home in Frankfurt. He had no proper closet for his and his wife's clothes— they were hung up along the wall on nails. His chair was a rocker—I thought I recognized it as his favorite chair in his former home.

Erding's hair was grey and thin. His collar seemed two inches too wide. When he looked up again, I saw the deep lines in his face; lines of bitterness, not wisdom.

He became suddenly very lively:

"You must excuse me a minute so I can put my jacket on and call my wife. You're the first to visit us out here, you know. This is a tremendous event for us. You have time to stay a while, haven't you?"

I assured him I had, and he conducted me across the hall into a small kitchen which also served as his living room. He brought his rocker from the other room and insisted that I sit in it—"you must be tired from your long trip."

The kitchen was even smaller than the bedroom. It, too, was overcrowded with furniture, a smell of boiled potatoes hung in the air. The window was closed tight, probably to preserve the warmth produced when Mrs. Erding had cooked lunch. Dishes were stacked in the sink. Apples and prunes in a bowl were the only food in evidence. A bookshelf along the wall contained a half-dozen big volumes of French and English dictionaries.

Dr. Erding came back in, wearing his jacket and shoes, his hair combed.

"My wife will be right back. She is probably standing in some food queue. I sent the downstairs boy after her. Just a few days ago we were talking about our Ebert school boys. And she wondered whether anyone would ever find his way back to us. Look how poor we are now. But I don't mind poverty—don't misunderstand me. I lost my library—you remember there were about 3000 volumes—in the bombing of March 22, last year. It was a terrible blow. Just before that bombing I had managed to get some things up here—you see all of it right here in these two rooms. But the library is gone. I miss it most. Everything else I can take. I had a stroke last January, you know. I'm much better now, although sometimes I think my memory is failing. But the doctor told me I would be all right for several years, if I could avoid excitement. I'm surprised I didn't have my second stroke when I saw you in the door."

He was talking fast and nervously. Next came a barrage of questions: where had I spent the past ten years, how quickly was I promoted to officer in the US Army, where had I fought the war, what did the crossed rifles on my lapel mean, was the US Army as horrible an institution as the German, and so on.

I had difficulty in keeping up with him, when he heard his wife coming up the stairs. He rushed outside and I heard him tell her not to get excited, but there was a visitor whom she'd certainly like to see. She screamed: "Well, who is it?" and rushed in. It was terribly embarrassing, for Mrs. Erding looked at me for a split second, then sat by the kitchen table, let her head drop into her arms and sobbed loudly. This time her husband patted her shoulders.

I wondered for a moment whether this was not an act. But I dismissed the thought quickly. She apologized for acting so hysterically:

"You must understand—we've been cut off so long. This terrible war. No news from anybody."

She wiped the tears from her face and tried to smile. But there was an expression of reproachful bitterness in her face which she could not overcome. She was pale and worn. Her blonde hair was disorderly; some strands had fallen across her face.

"Look what's happened to us. Isn't it terrible how we live now? You remember our beautiful place in Frankfurt, don't you? We're terribly poor. I can't even offer you a cup of coffee—we have none."

I told her she had, because I brought a pound—directly from the US by parcel post.

"Wonderful," she said, "the guests bring their own coffee. I still have a little milk left over, but we haven't seen any sugar in months."

"Never mind the sugar," I said, "I'm glad to see you both alive and with a roof over your head. I wasn't so sure I could expect that when I saw the ruins of your house in Frankfurt."

"You are absolutely right," Dr. Erding injected. "Women are so superficial. I know we are poor, and we can't even entertain a guest anymore. That's really the worst evidence of poverty. But we came through. Someday, books will be printed again, and perhaps we can buy one or two. The worst is over."

"That's not what you said this morning," she said, and an utterly dejected expression came over her face.

"Well," he answered, "it's easy to get into moods." He turned to me, "I was very depressed this morning, and I'm afraid I told my wife about it. Then we read in the Bible a bit—everything is in there for one who knows how to read. It helped us. I think we're over it."

The way these two people looked at each other made me wonder. The mood of depression in the morning, the hysterical reception, the emphasis on their poverty, the consolation they drew from the Holy Book:—nothing further was said about it, but I suspected that the whole picture added up to suicide plans. I would have to unpack my most optimistic set of arguments to give these people hope.

Objectively speaking, their living conditions, compared to the city, were not bad. They had two rooms, with windows in them, a kitchen stove which would keep them warm. They had the furniture they needed,—there would have been no room into which to cram more. They lived in the country, and food could not be as great a problem as in the city.

On this last point they corrected me. It was an ordeal, they said, to try to obtain food from the farmers. They had nothing to offer in return—the farmers wanted no money. Mrs. Erding was cultivating a small plot of land to raise some vegetables. It was a lot of work, and he, after his stroke, was of no help to her. She also had to stand in many food lines, and to keep house. Until a few days ago, she had spent her evenings teaching German to some GIs billeted in town. They had now been redeployed.

Meanwhile Dr. Erding was teaching English to some Germans employed by Military Government. The school was not functioning. And in his present state of health he doubted whether he could ever teach again. He was receiving a pension.

I realized that their desperation was not nearly so much caused by their actual physical circumstances, as by the relative decline of their standards, and by their view of the present. Somehow, they had kept plugging under Nazi rule, hoping for the better world that was to come afterwards. Now, half a year after the collapse, they probably realized that their reduced standards were there to stay. As far as they could see, the better world intended to exclude not only Nazis, but all Germans.

I asked Dr. Erding for particulars on his pessimistic outlook. His expression and gestures were those of a hunted man, rather than his former air of authority, when he begun:

"Germany has proven again that she is utterly incapable of ruling herself. We shall need foreign advice and guidance for a long time to come. I think most Germans would welcome it. But what's actually happening?"

Erding hesitated. Perhaps he wondered just how freely he should talk. I asked him to go ahead, letting the chips fall where they may.

"All right", he said. "I only hope that you have some positive things to say to me. I'm craving for a little encouragement. Right now, this is how I see our situation: You've split Germany proper five ways. There are four zones of occupation, and our breadbasket was ceded to the Poles. The French want Ruhr and Rhineland for good, just as the Poles now have Silesia and Pomerania. You've promised us at Potsdam to have some sort of German unity, so we can live, but there's no trace of it yet. You also say that we're to export enough to make up for the eastern breadbasket you've given the Poles, which means that we'd probably have to export more than before the war. The British also want to export more than before the war, and so do you. To whom?—In addition you dismantle plants which we could have converted to peace-time uses. You talk of our steel industry as though the smallest peace-time output would be sufficient for our needs. Haven't you seen all the destruction? There's no major bridge standing up. Whole cities need rebuilding. Our productive plant is shot. And you want us to produce just enough to cover the needs of a period in which hardly a plant, or a road, or a bridge, was built. Besides, how about the rest of Europe? Don't they need steel?"

Erding was talking excitedly. He had a well-trained, booming voice, too powerful for the small kitchen in which we sat. His wife reminded him of what the doctor had said—to keep calm. He went on:

"My wife is right. I have to be reasonable. Besides why should I pick on you—after all, you probably didn't write all those laws and treaties. You just happen to be the first man from the other side I can talk to. My trouble is that I just don't understand. Germany, after all, has always made a large contribution to the European economy. If you eliminate her, by parcellation and dismantling, all of Europe will be the loser. Don't ever let Germany govern herself again. Keep her under control. Keep your troops and your air force here. Keep industries and foreign trade under control. But let us work! Let us rehabilitate ourselves! All right, make us entirely dependent on imports and exports. See that we don't manufacture substitutes for goods that we can buy elsewhere. Don't permit us to pile up imported raw materials. Make Europe an integrated unit, and perhaps the old continent will show some life yet."

I told Erding that such ideas were beginning to make headway, if not so much in the United States, then in the liberated and neutral countries, and in Great Britain. That was news to him. He had despaired of reason getting the upper hand in Europe, he said.

"I'm glad you told me that. I have so many friends in France and England—if I could only write to them about these things. It looked to me as though a wave of nationalism was flooding Europe, almost putting our own Nazis in the shadow."

Mrs. Erding meanwhile was making coffee. Its smell interrupted her husband's political analysis, and he remarked on the miracle of having real coffee made of real beans. I never knew the smell of coffee could mean so much—both he and his wife appeared to have lost some of their accumulated bitterness.

But the pause was short. "Can you explain the Polish award to me?" Dr. Erding continued. "According to the Potsdam agreement, it is not final. Only an administrative arrangement until peace treaties are concluded. Meanwhile, the Poles evict all Germans living in their 'administrative' areas. There are so many refugees from the east expected here, that the population of our Kreis will be doubled. The land doesn't produce enough now to supply the surrounding towns. It will be terrible."

I told him that even now, food was being imported into Germany to tide her over until the next crop, and that no immediate payment was expected.

He came back with a question he might as well have put directly before the American electorate:

"This crop, and the next one, and the one after, won't be enough to keep us from starving. Is it your plan to feed us indefinitely without expecting anything to return?"

Erding sat back somewhat triumphantly. His wife had the coffee ready. She produced cups and saucers, no two of them matching. She apologized profusely—all her own things had been smashed in Frankfurt, and it was practically impossible to obtain chinaware nowadays.

Erding was much too well informed and widely travelled to be appeased with general statements of good intentions and instinctive optimism. There was no use pretending to him that our policies in Germany and Europe were entirely consistent, and perfectly coordinated with those of the other victorious powers. I frankly told him about the various conflicting theories held in the States on the future of Germany. He had heard of the Morgenthau Plan, the agrarianization of Germany. He was less familiar with the fact that our State Department's expressed policy was less radical in its economic aspects. Nor did he know about the debate over French claims for the Ruhr and the Rhineland. I also recalled to him that our policies always required some measure of support from American public opinion which was still overwhelmingly hostile to any, even the best-intentioned, German ambitions.

"Yes, I know," he said. "Your public opinion moves slowly. I used to despair of it once before, when they took years to recognize the world danger that Nazism presented. When they understood, it was almost too late. Now they'll take their time noticing that the chaos in Europe is equally dangerous. Meanwhile Europe goes to hell."

Erding was getting excited again. His face reddened and he almost screamed:

"Why in God's name don't you make a dominion out of us? We'll make you a good colony! Then you'd have an interest in our production, and in exploiting our resources and labor. We can't govern ourselves, I don't think we want to govern ourselves. Treat us like the Philippines, or India, or Rhodesia, instead of a colony of lepers. You know what I need most? A banner to look up to. An ideal to live for. Why don't you plant the Stars and Stripes in Germany—not as conquering temporary occupation, but as a permanent government?"

Again I had to take recourse to public opinion. Americans, I told him, did not wish to "colonize" Europe. They hoped that European countries, Germany included, would ultimately adopt democratic and neighborly ways of life which would insure peace.

"How naïve", he exclaimed. "That's typically America. It scares me. What scares me more is how Americans may ultimately answer the crucial question: Just how much of a stake do the United States have in Europe? I predict this: If the confusion goes on, if the suspicion continues here that sooner or later you will pull out of Europe, then the Germans will increasingly lean toward the east. I'm afraid the next election will already show a great increase of Communist votes. Supposing a Communist majority in Germany votes to become a part of the Soviet Union. Are you going to stop them?"

I told Erding that so far the Communist parties in areas occupied by Russia had not done very well. I added that it would do the German cause no good to wave the Russian flag before American noses, because we regarded good relations as a much more vital concern to us than the fate of Germany.

"That's all very nice," he persisted. "But the Russians want to take over the whole Continent of Europe. Are you or are you not interested in preventing that?"

With these two sentences he voiced both the fundamental conviction of vast numbers of Germans today, and their greatest fear. The first is that Russia is intent on expanding further into Western Europe, the second that the US may not oppose such a development. I had to go far afield to bring his views up to date, and I doubt whether I convinced him. I tried to explain Russian foreign policy to him in terms of their devastated country—a matter Germans persistently overlook,—their desire to rebuild and to develop their own vast resources, and their perhaps exaggerated desire for security. Erding, on the other hand, still judged Russia by the world revolutionary aims of the Third International. He could not believe that these had in any way been abandoned. He also took it for granted that the Elbe and Werra rivers were the dividing line between eastern and western spheres of interest, not merely temporary occupational zone boundaries.

"I'm so glad you came here," he said, "I want very much to believe what you said. Perhaps there is some hope. But mind you, I'm not the only one who has this feeling of uncertainty. That uncertainty itself produces Communists. The people say to themselves: Look, the Americans are going home. All they want to do is to go home. Someday they'll all be gone, and then the Russians come. If we join the Communist party now, we'll be better off. That's how politics work in Germany. I don't have to remind you at the people who were prepared for everything in 1933—with membership cards for both the Communist and Nazi party."

Indeed, I needed no reminder. German political conviction was always largely determined by what promised to pay off. There was no reason to assume a general change of attitude in the direction of pure democracy.

I complimented Dr. Erding on his comprehension of the interplay between American foreign policy and public opinion. After all, he could not have been in close touch with international affairs for several years.

"I had a radio", he said.

There was a small shelf on the wall. Above it dangled a piece of green wire with a plug, an aerial.

"Where is it?" I inquired.

"Well, you see, we had some of your soldiers at our house here quite often. They enjoyed themselves, my wife taught them German, especially the vocabulary they needed to talk to the girls. We liked to see them very much. One of them asked whether he could borrow our little set. It was an Emerson which my wife brought back from the States on her last trip shortly before the war. Well, those boys left. They must have been rushed, otherwise that soldier would have brought the radio back. I have no doubt about that."

Another thing I had not noticed before, was a small sign, about the size of a magazine cover, tacked to the inside of the kitchen door. It was in Erding's handwriting, in English, and read about like this:

"The few belonging you see in these two rooms are all a German anti-Nazi was able to rescue from his home in the city. He welcomes you, because you are his liberators. Please treat him and his property as you would your neighbors at home."

Erding was sipping his coffee. I pretended not to have noticed the sign. I was too embarrassed to comment on it, or on the loss of his radio which during the years of darkness had been his only contact with the people for whose victory he prayed.

It was natural that Erding would have wanted to discuss his present fears first, and then the past. I reminded him of our meeting in 1936, and his prediction of war. While it had stood out clearly in my mind, he had forgotten the incident. He remembered seeing me, of course, but he was surprised that he uttered the warning.

"Just goes to show how badly I was terrorized in these intervening years. I must have had some remnant of courage when I gave this warning to you after only three years of Nazi rule. The methods our tyrants used to prepare our youngsters for the blood bath, were, of course, my constant thought. But I wanted to keep my job. I wanted to have the chance to mould at least a few minds. I came pretty close to being thrown out a few times, of course, but generally I played their "Heil Hitler" greeting games to their satisfaction."

"Do you think playing their games, as you call it, was the right thing to do?" I asked. "Wouldn't it have been better to throw your weight into the other scale?"

"I thought that over carefully when I was offered a professorship at one of your colleges back in 1938. I decided then, and I still think rightly, that my place was here. I realize how infinitely better off I'd be today, had I taken that job. But I could have made no other decision. You must understand why. As an educator, I always strove to have an influence on my more intelligent students beyond teaching them English and French. I wanted to see them become human beings first, and Germans second. I wanted them to absorb some of the common elements of western civilization so they would appreciate it as a whole, instead of this stupid idolatry of everything German. Well, Nazis or no Nazis, that job never changed. While they were in power, I had to be careful in the selection of students I could take under my wing. But if I was successful at least to some degree, then there are a few more young Germans today capable of rebuilding our country, than there would have been without me. That is why I believe I was right in staying on my job, and making whatever pacts with the devil I had to."

The pacts, incidentally, did not include membership in the party.

He was looking at me intensely, expecting approval. I made no secret of the fact that his motives impressed me. At the same time, I asked myself whether Erding was not rationalizing his compromises with the Nazi school system. I had no reason to doubt his sincerity. Perhaps there is such a thing as sincere rationalizing. The dividing line can be very hard to detect.

Dr. Erding's brushes with the Nazis were bagatelles. Once during the war, at the end of a talk to the student body, he heiled just Germany, instead of Hitler. A grumbling went through the ranks, and Erding saw himself whisked off to the dungeons. But nothing happened. Stories like this are no rarity in Germany today. Saying "Guten Morgen" instead of "Heil Hitler" was more or less the extent of the opposition expressed to the Nazi regime. To do it, as least so people believed, was fraught with grave personal danger. More could not be risked.

In Erding's case, however, that was not the point. He consciously wanted to avoid these brushes which could have led to his dismissal, because he thought he had a mission to fulfill for which his job was essential.

"I was sure Germany would ultimately be beaten," he reasoned. "I was sure of it 10 years ago, when you were still passing neutrality laws. I looked beyond the war even then. Today the defeat is history, and Germany still exists. And if you come down to the essentials, what matters today is the same thing that mattered in the twenties, under the Nazis, and during the war—moulding the minds of the young into a pattern of peace and civilization. Only, now I'm too old to take a hand in it. This is a crucial time, because we have to start from the beginning. And I got so very desperate, because we're not getting any help from you. I've heard and read a lot about the reeducation of Germany that you planned. Your intentions are excellent. But then you apparently forget that people who haven't enough to eat, who have no home, who have no hope for a fairly decent living, and above all, who have no <u>faith</u>, are fit subjects only for radicalization not reeducation."

Erding had an immense reserve of vocal power. He put it all in the word "faith". It nearly shook the room.

Mrs. Erding had listened quietly to her husband's rhetoric. Now she intervened. Had I seen any of my former classmates?

I outlined my plan to find them. Then, with the list of names, we briefly discussed each man. One former student, Ernst Weller, had written to Dr. Erding from the Russian front three years ago. The father of another, Professor Arthur Rossert, had visited him in 1942, and left his address. For some reason he had evaded all questions about his son Paul, my classmate. Of all others, Dr. Erding had lost sight at the same time I did,—in 1931.

However, his memory of every boy's background and development was still fresh. He remembered having written the character sketches for our class at graduation time. I asked him whether it would be difficult to reconstruct them. No, he said, as a matter of fact there would be no reason now to be forbearing and diplomatic about it. He would mail them to me.

Mrs. Erding was getting the kitchen stove ready for supper. She insisted that I stay to share their meal, but I convinced her that I had another appointment in Frankfurt. I left after promising to keep them informed of the results of my search.

In his first message, Obrecht reported that Harro Wegener, according to his former neighbors, was killed in the war. His wife and parents were supposed to be living in Riesbach, a tiny village in the hills south of Frankfurt and west of Aschaffenburg.

It was Sunday, and the jeep was signed out for "recreational activities". This was no pretense. To leave the devastated city for a drive through the unharmed countryside is balm for the nervous system. Even the most confirmed cynic, who takes no interest in Germany, and has enough points to leave for the States the next day, will admit this.

The contrast is fantastic. I breathed more freely and regained some of my natural optimism as I left the last craters in the suburban parks of Frankfurt behind me. The farm country south of Frankfurt is not rich. Farm houses are old, not large, not in very good repair. Roads are narrow and bad. The people, even in their Sunday best, do not give the impression of wealth, as in other parts of Germany. But still—these people, living on the land, had maintained the basis and the meaning of their existence. Even after having lost history's most destructive war, they appeared to be better off than the French farmer in the Argonne, for instance.

Driving through a village, the eye involuntarily seeks evidence of destruction. I finally found a ruin—part of the medieval fortifications assaulted and taken by storm perhaps in the Thirty Years War and probably never rebuilt.

Across the street a ruddy-cheeked, pipe-smoking farmer sat on a chair outside his house contemplating the world. I asked him for directions to Riesbach. His description was somewhat complicated, except for his opinion that I'd never get through the mud. How were things in the village, I asked? All right, he said, they hadn't changed much in the last 50 years that he could remember. Only the foreigners were troublesome. They came through the village in bands at night, stealing and robbing. But the local policeman now had a weapon issued to him by the Americans, perhaps he could stop them. The village was short of horses and fuel to bring in the crops, he said, but they'd somehow manage. He was upset over the plans' people were talking about of settling thousands of German refugees from the east in the Kreis. There wasn't any room for them. People evacuated from the cities during the war had already taken all the extra space.

The farmer's prediction notwithstanding, the jeep negotiated the mired roads gloriously. In most of our German territory, the sight of this miracle vehicle causes the population only to run for cover, not to wonder. In Riesbach, however, it still seemed to be a novelty. A dozen open-mouthed youths quickly surrounded the jeep, dropping their jaws a little further, when I talked to them in their own German dialect. A boy eagerly volunteered to show me the way to the house where the Wegener's lived. He directed me up a near-90 degree hill, alternately over cobblestones and through mired farm yards. The jeep roared in low gear, with the four-wheel drive also in low. Ferocious dogs, straining their chains, barked themselves hoarse; geese and pigs scattered at top speed; all windows of all the miniature, timbered houses became alive with all the inhabitants' faces;—the jeep seemed to sense that the prestige of the United States as a world power was at stake, and made the hill.

Meanwhile, my navigator told me about the Wegeners. They were city people who didn't really belong here. Refugees, he said disdainfully. Thought they were too good for hard farm work. They had lived here only two years, and the sooner they went back where they came from, the better.

The Wegeners lived in a villa just outside the village. The house was larger, and of better construction than the farmers' houses, hidden in shrubbery in a big garden. It was probably built by a retired official or businessman who had chosen Riesbach, away from the worries of the world, as a place to spend the rest of his days.

I dismissed my pilot with a stick of chewing gum. He turned it up and down, not knowing what to do with it. After six months of American occupation, I thought. These were the back woods all right.

The bell at the entrance was out of order. Through the window next to the door, I heard a rattling of pots and pans. I put on an undertaker's expression, ready to face the widow of Harro Wegener.

A young, blonde German beauty, with a child on her arm, opened the door and eyed me suspiciously.

"Are you Mrs. Wegener?"

"Yes."

"Mrs. Harro Wegener?"

"Yes."

"May I talk to you about your husband?"

She showed me into a large bedroom which was crammed with enough furniture for three rooms. Clothes and bags were spread over the beds, tables and easy chairs. We climbed around one table loaded with toys, and found two empty chairs.

"What about my husband?" she asked.

"Well, I went to school with him 15 years ago, and I heard he was killed in the war."

"Oh no," she said. "Harro was never in the war. Perhaps you are looking for one of his brothers. They were both killed on the Russian front."

Then we straightened out her husband's and my identity by the years we had spent at the Ebert school together. She had met some of our other classmates at Marburg University, where both she and Harro had both studied.

I apologized for the mix-up. She was not offended—how had I found my way into this wilderness? I told her about the boy who had shown me the way, and about his remarks concerning the Wegeners.

"Yes," she said. "The villagers are not too friendly. As a matter of fact, we have to move to another house now. We'll have even less room there. It's a problem how to move our things. We rescued all this furniture from Frankfurt when we evacuated two years ago. It was a good thing—our house was destroyed a few months later. Now all we can do with the furniture is to barter it to the farmers for food. I wish we could move back to town. But Harro hasn't found an apartment yet."

I asked her where he was. He was a doctor, she said, at a tuberculosis hospital north of Frankfurt. He had worked there for several years now, and all this time he could come to see them only for a day or two every other week.

"Could you help him find a place for us, perhaps?" she asked. "Americans are so powerful these days. And I'd like so much to join him with the children."

A girl of about five with blonde pigtails came into the room. She curtsied when her mother told her to. The boy whom Mrs. Wegener had been carrying was about a year younger. He came over to me also to bow. Their mother excused herself—the milk was boiling over outside. I talked to the children.

The boy confided that mommy had told him he shouldn't say Heil Hitler any more. I asked him why.

"That's forbidden now," he said. "Our Führer is dead."

His sister blushed, put her hand over her mouth and ran out, probably to tell mother all about it. When Mrs. Wegener returned, I repeated her son's words laughingly. She seemed embarrassed. Perhaps she felt that her son had disturbed the family's denazification program. I asked her jokingly at how early an age she had taught her children to say "Heil Hitler". But she saw no joke in the question:

"I had to teach them early. After all, I was a Führerin in the Bund Deutscher Mädel."

That was the organization best known for its supply of unwed mothers to the SS. She insisted that this was a terrible exaggeration. The organization had other functions too. She had stuck to her post there only because she felt that in a small way she could maintain the morale and morals of the girls under her. She said that she had always disagreed with the extreme Himmler policies which were imposed only by a minority of brutal women who had positions of leadership.

"Harro and I were idealists. We were young, and what Hitler wanted seemed so beautiful for Germany," she said. "And who would have thought it could end this way?"

I found out from her that the road through Aschaffenburg was not as muddy as the one over which I had come. I left her and the children promising to visit Harro soon.

As I approached Aschaffenburg, relief at having escaped destruction for a while ended. A wrecked factory in the outskirts showed the way. Rusty scrap littered the yard. Twisted, rusted steel girders, which once supported the roof, pointed aimlessly at the sky. So did a heavy anti-aircraft gun a few hundred yards down the road. Children were playing with it. The town itself, dead as it seemed, was teaming with people. They hurried through its naked streets, carrying bundles of wood, pulling handcarts—always picking up things: a few lumps of coal dropped from a truck; a GI's cigarette butt; horse manure.

Who would have thought it could end this way?

"Friedrich Liedecke never really became a member of the class community which he entered late. A severe physical handicap (clubfoot) excluded him from athletic activities, and became decisive for the development of mind and character. He became abnormally sensitive, taking offense even at a casual glance in the direction of his withered leg. At the same time, he forced his body to performances only normal boys should have undertaken, refusing all consideration given him in view of his handicap. In the few contacts I had with his home, I gained the impression that here lay the main guilt for Friedrich's inability to find mental balance. His father was a typical middle-class civil servant, tyrant of his family. Friedrich's physical inferiority complex must have been reinforced by miseducation in his early childhood. An eccentric, disorderly, unharmonic character was thus formed, which fought incessantly for success and recognition. But his attitude remained hostile, even when he obtained the applause he craved.

In spite of his talent and remarkable energies, I am pessimistic about Liedecke's future course. He will feel compelled to compensate for the sufferings in his youth in some field in which he can find full expression and recognition. His mental development reminds of Lord Byron and Wilhelm II,—or Goebbels."

_____

Erding

October 23, 1945

O brecht traced Friedrich Liedecke's parents to Bad Soden, a small, slightly disused spa in the foot hills of the Taunus mountains north of Frankfurt. It took less than half an hour to get there by jeep.

It was evening, and the town hall offices were closed. I found a policeman on duty at the station who procured the key to the registration office. There was a card index of all inhabitants. Yes, the Liedecke's had lived here since March, 1944, probably after the bombing of Frankfurt. Friedrich Liedecke? No, he was not listed.

I drove to the address the policeman gave me through a park of tall oaks. It boasted fountains, statues, and a music shell where, two wars ago, military bands had entertained officers of the Imperial German Army, their ladies, and ailing, well-to-do burghers of the City of Frankfurt. Not even their ghosts enlivened the neighborhood. Bad Soden's warm springs, for the time being, went to waste.

Lights were burning on the second floor of the medium-sized apartment house where the Liedecke's were supposed to be living. The gate downstairs was locked, and for a while there was no answer to the bell. Then a gray-haired woman opened the window and wanted to know who was there.

It was Mrs. Liedecke. Considerable loud-voiced conservation took place between window and gate until I could persuade her to let me talk to her inside. She hesitated again when she came to the gate and noticed my uniform.

"An American?" she said. "I didn't know Friedrich had gone to school with any Americans."

Mrs. Liedecke had been engaged in roasting barley. There was a strong smell slightly reminiscent of coffee when I entered the apartment. She led me to a large, sparsely furnished room. A heatless stove stood in a corner, making the room appear even colder than it was.

"You're looking for Friedrich?" Mrs. Liedecke asked. "He is missing. He last wrote to us from Danzig. The letter was dated February 20, 1945. Since then we've had no word."

During the whole conversation which followed about her missing son, Mrs. Liedecke, a haggard, bent woman of about 65, never once dropped a kindly smile from her face. I don't believe it was a mask. There had been so much tragedy in her family, among her children and grand-children, that she seemed inured to it—perhaps even unable to show outward emotion. That's not uncommon in Germany and all of Europe today. Apparently, people can shed tears over just so much.

According to his mother, Friedrich Liedecke had become a librarian. He was afflicted with a club foot—a handicap which had its psychological effects in school days. Most of us made efforts not to notice it. He was a quiet fellow, studious, but not arrogantly so, greatly interested in his Lutheran faith. I had taken it for granted that he would study for the Ministry.

Mrs. Liedecke said, however, that Friedrich was afraid of it, because of his handicap. He did not want to limp up to the altar to preach—he always saw that picture before him. For the same reason, he did not want to become a teacher, a profession which would have been his second choice. He studied philology and went to a library school. After a year as a librarian at the Frankfurt City Library, he accepted a post in Berlin, and a few years later became chief librarian for the City of Danzig.

Was Friedrich an adherent of National-Socialism?

Mrs. Liedecke did not change the smiling expression on her face, but she hesitated a little. Perhaps she thought I had come for a political investigation.

"Yes," she finally said. "He was a member of the party. He joined it early—in 1932, I think. He was a great idealist. But as time went on, and certainly toward the end, he became quite bitter about it. Sometimes in his letters he wrote of the iron brooms that would be needed after we had won the war, to cleanse the party."

Friedrich married a Berlin girl—a teacher—with whom he had two children, the older one now six. It was an unhappy marriage, and had it not been for the catastrophic events in Eastern Germany early this year, he would have pushed his divorce. Mrs. Liedecke had just received word by mail that her daughter-in-law and the two children were safe in Schweswig-Holstein;—British occupied territory. They had fled on board a German minesweeper in February from Gotenhafen—the Polish-built Baltic port known as Gdynia before 1939, and after 1945.

And Friedrich?

Mrs. Liedecke shrugged her shoulders almost imperceptibly. When the Russians unleashed their fatal offensive in January, she said, the job of Chief Librarian in Danzig was not so important any more. Friedrich, according to his letters, took over the job of caring for the refugees which were streaming west by the hundred thousands to escape the dreaded Red Army. He wrote that he would stay as long as anything could be done for these people. He also told his parents to remain at home, no matter what army overran them. The misery he saw, he wrote, especially where old people and children were concerned, was frightful.

"What do you believe happened to him?" I asked.

"He must have perished. Some refugees say that all party members were driven east by the Russians. I don't know. But I'm sure he isn't alive today."

She took a family picture off the wall. It showed two couples and five children. I recognized one of the men as Friedrich. The other was in uniform—a German first lieutenant.

"My other son," Mrs. Liedecke said. "He came back here from a prisoner camp a few weeks ago. But he couldn't stand just sitting idly as long as he had no news about his wife and his three children. They're all in this picture. These are Friedrich's, and these are Wilhelm's. Wilhelm had evacuated his family from Berlin to Pomerania. We have heard nothing from them since January. I don't know how he'll get through the Russian zone and what he'll eat. But he just had to go."

"Have you some of Friedrich's letters?" I inquired.

"Oh yes," she said. "The house is full of them."

I asked her to be kind enough to pick some out for me which would reflect his ideas about Germany and the war. She promised to do that, but it would take her a few days because the room was so cold, the letters were in such disorder, and her eyesight was getting worse. Perhaps her husband could help her.

"Where is your husband," I asked.

"He went to see the doctor about his wound. The day the Americans came to Bad Soden, he was injured by the only artillery shell that was fired on the town. A fragment hit in the back. Gave him something else to complain about."

I expressed my sympathies and asked how long they had lived in Bad Soden.

"Ever since we were bombed out in Frankfurt. We lost everything in the great terror attack. We had to borrow these things here"—and she pointed at a china closet, a couch, a table and chairs. "All we have is my husband's small pension. He was a post office, director, you know. If we have to care for our sons' five children, I don't know what's to become of us." She was still wearing her smile.

I thanked Mrs. Liedecke for the trouble she was taking with Friedrich's letters, and said I would return in a few days.

Former post office director Liedecke seemed to expect me when I came to visit his wife again. She was sick in bed, but he did not appear to be very concerned. He said that all women always had something wrong with them.

Friedrich's father was close to 70. He was slightly cross-eyed, wore thick glasses, a once-stiff collar, a threadbare suit, and a head of grey close-cropped hair. Hollywood would have cast him as the typical, narrow-minded, pensioned low-level German bureaucrat—exactly what he was.

I needed no long political conversation with this man to know his views. As amiable as he now was, as interested as he appeared in the fact that I was engaged in finding old school "friends", I knew him and his type as the main support of Nazi rule. All he had to say were a few apologies:—nobody would have thought that the Nazis were such a band of gangsters as it now turned out;—weren't their original principles something quite admirable?—didn't they really abolish unemployment as promised?—and so on. The man's mental limitations were written on his face. I would have lost my temper talking to him. I disliked him intensely.

I asked him for some of Friedrich's letters. He went to see his wife, and returned with three sheets of paper. The letters were dated sometime in 1943. Not one of them contained as much as a hint that Friedrich had a political opinion. All they dealt with were family problems: the food situation, the difficulties of moving furniture, what birthday gifts he had presented his children, and the like. Not a word about "iron brooms" with which to clean out the party after the war was won, or any of the other things Mrs. Liedecke had told me her son had written to her.

Friedrich's father said that there were so many letters all over the house that Mrs. Liedecke had trouble, especially with her bad eyesight, picking out the ones I wanted, but he thought these were fairly typical. It was obvious that they had very carefully searched for some letters which would not give away Friedrich's ideas.

Next day I went to see Harro Wegener at his hospital. He and Friedrich Liedecke used to be friends at school, and I wondered whether they had remained in contact with each other. Yes, said Wegener, as a matter of fact he still had some letters from Friedrich.

Friedrich's letters to Harro were somewhat more revealing. They were written in Danzig, dated July 1943, Oct. 1943, and August 1944. The occasions were birthday greetings, or replies to Harro's best wishes. This is what I found in the letter of July 29, 1943, written four days after the ouster of Mussolini in Italy.

".... you picked a damn hot time for your birthday. Old Europe is fighting a desperate battle. Militarily, the air war seems to be decisive. They are trying to soften us up for negotiations. That means that in spite of all the suffering and destruction, we must above all be invincible from the air. My special hopes in this respect are with our old home town—Frankfurt. Other things that depress the soul these days can hardly be put on paper. It is good that our convictions provide us with an indestructible counter-balance against paralysing insight; against occasional bombshells, as the explosion of fascism from within and under the bomb terror; and against other depressing thoughts. Let us dedicate ourselves to these convictions, for better or for worse, and maintain our hopes. ..."

The next letter, dated Oct. 20, 1943, was written after an air raid on Frankfurt. (However, the 800-plane RAF raid which destroyed the inner town did not take place until March 22, 1944.)

"From a distance I have lived painfully through the destruction of our home town. In my heart, I have drawn consequences from it which do not even leave the egg shells of our strongly English-Western-Cosmopolitan-infected education at school. I believe that you too have discovered that these raids strengthen our will to resist, and increase our deeply rooted confidence in victory. In spite of it, and now all the more ... ... Perhaps they'll take me into the anti-aircraft home guard (Heimatflak). ..."

The last letter Harro received from his friend Friedrich was written on August 8, 1944.

"... I had little time to write, because the people are being mobilized for the security of the fatherland, over and above the requirements of total war. 200,000 men between 15 and 65 years of age will dig fortifications at important points of the eastern borderlands. All other activities are being cut to 80% to achieve this. I volunteered twice, but so far I have been ordered to remain in Danzig. Instead I have offered my service to the anti-aircraft home guard. Thus, literally the living force of our people will be committed for the protection of the homeland—and we shall never give way. . . . I shall not abandon myself to personal pessimism. But if death is to come, there remains, beyond life and death, my testament: We shall be victorious in the end, and all who love me should never lose this faith. You will understand me correctly if I ask you to tell this to my parents if it becomes necessary. With you I shall always remain united by the ties of our common ideals . . ."

It is said that the Russians wasted little time on Germans with Friedrich Liedecke's ideals.

"Harro Wegener is the typical son of a higher official's large family. He saw self-control and discipline as examples before him. An early, strong sense of duty and responsibility reduced the freedom of his development. Emotionally, his happy family life brought about a certain softness, and a need for affection. His intelligence was above average, but remained unobstrusive. Wegener developed characteristics of introversion, because he realized that his conscious, reasoned self-control was frustrating him."

Erding

Harro Wegener's hospital for tuberculars was located near Königstein. A friend, an American civilian girl employed by Military Government, accompanied me on this trip. She had worked for a newspaper at home and the human aspect of the occupation interested her intensely. Outside the I.G. Farben building which was her headquarters, and the large barbed wire enclosure which houses US personnel, she had seen little of Germany and met few Germans. Her knowledge of the German language was only fair, and she was too self-conscious to put it to the test all by herself.

A fog spread over the valley as the jeep climbed the straight, steep road into the wooded mountains. We passed the crest, leaving the fog behind us. Ahead lay the village of Königstein, topped by its ancient castle, in ruins for the past 250 years—a thoroughly pleasant-looking ruin for that reason. Beyond rose the pine-covered Feldberg. The view of Königstein's clustered old houses, nestling below, was marred by a large stone barracks directly before us. We drove into the town and stopped for directions to the hospital. Only the fourth person we asked could tell us. The others were "strangers here themselves",— evacuees from the city.

Leaving the village, we reached the hills. The leaves had fallen, spreading a dirty-brown carpet through the woods. Fall in Germany is not as colorful a spectacle as in New England.

Now the fog had lifted in the valley also. From the road we enjoyed a splendid view over the meadows gently sloping toward the city of Frankfurt. I remembered this view from childhood days: The silver band of the Main river stretched along the distance; the low rolling hills beyond it; the chimneys of the industries in the suburb of Höchst; the silhouette of the tall buildings of Frankfurt:—opera house, theater, cathedral, churches. The picture really had not changed. From the distance, through the haze, the destruction was invisible. But my mind did not let me forget the missing element: the shell of the gutted opera house, the burnt-out cathedral, the destroyed theater, the empty walls, the mountains of rubble.

Nor could I enjoy the view without being conscious of the ruined and decayed minds belonging to the men and women who brought this collapse upon themselves,—ruins which would be harder to rebuild than the physical ones; ruins which, seen from the distance, obscured by the haze of superficial personal appearance and studied good behavior, were not easily discernible.

We drove along slowly. I spoke to my friend about the direct connection I saw between the decay of a people's mind which accepted anti-civilized, anti-western, anti-Christian Nazism, and the physical end of a civilization which therefore no longer belonged to them. She listened with interest and exclaimed over the enchanting view.

We found the hospital on the side of a wooded hill, overlooking the valley. It was a large, modern brick building, with wide enclosed terraces facing south. A young nurse at the entrance said she would call Dr. Wegener.

Through immaculate corridors, we walked into the waiting room. After our cold jeep ride, we were glad to find it heated. Hospitals are among the very few German buildings which have coal this winter.

Dr. Harro Wegener came in. He had heard from his wife that I was looking for him, and was not surprised to see me. He wore a white doctor's uniform, a stethoscope appropriately emerging from his coat pocket. He was one of the few men whom I would have recognized anywhere after this long time. His sharp, pale features underlined his gaunt 6 ft. 6 frame, and his friendly personality expressed itself in a soft, warm voice. I recalled him as a quiet, unobtrusive boy, with an amiable sense of humor, and a consuming interest in the affairs of the former German colony of South-West Africa.

Harro took us to his room. He was on duty, and he notified the telephone operator where he could be reached. The room was almost as cluttered with furniture as his wife's in Riesbach. This, he said, was the more presentable part of his former household in Frankfurt. There were easy chairs, a couch, a modern and an antique desk, two or three lamps. The arrangement reminded me of a furniture store at home. Pictures of South-West Africa adorned the walls. His interest in that country had apparently not lessened. I asked him whether he had ever been there.

"Twice," he said. "I was born there, but my parents brought me to Germany shortly before war broke out in 1914, when I was a year old. Then, after we graduated in 1931, I started to study dentistry. After one semester at the university, I took the boat to South-West Africa. My uncle still lives there."

At the end of the first World War, the former German colony had become part of the Union of South-Africa. Harro still talked about it as an English colonial would about Rhodesia.

He invited us to sit down and apologized that he had no wine to serve us. I offered him a cigarette, but he refused. The room needed airing badly. It was loaded with a sweetish smell as though it had been slept in for a week with all windows shut. With Harro declining, I put the cigarettes away again. My friend, comfortably settled in a club chair, probably felt as strongly as I did that the air needed a change, if not an improvement, and smoked. She observed us in turn, ready for whatever fireworks might develop.

Harro spoke of his South-African trip. He stayed with his uncle for four months and toured as much of the territory as he could. He would have liked to stay and settle, but decided to complete his dentistry studies first. Returning to Germany, he found that he had contracted a stomach ailment. This delayed his studies and later kept him out of the army.

After obtaining his degree in 1937, Harro became an assistant to a number of dentists. Then the war came. The Germans decided they did not have enough physicians to carry them through, and offered dentists an opportunity to continue medical studies. Harro took advantage of the offer.

Wegener began to specialize in the problems of tuberculosis at medical school. In the course of a research project he contracted a lung disease. This made his physical unfitness for army service final, and after obtaining his doctor's degree in 1942, he joined the staff of the hospital at which we were now visiting him.

This brought me up to date on the external course of Harro's life since we graduated. His ambitions and ideas during that period, however, were more intriguing. I picked these up where I had left them 14 years ago—Germany's colonies. He had been an ardent proponent of the theory that Germany was entitled to a colonial empire just as much as other western nations, that she needed raw materials and markets there, that she had a right to a place in the sun, and that the Allies had unlawfully stolen Germany's overseas possessions after the last war.

He only smiled when I reminded him of his former opinions.

"You're rubbing it in," he said. "After all, we've just lost another world war, and I assure you our national ambitions have been toned down. We don't ever want to see Germany become a powerful nation again. Give us some sort of economic unity, and then let us live like the Swiss or the Swedes. They haven't any world power, and live very well just the same."

However, he added, if he were healthy enough, he would still like to go to South-Africa and become a loyal South-African citizen. Germany, he thought, was finished.

With his tall bones sprawled over an arm chair and a couch, he talked about the war. He had the air of detachment and objectivity of the non-participant. Anyhow, he said, he had opposed war. That is why he chose a very remarkable period in Nazi history to join the party—the week between the conclusion of the German-Russian non-aggression treaty, and the outbreak of war—the last week of August, 1939.

Personal recollection of that week flashed through my mind. I was then working for a newsmagazine in New York. When the news of the Nazi-Soviet pact came over the teletype on August 21, the world and its hopes seemed to crumble. Our writers and researchers looked pale and bitter. Hardly a word was said. Everyone worked furiously. The lights of peace were dimming. It was a more dramatic moment than their extinction ten days later. At first the Germans alone made the announcement, and some hope remained that Moscow would deny the story. Then confirmation came. The Communist Daily Worker was baffled, then switched to a triumphant "anti-imperialist" line. The day it performed this prize somersault, a friend sailed for Europe on a State Department assignment. We knew, looking over the day's papers in his cabin, that when his ship would dock across the Atlantic, the continent would be at war. Would Russia participate in the assault on the west?

It was during this frightful, blackest week, that Harro Wegener made up his mind to join the National-Socialist party. There were his reasons:

"Until the Russian pact was concluded ," he said, "I was afraid Hitler was driving us into war. Then this non-aggression treaty was signed. With one stroke, all of Germany's national aims seemed assured,—and without war. After all, what could the British do now? We felt sure the Poles would give up without a struggle, and the British would stand by as they did when we took Czechoslovakia. I talked the situation over with my father. He influenced me to join the party. Germany's world position, he told me, was now established. She owed this position to the masterful diplomacy of the National-Socialist party. We could express our gratitude only by becoming members. Well, after this conversation, my father and I both applied for membership. I was accepted, but his application was rejected because of his age. Today, I'm in difficulties, while he enjoys the privileges of those who never joined the party."

"The war came just the same," Harro continued calmly, "and that was a bitter blow. Father and I for a while thought of withdrawing our membership applications, but that would have been a dangerous thing to do. Then came the blitz campaigns of 1940, and the war seemed won. We were again convinced that Hitler's policies were right. But right or wrong, we were committed to them, and from then on we firmly believed in victory."

I asked Harro when he began to lose his optimistic outlook.

"Not until our troops were driven clear out of Russia," he said. "I knew from friends that there was a great deal of truth to the propaganda about secret weapons, and that some world-shaking invention was really in the making. As long as our own territory was intact, I thought we could still reverse the fate of war."

"Supposing you would have developed an atom bomb," I said, "would you have advocated its use on England for instance?"

"Of course," he answered. "It would have been the one means to give us victory. You used the bomb over Japan although you yourselves admit that you had victory practically in your hands. How much more would have been justified in using it, at a time when we were in danger of losing the struggle. Besides, I think, one or two bombs would have sufficed to end the war."

For a man who opposed war as such, I objected, the point was a little brutal. But he overruled this. War was war, and it was only natural that the German nation would have wanted to win it.

He used the customary superficial nationalistic trick of identifying his personal convictions with what he considered should be the people's collective aims. I made the point that by no means all Germans wanted to win the war, and that I had met many who had feared German victory more than German defeat.

Wegener seemed to dislike the idea. Outside, the afternoon was wearing on. Harro got up, climbed over the couch, and lit a desk lamp. It left most of the room in darkness. When he was settled again, he was thoughtful and deliberate.

"I'm afraid you are right," he said. "As a matter of fact, I don't believe there is another modern nation with such a lack of genuine national feeling as the German. The only Germans who really appreciate their fatherland are the ones who live overseas."

Although he had only four months in South Africa in which to form this feeling, it was a point which intrigued me. It was a good explanation for the ease with which Nazism could develop its fifth column. But if there was a lack of strong national sentiment inside Germany, what accounted for the forceful hold extreme nationalism took on the people?

"You shouldn't confuse extreme nationalism with genuine national sentiment," Harro answered. "The propaganda to which we were exposed was very clever. It said we were a superior people, destined to rule other countries. It promised us the good things of life, with Lebensraum to develop and expand our race and build our new world. That was nationalism. It also proclaimed, because the world denied these claims to us, that we had to go ahead by force. That was extreme. But supposing you had offered a simple German worker an opportunity to take his family to the United States, or to South America, or Canada, and there to work out his own life, he would have gone. That was a lack of national sentiment."

"What was your own attitude toward extreme nationalism?" I asked Harro.

"I'll come to that," he said. Then he pointed at the three letters from Friedrich Liedecke on the table, which he had extracted from the desk for me. "There is a man who had national sentiment, was convinced of our nationalistic aims, and went his way to the end. But I think there are only a few like him. You'll find his type in the middle class, among teachers and officials and educated people of small means. But for the masses,—look around. German women prefer American soldiers. The Werwolf was a complete failure. At least, I haven't heard of any subversive acts yet of the type we Germans encountered all over Europe. Nationalism should manifest itself most strongly when the country is under foreign occupation shouldn't it? Well, I ask you, where is it? Frankly, I'm ashamed of my people, especially of our women. But I'm glad we have peace and quiet."

"If sincere national sentiment is really that weak a part of the German character," I asked, "What was it that made the people so willing to support the Nazis?"

Wegener said he would answer that for himself.

"To be entirely frank with you: My reasons were purely materialistic. First, I hoped we would regain our colonies, because I wanted to go there. Then, the Nazi party program encouraged the family. I married six years ago. Without financial assistance, I could neither have married, nor raised children. After all, I was still in medical school. But even after a doctor had completed his university work, he had a terrific struggle to keep above water, as long as he had not made a name for himself. Our government recognized this. So, in 1943, it decreed a substantial raise to young doctors. There could have been no stronger argument for us to support the party and the war. This war seemed to be our only chance. After the last one, we had one economic depression after another. As soon as the party came to power, the situation improved. Our unemployment slowly disappeared. Our standard of living rose. People earned more, spent more, lived better. They raised families. That's always a sign of optimism. I think this is where you have to look for the reasons why the people supported the Nazi regime, not in the official nationalistic speeches and pamphlets. We were lied to, of course. Today we're aware of it. The propaganda was really excellent."

In part, Wegener's theory made sense. He only confused the excellence of the propaganda with the blind pleasure with which the German masses, he included, had swallowed it.

"Was your propaganda so excellent," I asked, "that you could overlook the by-products of your materialistic nationalism—the concentration camps, the slaughter of millions of human beings, the abolition of justice?"

"It's funny," he said. "You Americans always think we had been taken on weekly conducted tours through our concentration camps. We knew we had them, of course. But I swear to God that all I knew about them, was that they were places where critics of our national aims were kept for a few months at hard labor to cool off. Those who came out of the camps after their term was completed never said a word about them."

"You did know, though, that justice and human rights were abolished?"

"Yes, I did. That was only natural in war. And we were in sort of a state of war ever since 1933."

"Supposing," I said, "in view of your political reliability, the Nazis had given you a medical job at, say, Auschwitz, and you would have become a witness to the extermination there. Can you say how that would have affected you?"

"I think, I can," he said. "There would have been nothing I could have done. I was a little man in an enormous machine. I would have been a little man in such a terrible situation. Besides I could not have taken the risk to speak up. My family comes first."

At the mention of Auschwitz, my friend in her club chair perked up. Still, she continued to observe us quietly.

Wegener had been very serious. I said that his frankness impressed me. He smiled:

"In everything you Americans do and say about Germany," he said, "you simply forget that a man's instinct for self-preservation is still his strongest motive."

Clearly, I told him, the instinct of self-preservation had not played a role when Germans eagerly snapped the Nazi bait of a better life, in return for their acquiescence to a rule of injustice, blackmail, robbery and murder. He shrugged and looked at me as he would, as a doctor, at a hopelessly ill patient, beyond the pale of help. "You don't want to understand us," he said. That point of our discussion was closed.

I asked him some questions about the health situation in Germany. He did not believe that tuberculosis was getting out of hand. If present rations in the US zone of occupation could be maintained, he did not expect a catastrophic increase in the number of cases. And he did not believe that our well-fed American troops were in danger of being infected.

Then he turned to more personal, more pressing problems.

"We had an American investigation commission here last month," he said. "They talked to all our doctors. I could prove to their satisfaction that I was not a party activist, just a nominal member, and so they gave me a temporary license to practice at a common laborer's pay. But our chief physician, a great lung specialist, was deprived of his license by the commission. We found him dead in the woods out here two days later. He had given himself a morphine injection. The man had joined us only in June this year. The Russians killed our previous head physician."

I asked how that happened.

"It may have been revenge," Harro said. "We employed Russian help at the hospital. German help was rare, you know. This head physician of ours was not too kind to the foreigners. A few weeks after the Americans arrived, he was sitting one evening on the porch of his house across the street over there, with one of his assistants. Suddenly five armed Russians came up. They yelled: Hands up. The assistant physician raised his hands and was not harmed. But the chief tried to reach the house. He slipped through the front door and slammed it. One of the Russians fired a burst from his machine pistol through the door and killed him as he was trying to run upstairs."

The hospital was now running without a head physician, and not too badly, Harro proudly admitted.

He suddenly became serious. Taking his long legs off the couch, he bent forward toward me.

"Look," he said, "you're with the Americans now, maybe you can help me. He smiled: out in this mess. I can't live on this ridiculous salary they pay me now. I owe a decent living to my wife and children. Do you think they'll hold this party membership business against me for the rest of my life?"

I checked my desire to give him a plain, affirmative answer. The need for doctors in his specialty was now only too obvious, I said, and he should be patient about the reward. But he was not quite satisfied:

"The head of the commission was an American captain,—Smith, I think was his name. Do you know him by any chance? Couldn't you talk to him perhaps, so I could get my full license back? You know I wasn't an activist!"

It was my turn to put on a calm and superior smile:

"Harro," I said, "you know this American military machine is a very big one. I'm only a little man in it. There isn't a thing I could do."

He looked at me sheepishly, without, on the surface, taking offense.

My friend and I rose to leave. He politely conducted us through the hospital corridors into the night outside, to our jeep.

"Be careful when you back out of this driveway," he said as the engine started. "The road is very steep there. And do come back, won't you, when I move my family here. My wife and I would so much like to talk to you again. We'll leave out all that unpleasant politics then. You used to like to ski, didn't you? We'll have to show you our mountain pictures. We never missed a winter's skiing, not even the last one. Auf wiedersehen."

My American friend seemed thoughtful as we drove off.

"What a charming person," she said. "I'm so sorry I didn't get the full drift of the conversation. I really must learn German better. You got a little excited there, didn't you? And why did you have to bring Auschwitz into it? After all, he really had nothing to do with it, did he?"

"Wilhelm Recht is the only child of wealthy parents, born after 19 years of a childless marriage. Even as a boy, he showed traits of senility: he was surly and ill at ease, always suspicious of his surroundings which, he thought, infamously opposed his every step. He used his better-than-average intelligence to defeat this imaginary opposition by indirect, deviously clever means. Without a sense of humor, he lacked the playful freshness and unconcern of the healthy child. He was reliable and conscientious, but stubbornly opinionated and hard to convince. His actions were always carefully calculated, never impulsive.

Most repugnant to Recht's comrades was his caustic malice, a consequence not of a spoiled character, but of his senile view of the world. He is an asocial egoist who, with excessive prudence, intends to save and secure his own position."

Erding

The story of Wilhelm Recht is rather confused. I pieced it together from a visit to a police station, two to Recht's wife, and one to the prisoner of war camp from which he went AWOL during the last week of October. I did not find him.

According to Obrecht, Recht had been living as a physician at a small spa in the hills east of Frankfurt, Bad Orb, where carbonic brine springs reputedly relieve the pains of rheumatic sufferers. A duty trip on November 1 to a Bavarian headquarters gave me a first opportunity to inquire after Recht. It was noon as our olive drab, comfortable staff car reached the quiet, old town, and the colonel with whom I was travelling, was hungry. I left him at the sprawling, modern Kurhaus, where the Second Armored Division had set up its officers' mess.

My first stop was the town hall. Either the Bürgermeister's office, or the police would have Recht's present address. Across the street from the dignified, old building, a modern café had been converted into a Red Cross club. Hot jive was pouring over the square from an amplifier, reverberating from the surrounding hills. GIs were holding a beginners' baseball lesson in the parking lot for the benefit of half a dozen hot-cheeked, enthusiastic German boys.

The police station was alive with a loud argument as I entered. It was interrupted by an elderly, fat man with a Wilhelm II style moustache who rose from behind the largest desk in the spacious room. With a bass beer voice, he introduced himself as the Chief of Police. When I asked whether he had any information on Wilhelm Recht, he had everybody except one other police official leave the room. Secrecy was thus assured, although the Chief's gesture was undoubtedly more useful as a device to impress his subordinates and visitors.

When the room was clear, the Chief accepted a cigarette. He sat pompously behind his desk and told me in a hushed voice that the forces under his command had orders to arrest Wilhelm Recht, American prisoner of war, on sight. Another American officer, the commander of a prisoner of war camp, had come to see the Chief only a few days ago. Recht had disappeared from the camp, where he had served as a camp doctor.

"We've talked to his wife," the Chief said. "She lives with her children up the hill in the sanatorium they used to run. She denies knowing anything about his escape. Of course, we don't believe her. If Recht shows up in this town, we'll get him."

The Chief's eagerness to get Recht seemed motivated by more than the fact that Wilhelm had escaped from an American prisoner of war camp. I asked him about Recht's politics.

From school days I remembered that this quiet, rather fat, lethargic, unathletic man had developed Communist tendencies. He came from a wealthy family with which he never got along, and we usually considered his Communism a reaction to his home life. He very rarely talked about it, except for some rather abstruse, cryptic remarks during political arguments which often arose out of history classes. The details of his attitude then I cannot recall. All of us had given up making him out. He was generally disliked.

To the Chief, Recht's former Communist line came as a surprise. He thought he was a Nazi agitator. Recht had lived in Bad Orb on and off for the past 12 years, and the town had him labelled as a party activist. He had given Nazi speeches at party rallies from the very beginning of the Hitler regime, the Chief said. "That's why we're so glad to help the Americans recapture him. We can do without him in this town."

The large house where I would find Mrs. Recht, the Chief explained, was inherited by Wilhelm from his parents. He had turned it into a small sanatorium which paid him, as the doctor-owner, a nice income. The Chief took me outside to show me how to reach the place.

From a distance, the Victorian-style mansion seemed abandoned. It was surrounded by a large untidy garden, long untouched by hoe and sickle. Most windows were shuttered, and through the drizzle which had set in, the sanatorium looked like the place whence Charles Adams draws his ideas for New Yorker cartoons.

I had difficulty finding the entrance, when a part pigtailed girl of about ten who could have doubled for Margaret O'Brien, came out of a side-gate with a small milk can. She explained that I had to walk around the house to the little door in back, because the front door was nailed shut. Her name was Ilse Recht, she answered to my questions, and her mother was in the house. Her two younger brothers were inside too. She was only going for some milk.

I found Mrs. Recht mopping the floor. She was around thirty. Her thick glasses hid an intelligent but drab expression. By the window, the two younger children were eating a porridge—or rather smearing it across their faces.

This was not a very convenient time for Mrs. Recht, but I was not planning to stay long. I said nothing about the escape or my visit to the Chief of Police, merely explaining how I knew her husband. Was he at home?

"No," she said. "Wilhelm is still a prisoner. His camp is near Aschaffenburg. He is a doctor there, and they won't let him go."

She did not mention his escape, or the police enquiry at her house. Nor did her behavior indicate that she might be worried about him.

"Perhaps I'll have a chance to talk to him at his camp," I suggested. She said nothing to discourage me.

She told me a few things about Wilhelm. He had studied medicine, and practised all through the war. Only in February 1945 he was called into the army as a private. Before then, he was "UK gestellt"—4F—because of his poor health. Mrs. Recht said something about a stomach disease.

Why, Mrs. Recht demanded, could he not be released from the PW cage? Almost all of our prisoners had been sent home, except her husband. I said that probably there was a shortage of doctors to attend to the needs of the German prisoners, and that therefore his services were essential. She shrugged. Why didn't they take Nazi doctors for such jobs? Her husband, she said, had never belonged to the party, and had always been against Nazism.

From a desk, Mrs. Recht pulled a sheaf of paper, carbon copies of a petition, with annexes, for her husband's release.

"I took this to Wilhelm's camp commandant two weeks ago," she said. She thumbed through the papers: "These are certificates from police authorities. I travelled to three towns to obtain them. They prove that my husband wasn't a Nazi, don't they?"

There were only two certificates, and none from Bad Orb, where, after all, they and spent most of their time under the Nazi regime. I asked her what happened at the third town.

"The Chief of Police there was a Communist," she said using the term as an invective. "He refused to give me the certificate for my husband. He was once a patient of Wilhelm. Perhaps he had personal reasons I don't know about."

About Bad Orb and the report of her husband's early Nazi activities I still said nothing. I first wanted to have more information from Wilhelm's prisoner of war camp.

The boys were still stirring and smearing the food about. As I rose to leave, Mrs. Recht made them come over to make a bow until their foreheads nearly touched their knees. She seemed relieved that I asked no further questions.

Little Ilse Recht came back with her milk can as I walked out through the garden. She curtsied and smiled like a little lady.

The following week-end I drove through the ruins of Aschaffenburg. A policeman whom I asked for directions to Recht's prisoner of war camp, said that most of the town's destruction was due not to air bombardment, but to artillery. Last-ditch Nazi resisters were responsible for it, because they attempted to defend the town against General Patton's tanks last April. There was a rumor that the Nazi officer who had given the orders to resist was an Allied prisoner. The population, said the policeman, wanted to hang him publicly amidst the ruins he had caused.

I passed the sturdy provisional bridge across the Main river "by the courtesy of the umptieth Engineers." Down the road, a slow-down campaign was under way. Signs read: "Take it easy, dammit, our hospital is full! The so & so Medical Bn."

Further along, a German sign pointed to a "Kriegagefangenenlager." It was the camp I was looking for. Apparently, the Germans had used it for Allied prisoners before we took it over.

It was a small camp, with only some twenty barracks. Prisoners were cleaning the camp street and snapped smartly to attention as I walked by toward the office. The only places where Germans can still display their best military behavior are prisoner of war camps.

A sergeant at the office explained that this camp was inhabited by wounded German prisoners who had been returned from the United States for discharge. Hence the need for doctors.

When I inquired about Recht, the sergeant said that the camp interpreter was most familiar with the case. He had him called in.

The interpreter was a German Nordic giant of Africa Corps origin who had used the time he spent in a US prison camp to study English. He pulled Recht's file from a shelf.

"I don't understand why he escaped," he said. "Perhaps he has gone crazy."

In the file was the petition I had seen in Bad Orb. It had been returned to the camp by higher headquarters with a negative decision the day before Recht escaped. The indorsement, however, said that discharges would soon take place. The interpreter showed me a list of prisoners to be discharged which included Recht's name, dated five days after the rejected petition. It had just arrived. The escape, of course, invalidated the discharge.

The rest of Recht's papers consisted of his German army identification papers, a number of printed advertising pamphlets for his sanatorium, and a medical certificate dated August 20, 1945. It said that Wilhelm Recht had fallen out of a window and suffered a fractured skull. The interpreter knew no explanation. Recht only arrived at the camp in September.

"Dr. Recht was very unpopular among the prisoners," the interpreter said.

"Why?"

"He treated about a hundred patients daily. Out of these, he had to select 20 a day whom he considered healthy enough to go on work details around the camp. They resented it. Besides, his treatment of the men was rough and unsympathetic."

Going into further detail about the escape, the interpreter recalled that there had been difficulties recently over pass privileges enjoyed by German medical personnel, including Recht. Passes which had entitled them to travel within a 30 km radius once a week had been withdrawn by the commandant when a pass holder failed to return. Next day, Recht called a meeting of his medical personnel. He sternly pointed out the urgent need for them at the camp. Escape now, he said, was comparable to desertion in time of war. It was also an intolerable abuse of the Red Cross armband which all of them were proud to wear. He, Recht, would advocate severe penalties to the American Camp Commandant in all future cases of escape.

Less than two weeks after the meeting, Recht disappeared,—Red Cross armband and all—while making an evening barracks inspection.

Nothing else was known at the camp. I left, and turned north, back to Bad Orb.

Mrs. Recht was surprised to see me again so soon. She was fixing lunch for her children. All three were sitting around the table. Little Ilse was fixing her youngest brother's napkin. I waited and looked over some two-year old German magazines with pictures of the victorious Wehrmacht in Russia.

When her children had their food, Mrs. Recht sat down with me. She tried to be greatly surprised by the news that her husband had escaped from the camp. I mentioned that this was not a very nice thing to do, since after all I was not a criminal investigator, but one of her husband's former school mates. She said that she had been suspicious the first time I had visited her, and therefore not mentioned the fact of Wilhelm's escape. Actually, it worried her very much. But she knew nothing of his whereabouts.

There was still nothing in her expression or her behavior that would indicate worry. For a woman whose husband had been gone without a trace for over a week, she was the model of self-control and unconcern. I told her about my visit to Wilhelm's camp, about the rejected petition for his release, and the fact that he would be a free man today, had he not escaped. Perhaps, I suggested, if he surrendered immediately, the camp commandant would still consider giving him his discharge. Mrs. Recht continued to insist that she had not heard or seen her husband since his escape, that she had no news from him whatsoever, and would not know how to get in touch with him to advise him.

I suffered my next defeat at the hands of self-controlled, smiling little Ilse. I asked when she had last seen her daddy. "Mommy will remember," she said politely.

"You don't believe me," Mrs. Recht said. "I took the children to see him at his camp two weeks ago. After that I received a post card from him, and that's all."

I brought up Mrs. Recht's petition again and inquired why she had not obtained a certificate from the police in Bad Orb about her husband's anti-Nazi beliefs.

"I knew they wouldn't give it to me. We're not very popular here. Wilhelm once gave some talks for the party. Nothing political, you understand, only historic. He only did it because there was no one else in town who could."

The atmosphere of our conversation was now almost hostile. Mrs. Recht seemed anxious to come to better terms. When I mentioned the certificate in her husband's file about his fall from the window, she offered a full explanation.

"It will prove to you that my husband was on the Allied side," she said.

After the German collapse, Recht, as a prisoner of war, became a doctor at a hospital for wounded German prisoners in nearby Gelnhausen. One night three prisoners escaped. They had managed to hide a motorcycle, some civilian clothes, and enough gasoline to go quite a distance. With the general confusion among zones and even different army units then prevailing, they probably would have succeeded—had it not been for Recht. He pursued them in an ambulance together with another German prisoner and caught them. On the return trip to the hospital, the ambulance collided with a truck, and Recht was injured. All five, somehow, were returned to the hospital, where Recht now became a patient. The three escapees were placed in confinement.

For a man who had given "historic" speeches at Nazi party rallies, Recht had done a strange thing. Had he been as much as a German patriot, would he have gone out of his way, far beyond the call of duty, whatever that may be in such circumstances, to apprehend these prisoners? I asked Mrs. Recht why she thought he had pursued them. She said that he wanted to prove to his American captors that he deserved their confidence.

Very soon after, Recht, in his hospital bed, began to receive threatening notes from his fellow prisoners. The three frustrated escapees let him know that they would kill him as soon as he was well again. The other German who had helped Recht in the recapture, received similar notes. One night, he escaped. Recht was very frightened.

He was so frightened that one night before he was well enough to leave the hospital, he in turn undertook an attempt to escape. His room was on the second floor. He tried to climb down by the drain pipe which ran alongside his window. However, he was too weak to hold on. He slipped and fractured his skull. This was the story of his "fall from the window."

The threatening notes, Mrs. Recht continued, then ceased. Apparently the three escapees thought Recht had been sufficiently punished. As soon as he was well enough, he applied for, and obtained, the job as camp doctor at the prisoner cage near Aschaffenburg.

Mrs. Recht's account of his stay there confirmed that of the camp interpreter. She added that again his unpopularity had earned him threats of death from his German patients.

Wilhelm's pass privilege had just been withdrawn when Mrs. Recht last visited him. He told her of an interview with the camp commandant in which he attempted to have the privilege restored. As an argument, he cited the Geneva convention (which all German prisoners of war seem to have learned by heart). The commandant, according to Mrs. Recht, said: "You're forgetting that you surrendered unconditionally," and refused. Mrs. Recht stated that her husband was badly depressed by this reply and the fact that he could no longer leave the enclosure.

"Where do you think your husband might have gone?" I asked Mrs. Recht finally.

"Perhaps to another zone", she said. "We have some relatives in the Russian zone and also in the French. I don't know where else he could have gone."

This is as much as I could find out about the fate of Wilhelm Recht. When the Nazis won in Germany instead of the Communists whose chances he had favored, he secured his position by giving speeches for the party. After the collapse, he took a swift jump and, to please the victors, turned informer against his fellow-Germans. However, the bandwagon was out of his reach, and he missed. Somewhere in the Russian or the French zone, where his background cannot be investigated, he is probably exerting himself now to please his next boss.

"Erich Ingelmann is the only child of an extremely unhappy marriage. Emotionally he was bound to his mother, but mentally, and especially artistically, his father's influence prevailed. His instability and sensitivity caused him to shut himself off from the outer world, and complicated his relationship to it. Good, but not extraordinary intelligence led him both to insecurity and arrogance. He is talented for the study of law—his father's profession—but not capable of forensic eminence. He should be the law consultant of a large concern, working in the calmness of his office.

In the last analysis, Ingelmann is lonely. He is a pronounced skeptic, not by character, but because he lacks the willpower for decisions."

———————————
Erding

Obrecht sent a triumphant note with the full and exact address of Erich Ingelmann in Weilburg an der Lahn. The Frankfurt Post Office provided it. Its files on the whereabouts of those whose homes were requisitioned by the American occupying authorities, were complete. Erich Ingelmann had lived near the I.G. Farben building in the American compound of 50-odd blocks of apartment houses which was now enclosed by barbed wire and guarded by MPs.

To by-pass some of the mountain villages with their narrow, cobblestone roads, I took Hitler's luxurious Autobahn north part of the way to Weilburg. I suddenly remembered that I had been over that stretch of Autobahn once before, early in 1938, shortly after it was completed. I was then on a short visit to Frankfurt. A Jewish businessman wanted to give me some oral messages to his son in the United States which could not be entrusted to the Gestapo-censored mails. His place of business was not safe for a confidential talk. Some of his employees were acting as Nazi party informers,—he thought they had installed a microphone in his private office. So he invited me to ride through the ear- and microphoneless countryside with him—this particular stretch of the Autobahn, to be precise.

"Isn't this a wonderful road?" he exclaimed. "I wanted you to see it. I can now drive to Berlin in seven hours. Hitler has done some remarkable things for Germany. Business is good too. People have money to spend again. If only they'd drop this anti-Jewish nonsense. After all, I'm as good a German as any of his party followers."

About a year later, his family were offered an urn with his ashes for sale by the Buchenwald concentration camp authorities. Then they left Germany.

Near Bad Nauheim, I turned off the Autobahn for the bad and winding roads through the hills to the west. A few miles out, I left the road for a look at the underground headquarters stretching in milelong corridors underneath the old Ziegenberg (Goat mountain) castle. A Frankfurt architect had told me about it. "I figured it out," he had said. "The walls are a meter thick, the ceiling three meters. We poured enough cement into that place to build 10,000 one- and two- family homes." Construction had begun in 1939, and the general rumor was then that Ziegenberg would serve as Hitler's main headquarters, the architect had said.

Four bomb-destroyed farm houses marked the entrance to the area. On a hill lay the charred ruins of the castle. Bomb craters and seared trees surrounded it. A boy of about 14 volunteered to show me around. The bombing took place, he said, less than a month before the Americans took the area. The castle and underground installations were then Kesselring's headquarters, Rundstedt's successor as commander in chief of Germany's western front. The raid took place shortly after noon while Kesselring and his staff were having lunch at the castle. "Low-flying Yabos," (fighter-bombers) the boy said with awe in his voice. "But they didn't catch Kesselring." We had walked up the hill around the craters to the castle's court. The boy showed me the heavy steel trap door through which Kesselring and his staff had ducked into the safety of the underground shelter when the bombs rained down. "How did these Americans know at what time Kesselring had lunch up there?" the boy wondered.

Of the castle, only the charred walls remained standing. A chandelier stuck out of the rubble between them. In the court two American officers were taking pictures of each other with a stone bench as a background on which the castle's emblem, a goat's head, was sculptured. There was a lovely view from the platform over the green wooded hills to the south. Looking around, there was no indication in the landscape of the underground installations.

My guide took me down from the platform over a narrow stone staircase, and then into the underground corridor. With a flashlight, we walked along it for several hundred yards. Rooms on both sides were still partly furnished. In one room, remnants of hardware supplies were lying on shelves. A lonely, modern Frigidaire stood in another. German signs pointed to a movie theater and to the signal center.

When we left the corridor through another entrance, a shepherd outside was peacefully grazing his sheep in the sun-lit fields. His dog was sniffing on an unexploded 500 lb bomb which seemed to disturb no one.

"Before the Americans came," the shepherd said, "you couldn't come within two kilometers of this place. SS and army guards everywhere, armed to the teeth. It's good grazing now. I hope you're going to hang all the bastards who made war from here. The plain folks around here always thought so."

I couldn't help challenging his last statement. The "plain folks" in that particular area were generally known as rabid Nazis even 15 years ago. "Those were the young ones," the shepherd said. "I'm 68 now. I always told them they wouldn't get away with it. God has given us his Commandments to be obeyed. Now God punishes them. They deserve it."

My guide and I walked back to the jeep. As we passed some of the innocent looking farm houses in the valley, I saw that their walls consisted of three-foot thick concrete. "This is where the Stabshelferinnen (female army clerks) lives" the boy explained near what from the outside looked like an ordinary barn. A bomb had made a dent into the concrete in one corner. "They were safe in there," the boy said. "They never cared what would happen to <u>our</u> houses. Look at them."

Birth of a legend? In time, the boy's house would be rebuilt; moss would grow through the underground corridors of Hitler's headquarters, where his generals lost their war in the west; tourists would flock to the bench with the goat's head to have their pictures taken; and the boy's stories, as he grew older, were bound to improve. Note to Mr. Baedeker: the Ziegenberg is worth three stars.

A couple of cigarettes "for his father" were what my young guide asked as a fee. I turned the jeep into the hills again, through the villages in their Sunday quiet. A funeral procession stopped me. The priest set the slow pace at the head, followed by the coffin born by top-hatted villagers. The whole town seemed to have turned out. Behind the family of the deceased walked the men, in frock coats and shiny top hats, followed by the women and children in black. The procession turned off, up the hill, to the cemetery.

Then, after a stretch of straight road through well-cultivated woodlands, I reached Weilburg. Near the ancient tower which marked the entrance to the old city, a couple taking their Sunday afternoon walk directed me to Erich Ingelmann's address. The plain, three-story house was covered with shingles all around, enough to repair many Frankfurt roofs for the winter, I thought. A woman on the ground floor directed me upstairs. There was no bell. After some knocking, an old man opened the door wide enough to talk, but not to walk through. "What do you want?" he asked in English.

I asked to see Erich Ingelmann.

"He isn't here," the old man said. "What is it you want from him?"

I explained that I came neither from the Gestapo nor from any other organization to scare either him or Erich. He growled: "You can't tell these days who comes."

A man's voice from the inside asked who was there. "An American to see you," the old man said loudly in German.

Erich Ingelmann came out. He seemed taller than 15 years ago, hunched as though he wanted to avoid hitting the low ceiling with his head. His cheeks were shrunken, and his collar was inches too wide. Gold-rimmed classes and receding blond hair gave him an intellectual expression.

He recognized me immediately and gave me a hearty welcome. "Please excuse my father-in-law," he said, "he didn't know who you were. Americans scare him as much as the Gestapo once did."

Erich took me inside, where a young woman was helping a little blond boy of about five into his overcoat. Erich introduced his wife and child. He explained that since his Frankfurt apartment had been requisitioned by the Americans, he had been living out here in Weilburg with his in-laws.

"You take the boy alone," Erich said to his wife.

"Were you planning to leave? I don't want to disturb your plans," I said.

"Well, yes, there is a theatrical company in town playing Snow White for the children. But I'd rather stay here and talk to you," Erich said.

I asked whether I may come along instead—there would still be time to talk after the performance. Surely, they said, they'd be glad to have me come.

The play was being given in a dance hall which adjoined an inn. One end of the hall had been made into a stage. Erich explained that the town's theater had been taken over by the Americans for the entertainment of their troops. The hall was already jammed when we came. It was bitterly cold. Children of all ages in their best and heaviest winter clothes were accompanied by their parents, all dressed to survive two hours of cold enjoyment.

The company's manager insisted on giving us the best seats in the house, first row. There was an advantage to this, because behind us the chairs were placed so closely together that people had their legs wedged in tightly. Only the children were comfortable.

The disadvantage of the first row was that Erich's son at this close range to the stage, could absorb few of the intended illusions. He, and probably everybody else, forgot the hall's chilling temperatures as the play unfolded. There was a minimum of scenery on the stage, all crudely improvised. The wicked queen's throne consisted of a plain arm chair placed in a wooden box, covered by a very dirty rug. The box later doubled as Snow White's coffin. "But that's no mirror," Ingelmann Jr. suddenly exclaimed loudly. The queen's hand mirror, frequently consulted to determine who was most beautiful in the land, had her speeches clearly printed on its face.

Audience reaction at the play was loud and immediate. Indignation ran high at the queen's plot to have Snow White murdered. But the play's climax came in the third act. Snow White had entered the dwarfs' house. She found it empty, with seven little plates and cups on a little table, which was surrounded by seven little collapsible air raid shelter stools. Snow White said she was awfully hungry and thirsty and felt terribly tempted to eat of the beautiful food on the seven little plates, and drink from the seven little cups. Actually, Erich's son, who had climbed on his chair, commented that there wasn't any food on the plates, only a little bread on one of them. But Snow White had qualms of conscience. "That's stealing," she said to herself, "and I shouldn't steal." The audience was in an uproar of laughter. Youngsters from all corners yelled: "Go ahead, Snow White, eat if you're hungry."

Erich's boy was dragging his mother through the narrow streets, plying her with questions about Snow White and the seven dwarfs, after we left the teeming, cheering hall. Erich and I followed and began to fill in the past 15 years for each other.

Ingelmann's father was a lawyer, member of well-known old Frankfurt family. Erich too had studied law and was admitted to the bar in 1938. Without the slightest sympathy for Nazi party ways and aims, he said, he became a party member in 1937. He had studied law for a long time, and he was unwilling to throw his efforts away to avoid "that silly formality". He could not have exercised his profession, had he not joined the party.

It was somehow easy to come to cordial terms quickly with Ingelmann. In school days, I had considered him a snob. His associations then ran toward the sons of wealthy and influential families in our class. I could detect no trace of snobbishness in him now. He was an intelligent man. He was a humanitarian:—According to several people in Frankfurt, he and his family had proven it often when there was some degree of personal danger connected with giving aid to the persecuted. I found him to be a good-natured man with an open mind.

The disappointing fact was that in Germany even good-natured, intelligent humanitarians with open minds did not become open anti-Nazi revolutionaries, willing to give their lives in the cause of humanity. They became skeptics, not activists. Not only that—they became non-resisting, if unwilling, cogs in the Nazi machinery. Ingelmann had been a German army officer. Seeing him as a one-time friend, I could not accommodate myself to the technical fact that only an armistice, not peace, had a few months ago interrupted, not ended, his status as an enemy. I was deeply aware of the dual personality of the individual as a component member of his herd on the one hand, and as a human being, whose faults are forgivable, on the other. I faced the individual human being, but attempted to assess the extent of his commitment to the herd.

We reached Ingelmann's house. Erich's father-in-law said he had made a wood fire for us in the living room. Erich's wife apologized that she had no coffee, but she would make some tea. She thought that her son was showing an excessive interest in American uniform insignia and took him along to the kitchen.

Erich and I sat down. It was a cozy, comfortable room with heavy 19th century furniture. A fair-sized study lined with books adjoined it.

"It's not my library," Erich said. "I had to leave all my books in the requisitioned apartment in Frankfurt."

He didn't complain,—he merely stated the fact as something inevitable. He was skeptical of my assertion that ultimately his property would be returned to him. Then he talked about the war.

"I had six years of it," he said. "We were married in August 1939. A few weeks later, I was drafted. Do I have to prove to you that I did not like to go?"

Ingelmann said flatly that he had never believed in the German cause. However, he did what was demanded of him, and in 1941 he was commissioned. He said he did not believe at any time that Germany could win the war, not after the swift Polish campaign, nor after the successful blitz in the west. He had travelled. His family had many friends in England and the United States, and he knew better. Yet, to judge by his record, he was a good German officer. After a short time with a rear-echelon Anti-Aircraft artillery unit, he was retrained for the infantry, and stayed with it to the end, rising to the rank of captain. He saw action in Russia, the Balkans, Italy, was in France with the German occupation army for a short while, and ended up running away from the Russians into the safety of an American PW cage. He had no intention of dying for the Führer, the fatherland, or anybody. He said he stuck to it for no particular cause, but because of his men who seem to have placed much confidence in him and his philosophy of surviving.

"Tell me frankly, Erich," I said, "What did you think when you saw me in American uniform?"

"Frankly," he answered, "I envy you. You knew you were fighting an evil thing. I was caught in a machine which made me fight _for_ it. All I could do was try to stay alive. Now I wish I had had the courage early enough to join you."

It was a rather disarming statement to one who came to find out what kind of mental gyrations the supporters of Germany's war were now going through.

There was, of course, a limit to Ingelmann's pro-Allied sentiments. A German communist editor of the Frankfurter Rundschau, American approved German newspaper, had just editorially branded all German soldiers and officers as murderers and robbers. That hurt. It started Ingelmann on a protest against our information services "which give you nothing to read and hear but concentration camp stuff and our atrocities abroad."

"My unit never harmed any civilians anywhere," Ingelmann insisted. "And for a whole year we were committed against the Yugoslav partisans who cut my division down from 15,000 to 2,000 men. Restraint wasn't easy. But we behaved as soldiers. I know damn well what the SS has done. In the end, they stole our vehicles to get away faster. But you shouldn't be blaming the Wehrmacht for the criminal behavior of the SS."

I said that he would have to get used to the fact that, as far as the outside world was concerned, they were all fighting for the same Führer. He agreed that all of Germany now had to take the consequences for all crimes, and for the war as such. He did think that was not entirely just:

"You say we were responsible for having the Hitler government, and for not getting rid of it. How about the rest of the world? In 1936 some English friends visited us in Frankfurt and we discussed the situation. I said to them they ought to watch out, because Hitler was preparing for war. Instead of negotiating naval treaties with him, they ought to be making airplanes. After all, the whole world treated the Hitler government on equal terms then. Instead of marching into the Rhineland when Hitler introduced conscription and tore up the peace treaties, the French introduced holidays with pay for their workers. And you in America? You passed neutrality legislation. Ribbentrop interpreted it his own way—as a green light for his aggressive policies."

I granted Ingelmann that Allied policies up to the outbreak of war, given Germany's inflexible intentions, had made war inevitable because they tried at all costs to avoid it. "But," I said, "supposing Allied forces had actively intervened, thus denying Germany the right to its own sovereign internal and foreign policies—would that not have made Nazis out of all Germans?"

Ingelmann thought this would have been a secondary danger compared to the much greater one of unchecked Nazi militarism. "Besides," he continued, "you underestimate the number of Germans who would have welcomed intervention, who would have taken courage from it to act against the Nazis. They felt abandoned by the world, and resigned themselves to the terror. Meanwhile the foreign powers sent their diplomats to the Nuremberg party rallies. I grant you that we've lost the war, and that therefore our war criminals will be tried. But we are not guilty alone."

"Don't you believe," I answered, "that any people is itself primarily responsible for the composition and behavior of its government? Other nations today realize they must share in the responsibility. This is quite clearly recognized in the charter for the Security Council of the United Nations. It is intended to deal with aggressive intentions before they can be let loose."

"Fifteen years too late," Ingelmann said. But he agreed that the German people as a whole had permitted themselves to be fooled and to acquiesce. "As a modern political body, we were not mature enough. I'm afraid we are even less mature today."

Inevitably, Ingelmann raised the question whether other modern nations had reached the political maturity to resist a situation such as the Germans faced in 1933. I said that I drew my optimism in this respect primarily from the fact that by far the greater part of humanity in the war just past had answered Cain's eternal question in the affirmative.

Erich called me an idealist. Going through the list of major nations ranged against Germany, and examining their motives in entering the war, I found that Ingelmann's admiration for Britain was almost boundless, not for going to war over the liberty of Poland in honor of her treaty obligations, but for her determination to remain a great Empire. "The irony is," he said, "that the British lost the war and their Empire not to us, but to the United States." The United States, he thought, had entered the war only when she was menaced with the loss of the British fleet. Russia, Ingelmann felt, had fought only because of Hitler's stupidity in attacking her. His outlook on past and present was determined by his dogmatic conviction that positions and ambitions of power were solely responsible for the course of history.

"I'll give you an example," he said. "You conquered Thuringia and Saxony. But you did not possess the strength to hold them. The Russians had their armored strength concentrated near that area, and you had to evacuate it."

I had heard this story many times. The German belief last summer that the Western Allies would immediately come to blows with the Red Army was not the only contributor to its circulation. To prevent a mass exodus of Germans from these provinces into American-occupied Germany, the facts of the transfer to Russian control, which had been agreed upon months before, were kept a secret from the German population. The transfer thus came as a surprise, and was generally interpreted as a sign of American military weakness. Stories about fortifications along both sides of the new demarcation line were only a logical sequel in the rumor mill.

It was not easy to convince Ingelmann of the basic facts. He thought in terms of tanks, planes, and divisions. That statesmen were capable of agreeing, and compromising even on matters affecting national power, that such agreements and compromises could then be kept and fulfilled, was an idea foreign to his mental processes.

The fact that we were redeploying all but occupation troops made an impression on him. He had been largely ignorant of the extent of the movement, and suspected that we were not telling the whole story in our frank publication of redeployment movements. He then wanted to know whether we were going to leave Europe to Russian expansionism.

Again, as with many relatively well-informed Germans to whom I have talked, his interpretation of US—Russian relations had run full circle. Having troops here meant to him that we intended to fight the Russians. Sending them home showed our disinterestedness in the affairs of Europe. The alternative of agreements taking the place of military power displays met only with his incredulity. Erich again accused me of being a blind idealist.

Mrs. Ingelmann had returned meanwhile with a tray of tea and cookies. After she had served us, she sat down and listened to the discussion. She emphasized her husband's points by nodding her head, adding an element of argumentative excitement to her husband's calm, almost resigned voice.

Mrs. Ingelmann felt she had to apologize for the fact that the cookies contained no sugar. Luxuries like sugar apart, it was very hard to get enough food for the boy and for themselves. Erich added that he had come out of the German army and U.S. captivity a quite well-fed man. He had lost 25 pounds since he returned home.

"You're not far from the farms in the neighborhood," I said. "Can't you scrounge what you need?"

"These farmers are tough," Ingelmann said. "Money won't impress them. And we have no clothing or cigarettes to barter away."

Ingelmann was bitter about the selfishness of the farmers. They had not reduced their own food standards. They knew they had a strong bargaining position, and exploited it fully. Having suffered comparatively little in war and defeat, they had preserved a spirit of nationalistic egoism. Erich had often overheard them freely criticizing Military Government and their new German officials. Things had after all been better under Hitler, they said. The facts of the breakdown of the German economy with the political collapse had so far escaped them.

We talked about some of our classmates I had seen or intended to visit. "Do you remember Blunthead?" Ingelmann asked.

"Blunthead", the banker's son, had left our class several years before we graduated, and I had lost sight of him. Ingelmann had seen him quite recently.

"He wasn't as lucky as you and I in the war," he said. "Was injured twice on the eastern front—the last time quite badly. He was shot through the leg. Walks on a cane. Do you know what he does now?"

I supposed that he was probably engaged in some phase of banking.

"You're right. He makes a lot of money, too. He goes back and forth between the stock exchanges at Hamburg, Munich and Frankfurt, exploiting the difference in stock prices. If I.G. Farben shares are 10 points higher in Hamburg than in Frankfurt, he buys them up and takes the train to Hamburg with them."

"With present travel conditions that can't be a pure pleasure."

"That's exactly the point. He has a special permit as an injured war veteran and is entitled to ride in a reserved compartment. He said he is usually quite comfortable."

I asked Engelmann whether this kind of business was legal. He didn't think it was. "Blunthead's father was active in the party," he said. "He has been prohibited from taking any part in his business. So Blunthead is carrying on. He said he had to make money some way."

What a grotesque picture. The son of a Nazi banker who was put out of business by Military Government, was taking advantage of his war injury to profit illegally from price differences in stocks of corporations, like I.G. Farben, which had been dissolved by the Allies.

"We have a lot of people now who live on such paper money profits. Black market, stock speculations, all kinds of shady deals. It's not too difficult to get rich. But all the marks in Germany can't buy me a pound of butter at the farm down the valley. I don't think our currency will last much longer. People around here are hoarding your Allied mark notes because they think they're backed by dollars."

Suddenly young Ingelmann burst into the room, changing the subject violently. "Snow White wasn't dead at all, when she was in the coffin," he exclaimed. "She was laughing all the time! I saw it."

It was time for me to leave. I wished Ingelmann luck in his paper war for readmission to the bar in spite of his party membership.

"What I'd like even better than that," he said in parting, "would be a visa to Brazil."

"Albert König's early environment was that of the mentally narrow, decent, colorless, artless small merchant. In spite of considerable material wealth, this small bourgeois influence produced in Albert a somewhat frightened insecurity, frustration, and a need for guidance and authority. Of medium intelligence, this average boy felt most secure among the mass of average people, moving ahead steadily avoiding conflicts and important, independent decisions. Under strong influence, he has been able to develop considerable energies, but not initiative. His faultless, upstanding decency was not attained through experience, but is the result of a frustrated character."

Erding

Obrecht's tracing successes continued. He brought me the address of Albert König,—the first classmate to be found still living in Frankfurt. His home was on Mendelssohn Strasse. During Hitler times, it was probably Göring or Goebbels Strasse. It was a doubtful honor for the old non-Aryan composer to have his street back after its houses and the life in them were destroyed. Perhaps the city would have done better to leave some streets named after Nazis, as a permanent memorial to the fury they brought over the city,—the ruin they caused.

I took a long walk through the darkness of Frankfurt, trying to remember Albert König. I pictured a short, wiry, decent, fairly intelligent boy. Nazism must have been foreign to his ideas up to the time of our graduation. I was certain of that. I could not think of him as going out of his way to be brutal, or to condone brutality.

I had reason to know König a little better than most of my class mates. In 1926, we had been to a four-week boy scout camp together in France, organized by idealistic French and German educators as an experiment in practical rapprochement.

Details of this camp, long lost in my semi-consciousness came back to mind. We were thirteen then. French and German boys pitched tents together in the forest of Compiègne, near the site of the 1918 (and the 1940) armistice. We played soccer, learnt a lot of French, and concluded international friendships which, we swore, would last forever. Our fathers might have fought and killed each other in this very forest, but we, the brave new generation of democrats would never let it happen again in the age of the League of Nations.

We hiked to the monument erected in the armistice clearing in honor of French victory—it showed the German eagle's throat cut by the French sword. At the time, I believe, I thought the idea had its merits, although it was perhaps too vividly expressed. I feared that some of my fellow boy scouts might develop thoughts of revenge at seeing it. I don't know what their reactions were. Our French guides said they abhorred the monument.

Somehow, König and I managed to go to Paris. Our French was fair. After a month with French boys in the forest of Compiègne, it contained a considerable element of Paris slang. The Capital made an overwhelming impression on us. We rode the Metro, climbed the Tour Eiffel, were fascinated by life on the boulevards.

Only once did we lose faith for a moment in the ideal of rapprochement: We wanted to climb the Arc de Triomphe for a view of the city, and of the great avenues converging on the Etoile. Downstairs by the gate, near the eternal flame for the French Unknown Soldier, a guard stopped us. He was a one-armed war veteran, with medals across his chest, and a ferocious moustache. He took one look at us and barked: "Trop jeune." The Arc de Triomphe was closed to us.

Now, nearly 20 years after our common visit to Paris, I wondered whether Albert König would remember the guard at the Arc de Triomphe.

On my way to see him, I passed the Frankfurt railroad station, once Germany's second largest, the city's pride. In the dark, it looked as though nothing much had happened to it. GIs were strolling about, and crowds were entering and leaving as though it were still the great traffic hub of prewar days. But the baggage of the travelers betrayed the times. A shabbily dressed woman who looked 60, carried a bulky rucksack and a large fiber bag. The load seemed almost too much, but her haggard face expressed no expectation of help. A man in his forties carried a paper-wrapped bundle,—hoarded food by the looks of it. A boy carried a GI's duffel bag. He would get a cigarette in return. A discharged German soldier in a torn, dirty-grey uniform had his mess gear slung around his shoulder, and carried his pack and blankets. He emerged from the station and looked blankly around, apparently not knowing where to turn. Two German girls strolled past him arm in arm, chewing gum like cows in a stable, intending to be noticed by American soldiers.

I walked on to Mendelssohn Strasse. The small cone of light from my flashlight isolated and grotesquely emphasized bits of ruin which the darkness wanted to hide. On the third floor of a house whose front wall was missing, a chandelier hung from the ceiling, its bulbs in place. Next door, the staircase only was still standing. On the second floor, a gasometer seemed to await the man from the gas company for the month's reading. In the next house, a rusting bath tub hung over the partly demolished floor.

I found König's house. Buildings on either side were bombed to rubble. His own was badly damaged. As far as I could see, no window pane was intact. The frames were filled with cardboard, wood, or some sort of ersatz glass. The stair lights worked. They were still painted dark blue for air raid protection.

König's name plate was on the door of the third-floor apartment. After a while, a young, thin, brunette woman answered the bell—König's wife. She seemed bewildered that an American would come in the evening to ask for her husband. When I mentioned my name, a door inside opened, and Albert came out.

"Gosh, what a surprise," he exclaimed. "Come in,—I think it's great that you're looking us up."

Albert König had become fat. The wiriness of his boyhood had gone. His short stature, his straight, partly grey, accurately parted hair, his striped business suit with a silver watch chain across the vest, made him appear a prosperous member of Germany's middle class. But the pallor of his face and the uncertain stare of his eyes belied his well-being.

They took me into a nicely furnished room, its appearance marred by cardboard in one of the window panes, and by a roughly repaired, unpainted plaster ceiling. The furniture, as Albert's appearance, served to create an impression of wealth, without quite succeeding. It seemed quite new and too prominent to be comfortable.

Albert's wife said the occasion called for a bottle of Rhine wine: "We just smuggled it out of the French zone."

She left the room and returned with a dust-covered bottle of white Rüdesheimer 1925. So the label said. Out of a round-corner, highly polished, modern cabinet came three lovely wine glasses. Albert opened the bottle and filled our glasses with ceremony.

I produced some cigarettes. Albert took one with a deliberate, slow move, as though he was handling gold. He said: "Ich bin so frei". A good translation would be: "Permit me the liberty of taking one." A better translation: "You know damn well I haven't had a good cigarette in months. I'd be a sucker to miss this chance. Hope you leave the whole pack." Nine out of ten Germans, when offered a cigarette, will say: "Ich bin so frei."

There came the embarrassing pause in which all three of us were thinking of an appropriate toast. Germans usually picked something more specific than "happy days". Mrs. König finally solemnly said: "To peace on earth." We all agreed. I am not a Rhine wine connoisseur, but I did my duty as a guest, and uttered proper epithets of appreciation.

As I proceeded to ask them about their life in the past 14 years, I was struck by their readiness to answer. Albert and his wife eagerly took turns at reviewing the past as though they had waited for a long time for an opportunity to unburden themselves—or perhaps to justify their conscience in the face of theories of German guilt which, they may have felt, I represented.

König had worked in a factory for a while after he left school, then studied engineering. He had just received his diploma as an engineer when he was mobilized to defend the West Wall during the Polish campaign. His was a horse-drawn artillery outfit, and when the French blitz campaign was staged in 1940, his unit was left a long way behind the front by the slashing and victorious tanks.

"I was a forward observer the one time we did get to the front. It was near Montmedy and the French treated us to some wonderful loudspeaker propaganda. They played 'Parlez-moi d'amour' for us. A lovely tune. I must get that record for you, dear," he said to his wife.

"What was the effect of the propaganda?" I asked.

"Oh, well . . . we were amused. We thought the war was just about over."

After the French capitulation, König's unit was quartered in a French village, on occupation duty. He became an officer. Life was pleasant and the villagers were easy to get along with. Especially for König who knew French, and liked the language and the people who spoke it.

"Did you get to Paris?" I asked.

"Yes, but only once," he replied. "I hadn't been there since 1926."

He remembered our common trip to the French capital. The incident at the Arc de Triomphe, the curt refusal by the guard to let us go up, had remained as vivid in his mind as in mine. Except that he interpreted it, perhaps immediately, perhaps in time, as a deliberate hostility on the part of the guard, because he had recognized us as German boys.

I asked Albert whether he had climbed the Arc when he saw Paris in 1940.

"I made a point of it," he said. "I felt rather pleased that no French guard was there to stop me!"

König tried, I believe honestly, to recall his political ideas of the time—the spring of 1944.[1] He was an officer in the Wehrmacht. The war had gone extremely well up to that point. He hoped that the German New Order would now unify Europe and that the rest of the world would give up its opposition upon seeing it work. He also hoped, now that Germany's foreign political aims had been realized, that the more ferocious Nazi leaders would be sacked.

In May of 1941, Albert's unit was transferred from France to Stettin—perhaps to guard Norway, he thought. There was some talk about possible war against Russia, but he said this was considered harebrained nonsense. Then he had an accident. He fell ingloriously, nowhere near the enemy. His injuries were nonetheless severe, and nonetheless caused by the war—because, Albert said, without the war he would never have had to ride a horse.

---

1 Given the context of this passage it is likely Jessel meant 1940 or 1941, not 1944.

König then gave me a 15 minute detailed description of his wounds, the healing process, the characters of his doctors, and the location and advantages of the various army hospitals in which he spent four months after the accident. After he was released, he was sent home, classified the German equivalent of 4F, and got married. The accident may have been painful, but it saved him from participation in the Russian campaign, and he now sincerely considered it due to the personal intervention of his guardian angel.

His wife nodded her consent to this relative appreciation of horses, God, and the Russian campaign.

"You've been married about four years?" I said.

"Yes, almost."

"Do you have children?"

"No. That had been our great worry. But now we think it's better like this."

I looked around the room. "You must be glad that you saved your things through the bombings," I remarked.

Their faces brightened. "I had most of our furniture hidden in a small village on the left bank of the Rhine," he said.

"That's in French territory, isn't it? How did you get it back here?"

"We got it, that's the main thing", Mrs. König said. "Somebody took off at midnight with a truck. How he got across the line is his trade secret. Perhaps the guards are sleepy after midnight. When you get a chance like this, you don't ask questions."

"We are rich, very rich, Walter," Albert added. "Few people in Frankfurt kept their possessions."

"Except for this, you see," Mrs. König said, pointing at the cabinet in the corner, "the lock was broken. And you can't get a thing repaired these days. It's really terrible now how people handle beautiful furniture. Don't you know anybody, Albert, who could repair the lock? It's such a nice cabinet. Perhaps for a few cigarettes you could get a carpenter?"

The cigarettes were undoubtedly mentioned for my benefit. Albert seemed embarrassed at his wife's preoccupation with the slight damage her cabinet had sustained. "Look, dear," he said, "we really ought to be glad we have it at all."

We turned back to the war years. König said that after his discharge from the hospital and the army, he had little difficulty in finding a job.

"Were you a member of the Nazi party?" I asked.

"Yes," he said. "I joined up while I was still at engineering school. Industry was swamped with rearmament orders then, and there were excellent job chances. I had to be in the party. Otherwise such jobs would have been closed to me. A man wants to get ahead."

König became an engineer in a chemical plant. His work with sulfuric acids was appreciated. After a year, in 1942, he was appointed the plant's representative on an industry-wide coordinating committee. These committees were being set up in the Speer Ministry of Armaments to standardize German industrial methods and increase production.

"As long as competitive engineering continued," König explained, "every manufacturer made his machinery to his own specifications, so that only his own spare parts could be used and only his own pocket would be lined. Our committees were set up to study these competitive abuses, eliminate them, and get war production properly under way."

"Hadn't all this been organized longer before the war ever started?"

"By no means," König said. "The industrialists considered the war good business, and they wanted to maintain any real or imaginary competitive advantages they had. There was much wailing when we cut across this thing. Real mass production didn't get going until 1943 and 1944."

"How do you explain that?"

"I'm only a little man. I can't understand it. Perhaps the bosses who planned it all thought as I did in 1940, that the war was about over."

In August 1944, König vividly realized that the war was not over. He was redrafted, this time as an administrative officer with a stationary artillery unit on the eastern front. He was again located at Stettin, and when the surrender came, he and his commanding officer saved themselves by fleeing in a staff car into British captivity. The British discharged him in July.

Albert refilled our glasses. He didn't like to think back to the time in the prisoner of war camp, he said. But he realized that he was lucky in being discharged so soon. Other prisoners, rumors had it, were to be sent to France, Holland and Belgium for forced labor.

Mrs. König looked at her husband seriously. "I don't know what would have happened to us if he hadn't come back in July," she said to me. "Mother and I were both ill. Mother is still in bed. We had no one to take care of us. God has been good to us."

"What are you doing now?" I asked König.

He shrugged his shoulders. "My company can't use me." he said. There were several reasons: First,—war contracts were the plant's chief business until the collapse. It was operating now only at something like 5% capacity, making pharmaceutical products. There was practically no work for chemical engineers.

Besides, the plant told him, he had spent most of his time before he was called into the army again, in the Speer coordinating committee, not in the shop. Albert's Nazi party membership had not entered into the discussion, probably because the other arguments were good enough, he thought. However, in view of past services, the company was as generous as to keep him on the pay roll until the end of 1945. Their accumulated war profits allowed this.

"Have you tried to get another job?"

"I've written to the Rhine river regulation commission. It's run by Americans now. They advertised for engineers. I received a very brief reply: 'Your services will not be required.' Probably because of my party membership."

I said I thought this might well be the reason why an American-controlled organization would not employ him.

"Yes, but don't you Americans realize that anybody in any kind of an essential position <u>had</u> to be and was a party member? How are you going to run this country without all these people?"

I said I didn't know, but our officials apparently felt it would be better to risk some further confusion than to trust Nazis.

"But we weren't Nazis," he exploded. "Most of us were Karteigenossen (card index members), and not Parteigenossen. I never supported the Nazis. Their excesses were obnoxious to me."

"It's terribly unjust," Mrs. König said in a low, resigned voice. Albert sat back, looking into space. His flushed cheeks resumed their former pallor.

It was Mrs. König's turn to protest anti-Nazi convictions.

"I had a job with the German Labor Front before we were married," she said. "I saw the Nazi swindle from the inside. Our bosses were draft-dodging young rascals who made patriotic speeches to the workers, but never exposed their precious skins to enemy fire. They treated us like dirt. I'll give you an example. Winter before last the windows in our office were smashed in an air raid. We couldn't get them repaired right away, so three of us girls moved into another office across the hall where one of these boys had his desk. When he arrived with his customary hangover at 11 in the morning, he simply threw us out. We told him our office was too cold to work. But all he said was: 'If you don't like it, we'll find jobs for you in an aircraft plant.' Finally, I couldn't stand it any longer and asked to be discharged. That was last year. My husband was away again in the army. At first, they didn't let me go. Then they forced me to work in a ball bearing plant. I took sick. My husband tried everything to obtain my release. He even risked writing to Gauleiter himself. You still have that letter, haven't you, Albert? There were some quite frank opinions in there about the German Labor Front.

But it was no use. You see, the people in concentration camps weren't the only ones who suffered under the Nazis. Plain people like us did too."

I did not ask to see Albert's letter. Sight unseen, I felt safe in taking it for granted that the "frank opinions about the German Labor Front" were guarded allusions at the very best. But Albert and his wife were certainly sincere in counting themselves among the victims of the Nazi regime.

They looked at me expectantly for words of approval and understanding. I did not feel capable of convincing them that the world would hardly place their sufferings on a level with that of the true victims of Nazism—those who suffered because they never abandoned the fight against it. I tried to make them understand that they, like the great majority of Germans, had contributed to the Nazis' war effort, Albert by producing more and better sulfuric acid for high explosives, his wife by working for the agency which kept German labor docilely at work. I wondered whether they expected the world to overlook their share in Germany's struggle to enslave it.

"But that was our job and our duty as Germans! What else could we have done?"

It would have been hopeless to attempt to answer their question.

To kill the silence which remained, we drank wine and lit another cigarette. Albert asked a few questions about other class mates, and about myself. Then we discussed his future plans.

"No point in talking about plans," Albert said. "I won't be able to find a job as a chemical engineer. Our industry is dead. America and England are rid of a serious competitor in world markets. That's why the plants that survived the bombings are now being dismantled as reparations."

Thus, to Albert König, reparations in plant were no more than an economic device on the part of US and British industry to dominate world markets. To the industrial devastation of Europe deliberately carried out by German armies, to the simple thought that damage caused by Germany's war would have to be repaired by Germany to the limit of her ability, his mind was closed tightly. Again, I saw myself confronted by something more than an insidious argument. When a German is at work rationalizing the consequences of defeat away from his own responsibility, no array of facts and figures will prevail. For the individual rationalization is only a product of the basic complex which consists of a semi-conscious realization of guilt, and the conscious refusal to accept it. No refutation of a single deliberately misconstrued, misunderstood, twisted line of thought, which many a German is now producing in order to come to a superficial but livable harmony with his own conscience, will make a dent in the basic complex. There, only the compulsion of history, of defeat, occupation, foreign tutelage, can act as teacher.

Albert continued to speak of his own future. "I don't know what's next. We have saved some money,—I guess we can continue to live on that for some time."

The prosperous silver watch chain across his vest seemed to blink in agreement. Albert sat back and sipped from his glass. His wife looked worried, cornered, resigned.

"Look, Albert," I said. "Frankfurt is a city of ruins. Cleaning it up, and rebuilding it will keep thousands of people busy for years. Have you thought of switching to the building trades?"

"All my training," Albert answered, "was in chemical engineering. I would have to start from scratch. Probably as an ordinary unskilled worker. If my savings run out, I may <u>have</u> to do it. But right now? I'll wait and see."

"Do you think many people who can't find exactly the job for which they are trained, feel as you do?"

"I'm sure of it," Albert replied. "Workers too. Almost everybody accumulated some savings during the war, what with overtime, high wages, and no chance to spend. My banker told me that the average German worker has probably 1,000 to 2,000 marks in the bank. He's in no rush to earn more. The price of our food rations has not gone up much. There is practically nothing else to be bought, except on the black market. So, for them as for me, there is really no reason to go to work on just anything. Then, there is another point. How long is our currency going to remain stable? <u>Something</u> will have to be done to bring it in line with what little remains of our real wealth. We believe there will be a depreciation. The best thing to do then, is to spend our savings now, or as we do, to live on them. That way we can at least buy some leisure and rest for them after the terrible strain of six years of war."

König had given sound reasons for the general apathy of Germans— toward their national life as well as their personal—which all observers were reporting. If he was right, it would be accurate to conclude that on the whole Germans have no common enthusiasm for rebuilding their country, which would provide an incentive to work; to work even if the nature of the job was not quite up to the dignity of a man's training and social position. Next thought: If German workers have to be forced into jobs by a currency devaluation wiping out their savings, and by impending hunger, what hope could there be for a sound political and economic German community, which, after all, has to be based on the common man's desire to have it, and his willingness to make some personal sacrifices for it?

I felt that the mood of Albert König and his wife was sufficiently despondent without exposing them to these wider implications of their attitudes.

He had mentioned the black market, and I asked him about it.

"Would you like to see it?" Albert said. "I was planning to go down-town tomorrow to try and make a deal. My mother-in-law is pretty sick, you know, and we don't think she'll be able to do much more walking. She has a pair of shoes which I may be able to trade for some coffee."

I arranged to meet Albert at the railroad station the following afternoon. The black market did business in a side street near there. Then I left.

Albert was waiting for me at the appointed time and place in front of main railroad station the following afternoon. The small brown ersatz leather brief case he carried bulged with what I expected were his mother-in-law's shoes.

We dodged between fast-driving jeeps and trucks across the square. A large store, now a Post Exchange, was beleaguered by children who begged chocolate, cigarettes, and chewing gum from soldiers who left it, their arms and pockets loaded with these treasures. Further down the street we saw clusters of people, like Columbus Circle in New York without soap box orators.

Men and women, some shabbily, some well-dressed, walked slowly about, talking furtively to someone here, then joining some other group. Nearly all of them carried briefcases or satchels, but no merchandise was displayed.

Albert said that articles are not actually exchanged on the spot. "It's an exchange for futures. You arrange your deal or barter here, then make an appointment for the actual time and place of the exchange itself. Makes it a little more difficult for the police and your MPs."

Some of the traders had the red and white Polish insignia in their lapels. Others wore the dark-blue dyed US Army clothing issued to displaced persons by UNRRA. But most of the black marketers were German civilians. A German policeman, armed with a truncheon, stood at a corner.

Albert seemed to know one of the traders. He left me and crossed the street to speak to him. While I waited, a boy of about 12 approached me and showed me a well-preserved 5-inch long Hitler youth dagger, with an enameled black swastika on a red and white background in the hilt. He wanted me to buy it for two packs of cigarettes.

"Look at the policeman over there," I said. "If he sees you with that dagger he'll put you in jail."

"He won't see me," the boy said. "One pack of cigarettes? Yes?"

I faced a triangular dilemma. First, the boy should have been arrested for having the dagger. Second, if he were potential Werwolf material, he would not be selling his murder weapon for a pack of cigarettes. Third, just the same, I did not want him to keep it. The deal was closed. The boy disappeared.

A man had been standing nearby, watching the transaction. Now he came over and said: "Cigarettes," flashing an Allied 50 mark note in front of me. Several other people took notice, and slowly joined us. I asked the man why he was willing to exchange so much money for blue smoke. He said:

"What else can I do with it? I've got enough money. These 50 marks will buy the food I can get on my family's ration cards for a month. But that isn't enough to eat. The rest I can get for cigarettes. That's what the farmer wants."

The policeman had been watching the assembly. Now he walked slowly closer. Perhaps he thought I needed help. Meanwhile everybody talked at once, bidding up the price for cigarettes. A tobacco auctioneer would have been of better use. The crowd took no notice of the policemen. Except for one man. He said:

"These cops. When they haven't got enough to smoke, they stage a raid on the market and confiscate our cigarettes. Then they smoke or sell them themselves."

The crowd dispersed when I showed no interest. Only the man who had first come over with his 50 mark note persisted in holding it under my nose. When Albert returned with his black-market acquaintance, he left grudgingly.

Albert said he had obtained half a pound of coffee for his mother-in-law's shoes. He seemed quite satisfied with the bargain. A pound of coffee, he said, sold at about 200 marks, and the shoes, really not in very good condition, were estimated at about half that.

Albert's trading friend said that sugar sold at 40 marks a pound, cigarettes at 40 to 70 marks a pack, and Allied issued German marks at 2 German issued marks apiece.

"Where do the cigarettes, and the coffee, and the sugar come from?" I asked.

He looked at me sheepishly. "From the Amis, of course. Also from the Poles. And from youngsters who probably steal the stuff. If you'd come half an hour earlier, you could have seen a jeep pull up. A soldier had 20 cartons of cigarettes. He wanted 5000 marks in Allied notes ($500). Half a minute later he was gone. He drove around a corner. One of the dealers here walked over and the transaction was completed."

Allied issued mark notes were wanted for two reasons, he said. First there was a superstition that when German marks would be depreciated, Allied marks would retain their value, because people thought they were backed by the dollar. Secondly, and more important, American soldiers dealt only in Allied notes in return for cigarettes, coffee etc., because their finance offices accepted no German issued currency.

A pair of MPs in white helmets and belts had passed our group and listened for an instant to our conversation. Perhaps they understood some German. A little while later a soldier joined us. He also listened for a while, then he said:

"Can you help me out, sir? I don't know any German. I want a camera, a good one, see? A Leica or something like that. I can pay for it in cigarettes."

I had to disappoint him. Then Albert said he had also bought himself an additional ration card from a Polish displaced person. It cost him 25 marks. The food he could buy for it would cost about three marks. The cards were not made out in the owner's name, and there was a brisk trade. It appeared that not only displaced persons, but also Germans with large families were in a position to sell them.

Albert had completed his day's business, and we turned away. I took the bus back to headquarters. Two GIs who sat in front of me had just returned from leave in Switzerland and compared notes.

"Look at this watch," one of them said. "Cost exactly 50 Swiss francs. Black face and gold numbers, see? It's going to be worth all of 500 bucks to some Russian in Berlin."

Ernst Weller was the youngest of four children—the spoiled family darling. His father was a creative musician and composer, emotional, faithful, helpful, eager,—and unpractical. His mother was much younger than her husband, a splendid, deep, quiet, patrician personality. Ernst developed well in the warmth of his home which was marked by an atmosphere of physical and spiritual cleanliness, and by a nobility of thought and attitude.

After a slow start, Weller's performance at school rose to average and above, and to a quite successful record at graduation. His emotional softness remained unchanged. As a lover of nature, he eagerly accompanied his father on hunting trips, but when a shot rang out and hit, Ernst came close to crying over the sight of the dead animal. He remained a dreamer and an introvert, but his strong imagination often led him to sudden, surprising decisions, and to dangerous feats of courage. As friends, Weller sought our fellow students whom he considered better than himself. He did not look for convenient friendship, but for examples of growth. This precluded full mutuality—here rarely confided in anyone.

In time, Weller developed a strong sense of justice. At the sight of injustice, this correct, quiet boy was capable of exploding unexpectedly, no matter whether he was concerned or not. His sensitivity developed in the direction of art. Beauty in all forms, books pictures, objects of daily use, attracted him. Ugliness, be it moral or physical, caused him bodily pain. The good and the beautiful, to him, belonged together."

Erding

The only trace Obrecht could find of Ernst Weller was the address of his sister-in-law. I had hoped to find Ernst. He was one of the boys I had liked best at school. He was not too bright, but there was a spirit of sincerity and friendliness about him which few of our class mates, most of them budding cynics, could match. From him, I thought, I might have obtained a picture of what happened under the Hitler regime to the best element in the Germany of our generation.

About Mrs. Weller, the wife of Ernst's older brother Arthur, I knew nothing. Obrecht said she lived on Eckenheimer Landstrasse, a street which borders the American compound. "Just follow the barbed wire fence on the outside," he added.

I went to visit Mrs. Weller quite late in the evening. When I rang the front door bell in the apartment building, a light appeared in a fourth-floor window and a woman asked what I wanted. I yelled up that I had been a friend of Ernst's and that I would like to speak to her. She came downstairs to unlock the door.

Only half the house was still standing. Mrs. Weller led the way up the staircase, one side of which was boarded up, the other giving access to the still inhabitable apartments. The hall of her own apartment on the top floor of the building was partly charred. "A phosphorus bomb," she said. Most of the wall paper was burnt, hanging in blisters and shreds from the walls. The ceiling was nearly all blackened. To show me what happened to the other half of the building, Mrs. Weller opened a door to a room—it led into space.

"Part of the floor outside is still quite safe," she explained. "I use it to dry my laundry."

She showed me into the kitchen, and we sat down by the table. In a corner was a bed in which two young children, her boys, were sleeping; at least they should have been. After Mrs. Weller and I had exchanged a few words, they were wide awake and listening. Next door was her only other room which was still intact. Mrs. Weller used it as a bedroom for herself and her eight-year-old daughter.

Ernst's sister-in-law was a dark-haired, slender woman of about 35 who, ten years earlier, must have been beautiful. Worry, bitterness, and lack of food were now written on her face. She had great difficulty scraping enough food together for her children, she said. She had to take care of them all by herself.

Her husband, Ernst's brother was a sergeant in the German army. He had been fighting Yugoslav partisans in the Trieste area. She had not heard from him in nearly a year, and had given up hope that he was alive. Tears came to her eyes as she told me this, but she kept herself under control.

I asked her about Ernst.

"We believe he's doing forced labor in France," she said. "He gave himself up to the Americans in April, and we've had no news from him since. He may not be alive either. He had malaria."

Before I could ask her for details, she bitterly related the rest of the family tragedy:

"You know that his father was dead, didn't you? Died in 1934 of a heart attack. Now his mother died a month ago also. All her children were gone. It was too much for the poor woman. Ernst's oldest sister Else was married to an airplane construction engineer who worked for Junkers in Dessau. The Russians took him away. Something dreadful must have happened to Else, because we heard six weeks ago that she had killed herself. Fortunately, they had no children. Then there was Anna. She was killed in the terror raid a year ago last March. I told you about Arthur. And now no word from her youngest, Ernst. It's terrible,—the whole family ..." Mrs. Weller let her head drop in anguish. Her voice shrank. One of the boys in the bed began to cry.

That pulled Mrs. Weller together. She went over and told the boys to sleep. She apologized to me that she had no other place where she could talk to me.

"In a way, I'm glad I have the children. Otherwise I wouldn't know what I'd do."

Mrs. Weller was close to despair and hysteria. It was at first difficult to get clear answers from her to my questions about Ernst, but then she calmed down.

"I wish I knew more about him," she said. "If his mother were still alive, she'd tell you. He loved his mother very much. Did you know he took a trip to Italy right after you graduated?"

"No," I said, "I have not seen him since March 1931."

"Well, he was a bit of an adventurer, you know," she continued. "He had no money for the trip at all. He got as far as Rome. I still don't know how he got back, because his father refused to send him a train ticket. When he came back, he went to the University of Berlin to study medicine."

According to his sister-in-law, Ernst did well with his studies. At least that was all she knew of him at the time. She saw him only rarely. Then, suddenly, after four years of work, he returned from Berlin one day and announced to his family that he had given up medicine.

It took the family some time to find the reason for Ernst's decision. At first, Mrs. Weller remembered, there was talk that Ernst felt revolted by his anatomy classes. To dissect the human body was more than Ernst's soft nature could stand. This may have been part of his motives. But the full story came out when Ernst returned to Berlin and took up acting—together with the divorced non-Aryan wife of a former friend.

I remember this man by name. Mrs. Weller said he was a lawyer, and Ernst's closest friend at the Berlin University. He was intelligent and ambitious—two qualifications for riding the crest of the Nazi wave. Only one thing stopped him,—his half-Jewish wife. She was a prominent actress, and in pre-Nazi times an asset to his social and business position. In 1934, he divorced her on racial grounds.

Ernst was a close witness to the development. He fell in love with the woman. Had it not been for the Nuremberg racial laws, he would have married her.

It took the Nazi student organization little time, Mrs. Weller said, to hear of the affair. They gave Ernst the choice of giving up his "Jewish mistress", or leaving the university. He took the latter course, and under the guidance of the woman he loved, became an actor.

Mrs. Weller had seen Ernst on the stage only once with a small stock company, in the role of a young lover in a classical play. She forgot what it was. She thought he was a very good actor. Companies in the larger cities were closed to him, because he refused to join the party.

In 1940, the Nazis forbade Ernst's friend to appear on the stage. Ernst was drafted into the army at about the same time.

"He came to say good bye to us," Mrs. Weller said. "I remember the day very well. The radio was going, and suddenly the great news came that France had capitulated. Ernst left the room. I think he cried. When he came back he said plainly that he hoped Germany would yet lose the war. We were horrified. But we said nothing, because we knew he'd be in uniform the next day. I don't think he was a good soldier. At least he never got to be more than an Obergefreiter (corporal)."

Ernst's unit spent the winter of 1941 to 1942 in the snows of Russia. In summer of 1942 he returned on furlough with both his legs frozen.

After he recovered, he was sent on occupation duty to France for a year. During the fall of 1943, he was again transferred to the Russian front. The following spring he returned. As souvenirs, he brought a very ugly skin ailment, some other illness which had made him lose all his teeth, and malaria.

When he left the hospital in the summer of 1944, Ernst was made an instructor at a replacement depot. He was to help drill and train what was left of German manpower for the defense of the fatherland. But his malarial attacks were so frequent and violent that he was hospitalized again.

His hospital was about 50 kilometers from Frankfurt. He was still there when the Americans moved in in April, Mrs. Weller said.

"If he had only stayed there! But he did a very foolish thing. Knowing that his mother was worried about him, he left the hospital without permission, to see her. He stayed two days at home. Then he reported to the Americans at Military Government as a German soldier. Since then we have not heard from him directly."

"You had no news at all?"

"Only through one of Ernst's comrades. He came back from a French prisoner camp in July because he had his foot squashed in a railroad accident and could not work anymore. He told us that Ernst was doing forced labor in France. Ernst was a very sick man. I just don't think he could have lived through it."

If the report from Ernst's comrade was true, then Ernst was one of the several hundred thousand German prisoners we turned over to the French authorities for forced labor.

She knew nothing else about him. From a desk in the corner she produced a small leather box with pictures. There were some of Ernst in various disguises—one as Hamlet, another in a modern role, a third as a German Obergefreiter in the Wehrmacht.

I hoped he would return from France where, if he was alive he was now atoning for Hitler's sins. After experiencing the wrath of Nazidom in his private affairs, after returning broken in health from a war he hated, a war which wiped out his entire family, he of all Germans had to rebuild France.

Was this poetic justice? Or was it the tragedy of the non-political man of good will?

It is tempting to think in terms of poetic justice where Germany is concerned. Germany brought untold misery over the world, therefore Germany is a shambles. It is so logical. It is so comforting to accept Germany as proof that poetic justice operates. It is good to know that those who sow the wind will reap the whirlwind. It relieves you somewhat of the responsibility for keeping a wind meter in good condition at all times, and for hoisting the storm sail when the wind begins to blow. For the whirlwind will surely come. Also, when circumstances make you an infinitesimal part of the whirlwind machine, it is balm for your conscience that you are only a tool of poetic justice, and not of man's inhumanity to man.

Should millions of men, women and children be deprived in mid-winter of home and property, of health, happiness and liberty, and often of life, that Silesia may become Polish, and the Sudetenland Czech? Should Ernst Weller do slave labor because a man he hated usurped government power in his country?

If the answer is no, then the world has yet to take notice and act. By its very silence and unconcern, the world has shown that, for all practical purposes, the answer is yes!

Every man, woman and child, the unborn even, who bear the mark of German, are being held to account, some with extreme suffering, some lightly, as accident will have it, for the deeds which were committed in the name of their nation. No one has risen to speak for them—no one with a voice loud enough to be heard. Is it not clear then, that Ernst Weller, the nonpolitical man of good will, is doing penance today not for any positive personal guilt, but simply for his failure to be a responsible citizen? Unless he were to accept his fate as inevitable and unalterable, there would have been for him and those like them only one alternative: Active revolt, at no matter what risk, at a time when Nazism could still have been stopped.

To me, the three pictures of Ernst Weller I was contemplating contained these lessons: The nation whose citizens do not consider themselves individually and personally responsible for basic human rights everywhere, is headed for ruin. It thus becomes the duty of the citizen toward his nation to disobey any law, no matter how legally enacted, which is in violation of human rights. For no man may render his brother's right unto Caesar and go unpunished. Liberty and justice, as peace, are indivisible.

Perhaps the answer to the question whether there was justice in the suffering of millions of personally guiltless Germans, as in the slavery of Ernst Weller, is both yes and no. The world, if it drew the consequences, would then continue to exist on a safer margin.

Mrs. Weller put the pictures away and sat down again. The boys in the corner bed had finally fallen asleep. Their mother unburdened her own worries.

There were two other undamaged rooms in her apartment, she said, which the housing authority had requisitioned. They assigned the rooms to a Spanish Falangist whose son had been a member of the SS. The Spaniard led a life with women and alcohol of which Mrs. Weller did not approve.

"Can't you get rid of him?" I asked.

"No," she said. "He says he has diplomatic immunity. And he has threatened to have <u>me</u> evicted because my husband was in the party. My husband was not active, you understand. He was forced into it, because of the position he had in his publishing firm. I'm going to complain to Military Government. Perhaps you Americans should do something about it."

I asked her how she was earning a living.

"I'm a seamstress," she said. "There is plenty of work. Only getting paid for it in money doesn't really help in feeding the children. Before Hitler came, I used to work only for Jewish employers. They were wonderful to me. They were rich people, and you can ask anybody, I never had anything against them."

"What happened to them?"

"I don't know. Some of the Jews I knew emigrated to the United States. When are they coming back?" she asked.

I said that was little likelihood that any of them intended to return.

"Don't they want to come home?" she asked again. "That's terrible for Germany. I don't think Germany will ever be rebuilt again without the Jews. They are the only ones who have the money to do it."

This was German anti-semitism, shifted from high gear into reverse, but powered by the same engine. I made some attempts to enlighten her.

"Yes," she said, "you are absolutely right. I always said that Hitler made a terrible mistake when he antagonized the Jews. They are an unbeatable world power. Consider the things they did for Germany, and especially Frankfurt. If only they'd come back."

I gave up and excused myself;—my last bus was almost ready to leave.

"Heinrich Hirth's personality must be seen in the light of his narrow parental environment. His father was an extremely dutiful and conscientious, but altogether dependent official. Heinrich believed in, and needed authority. His way of life was painstakingly regulated and standardized. The Catholic faith of his home environment became a decisive influence. However, as a boy, as long as his faith was not subjected to attack, he was open to other influence and guidance. Once he had adopted an ideal, he was capable of considerable sincere enthusiasm and energy in its propagation. His many good qualities and his sense of decency are not sufficiently strong to make him an independent personality. Within the family, professional advancement is the strongest determinant of action. This may require sacrifices in terms of convictions.

Hirth is the raw material for the typical, responsible, dutiful civil servant, whose respect of authority will always overshadow his own opinions. He will never be more than a subaltern."

————————

Erding

November 25, 1945

A message arrived from Obrecht to the effect that Heinrich Hirth lived at Lorch, on the Rhine river. I was lucky in choosing a splendid day for the trip. The road ran west through Wiesbaden, then following the Rhine. The broad valley narrowed down-stream, and the river seemed to gather speed. A slight haze lent a ghostly atmosphere to the castle ruins—honest-to-goodness ancient ruins, not the hideous air raid wrecks,—which topped the vine-covered hills.

On the green-brown river, the Willem III, a decrepit Dutch paddle steamer, was taking a boatload of Americans on a sight-seeing tour. Its dance band outroared the jeep's engine. Ashore, under neat rows of elms and oaks, GIs strolled with their German girls. Over a 20-mile stretch I counted 14 GI-Fraulein couples against three all-German idylls.

It was a beautiful, peaceful, restful scene. Because they were so quiet and inactive, even the beached hulls of ships and barges, bombed or scuttled months ago, fitted into the picture. Uglier were the bridges—the dropped, twisted, unconnected, useless spans which cluttered the river.

A GI by the roadside stopped me and asked for a lift to the next town. He knew a girl there, he said. We commented on the beauty of the much-romanticized scenery.

"It's beyond me," he said. "With a beautiful country like this, why did they have to go to war?"

GIs in many parts of Germany, from the broad Elbe through the low, rolling hills of central Germany, in the charming Swabian and Bavarian farm lands, and down toward the snow-capped Alps, had asked the same question. How could anyone who lived in such lovely surroundings want to occupy other lands, enslave other people? The soldier expected no answer.

He told me he had recently been transferred to this area from Berlin. I asked him what he thought of the German capital.

"It's a dead city," he said. "People walk around and you can't imagine what they live on. But there's a lot of money to be made in that town."

"So I hear. Did you do all right?"

"I guess so," he said. "Before the new currency control book was introduced, I sent my wife about $3,000. She's had a rough time since she lost her job, and we can sure use the dough."

The currency control book was instituted to prevent army personnel from transmitting more money to the United States than they had earned in pay and allowances. Before the books were issued, money sent home exceeded the sum total of pay given Berlin troops by several million dollars.

"Do you know who paid you that $3,000?" I asked.

"Who?"

"The taxpayers did."

"What do you mean, Lieutenant?" he asked. "I sold a couple of watches to Russian officers, and some cigarettes to the Krauts. They paid me for the stuff, and I sent the dough home."

"They didn't pay you," I said, "they just gave you some paper with figures printed on it. You took the paper to the post office and bought money orders. For the money orders your wife received dollars. The Russians have your watches, the Germans your cigarettes, your wife the dollars, and the US treasury the paper money you received. The treasury paid you, not the Russians and the Germans. You see my point?"

"Gosh,—I hadn't thought of it that way. Quite a racket, wasn't it? Well, it's all over now. The currency control books stopped it pretty much, I guess. At least I can't send any more money home than I get paid. But I can still send things. I just mailed the most beautiful Leica camera to my wife you ever saw. Cost me four cartons of cigarettes. The treasury doesn't pay for that, does it?"

"No."

"How does it work?" he wanted to know.

"Well, there are a lot of Germans who have wads of paper money stuffed away some place. They saved it during the war, or earned it in black market deals. Anyhow they're rich. There isn't anything they can buy for their money, except the few rare and expensive things offered on the black market. Cigarettes for instance. And many of these so-called rich Germans can't give up smoking. They're the customers for your cigarettes. At the same time, there are other Germans who're broke and haven't any work. Like war widows with children and no money in the bank. If they want to eat, they have to sell their possessions. So one of these war widows sold her Leica in the black market. In return she received money or food. The black-market operator sold you her Leica for cigarettes. So there it is. You got a Leica which is worth a few hundred dollars; some Germans, thanks to you, have smokes to last them for a while; and a German woman has enough food for her children for another few days. The food, of course, only changed hands inside Germany. The German economy as a whole has a Leica less, in return for smoke. You follow? From now on not the US treasury, but the Germans pay for your black-market profits."

"Well, that's all right, isn't it?" he said.

"Perhaps. Supposing you take a starving man's wallet before feeding him. He'll be glad to let you have it, won't he? He'll offer you his watch in addition, if only you give him something to eat and drink. Think that's all right?"

"Gee whizz," said the soldier. We had reached his destination and he stepped out of the jeep. He thanked me for the lift. A blonde girl waved to him from a third-floor window, and he waited for her.

Another few miles along the banks of the Rhine, and I reached Lorch. The address Obrecht have given me was on Rhein Strasse. The house was hard to find,—a whole row of buildings along Rhein Strasse was destroyed. This was unusual for a town the size of Lorch.

An elderly woman had been watching my search from a window across the street. She directed me to Hirth's house which lay behind the destroyed block of buildings, away from the Rhine. On the stairs I met a boy who said that Herr Dr. Hirth was not at home. But he knew where to find him and would ask him to come right over.

I hardly recognized Hirth when he walked up the alley to his house where I was waiting. With most of his blond hair gone, he looked at least 40. He wore a well-pressed dark-blue striped business suit with a stiff collar almost as high as Dr. Schacht's. His eyes were narrow, as though he was constantly looking into the sun, and he wore thick glasses. An artificial smile covered an apparent lack of self-assurance. Hirth was greatly surprised to see me. Remembering his ardent Catholicism, I had expected to find him a priest. Instead, he looked like a school master, although perhaps a little too prosperous for that.

"I'm sorry I wasn't here when you came," he said. "Did you wait long? What brought you out here? We were just having our Sunday Kaffeeklatsch at my in-laws. Excuse me if I won't ask you over there—they have all kinds of people visiting them. I don't know what they'd think if I brought an American along."

We walked up to Hirth's room. He was living in the house of a wine merchant, and he suggested that we celebrate this reunion with a sample of Lorch Rhine wine from the cellar.

Hirth's room overlooked the row of ruins which spoiled the charming view of the narrow Rhine valley and the vineyards on the opposite bank. The room was poorly furnished with a large and a small bed, a clothes closet and a desk. Baggage was piled in a corner.

After Hirth returned with the bottle of wine and had toasted our class of 1931, he told me that he was twice bombed out in Frankfurt and that he had lost all of his furniture, books, and most of his clothes.

"That's why we came out to live here in Lorch," he said. "It's nice living along the Rhine, but there's nothing for me to do. You know I'm married, don't you? Yes. And we have a little boy. They're over at my in-law's house. Sorry you won't meet them today. But you must come back some other time."

The furniture in the room in which the three of them found refuge after the great air attack against Frankfurt was borrowed, Hirth explained.

"At that we were very lucky," he said. "You see the ruins outside? Well, our house was just missed. I wouldn't have known where to go next."

"Do you know why we bombed this town?" I asked. "Was there any industrial plant of importance?"

"Oh no," Hirth answered. "This wasn't done by planes. These ruins are a memorial to your excellent artillery. At the end of March, the SS tried to defend the river bend. You can see it from the window. Then your artillery got the range and the SS took off. These piles of rubble are what's left of the incident."

I suggested that in that case the ruins were a memorial to the SS rather than our artillery. "That depends how you look at it," Hirth replied.

We stepped away from the window and sat down.

"What happened to your interest in theology?" I inquired.

"Come to think of it," he said, "perhaps I should have remained true to my school day ideas, and studied for the priesthood. At least I'd have a job now. Well, I took up law instead. I've been an Amtsgerichtsrat (district judge) since 1941, but I've acted as judge ever since 1937. Of course, under your new denazification laws, I can't get back to work."

"Didn't you have to serve in the army?"

"Oh yes, of course. I did my duty as a soldier as everybody else. I was drafted in 1940."

"Were you on the eastern front?"

"No. You know, I wasn't really much of a soldier. I'm shortsighted and not very strong. They had me taking care of the men's legal affairs in an anti-aircraft unit near Berlin. I stayed there for five full years. Never moved until the Russians came."

"Were you an officer?"

"No. All I got to be was Unteroffizier (sergeant), and that only in 1944. I just haven't the knack for military matters. Well—I lived through it. That's the main thing. When the Russians came, we moved west, and became American prisoners. After a month in a terribly uncomfortable camp, we were turned over to the British, where we were even more uncomfortable. Then I was lucky enough to be discharged. I'm a lucky man, I know. Can't say that I sought action. Never saw any."

"Where did you act as judge?" I asked.

"In Frankfurt."

"And you can't return there now and take up your duties once more?"

"I'm afraid not," he said. "I told you the Americans kicked me out. I was a party member since 1933."

"That early?"

"Certainly. I liked law and I wanted to become a judge. You know very well that nobody could get any place if he wasn't a party member."

"That may be, but in 1933 you were still a student. Did your job prospects compel you to join the party as early as that?"

"No. I could have continued to study without joining. But it seemed like the thing to do to be on the right side from the beginning."

"What happened to your religious beliefs?"

"I feel as strongly about them as ever."

"Was your faith no obstacle in joining the Nazi party?"

"No. in 1933 there was no apparent contradiction to my religion."

"How the Nazis would deal with human rights was as apparent then as ten years later. Didn't you consider that a contradiction to your faith?"

"I did not think so at the time. To you as a Jew, this may have been clearer. We thought there would be a difference between a party program and a responsible government in power. Nobody imagined that they could possibly carry out all this nonsense. And everything else they promised was very sensible. We had 10 million unemployed and you can't deny that Hitler gave them work."

"Wasn't the price a little high?"

"We lost the war. That's true. And our cities are in ruins. That's probably what you mean by the price. But don't forget—we came very close to winning the war. Then the price wouldn't have been too high."

There was a note of pride in Hirth's voice, as he said this. His mind impressed me as being made up of a mixture of unscrupulous, frank opportunism and a specifically German brand of arrogance—the ingredients of the Nazis' essential middle class support. The type is anything but rare. Only, it is usually not camouflaged by apparent sincere religious faith.

In self-justification, Hirth exposed Germany's well-known and well-worn pre-war grievances—especially the injustice of not permitting Danzig to join the Reich in 1939 if it wanted to. And, he added, Germany victory was practically certain in 1940, when England was defenseless. This, in Hirth's frank opinion, showed that Hitler was right—until the day he marched against Russia. That was a mistake.

I asked Hirth how he could reconcile his religious principles with support of aggressive war.

"You are right in stressing the role of my church in proclaiming universal peace, and in defending human dignity and natural rights," he said. "But you forget another part of our faith. We are taught absolute obedience to the State. Paul said so, and Thomas Aquinas said so. Paul had every reason to preach revolt against the pagan Roman dictators. Instead he taught submission and suffering. And then, if you think back to the thirties, you'll recall that the Holy See took a conciliatory stand toward the New Germany from the beginning. There were some protests, but they were confined to pastoral letters against specific Nazi measures. Then the Holy Father concluded a Concordat with our new government. Our German volunteers in the Civil War in Spain found themselves fighting alongside our Church. Then came the victory over Poland. Our government insisted that German bishops be appointed for Poland. And although the Polish clergy was always closely linked to the Holy See, our government's demands were fulfilled. These things are too easily forgotten. In a situation like this, how can you expect a simple Catholic layman to revolt?"

"You're forgetting," I said, "that among the few who did revolt were a high proportion of simple Catholic laymen who looked at the signs of the times from a different point of view than yours. But I grant you—if you're looking for excuses for having obeyed the authorities you wished to obey, you don't have to go far to find them."

There was a pause in which Heinrich Hirth, for a moment, appeared to lose his composure. But his forced smile reappeared quickly.

"That's putting an unpleasant interpretation into what I just said," he retorted. "You asked me whether my German convictions collided with my faith. I answered you that they did not, and I told you why. I looked for no excuses. Anyhow, let's drop this—how about another glass of wine?"

He picked up the bottle and poured again. Although he would plainly have preferred to talk about the weather, there were a few things I still wanted to ask him. For instance, what the attitude of the Catholic clergy was in Germany when the Nazi party came to power.

"Many of us consulted our confessors when it came to a decision on party membership," he said. "I know of several laymen, apart from myself, who were advised by their priests to join. The clergy probably thought we could exercise a moderating influence on the party radicals once we were inside. The Austrian Anschluss is a good example for what I want you to understand. The Austrian clergy were opposed to the Anschluss. Then Schuschnigg fell, and Austria became German once again. Once the union was established, the Austrian clergy welcomed it,—at least I never heard anything to the contrary. And we here in Germany felt that the inclusion of Austria would lend the Catholic voice more weight against Protestant Prussia."

"Did that apply to the Sudeten country and to Danzig as well?"

"No," he said. "The Sudeten country is German. When it returned to Germany, I was naturally happy about it. I am a German. Today I realize what I couldn't have known then, that the Munich conference was only a prelude to war. Then we asked for the city of Danzig, and the world refused. Well, to us, it looked like a reasonable demand. Danzig was a German city. It was shock, of course, when war came. But then, after the blitz campaigns in the east and in the west, it seemed won and finished. Now you Americans are surprised that nearly all Germans supported Hitler."

"How long did this general support last?"

"The winter 1941/1942 was the turning point. The Russian war was not popular. Our men in Russia froze, and the people at home realized that this was not like the walk into France or Denmark. Russia was too big and too rich in resources."

"Do you think he could have had peace? Hitler should have knocked out England and then made peace."

"Perhaps. I don't know. I'm beginning to doubt it. But at the time, after all, we were completely under the spell of our propaganda. In the papers, we read the speeches of your isolationists. We were sure Americans would never interfere. I'm afraid we know now that the democracies weren't quite as decadent as we were told for 12 years."

I was glad to find that if not our ideals, at least our power had made an impression on Hirth. I wondered how deeply the lesson had sunk in: "That was one of Hitler's fundamental miscalculations," I said. "But I'm afraid it was only one mistake of many. The thought that he could force the world to accept his concentration camps, occupation rule, and enslavement policies, was perhaps the greatest. Germany has to pay for it now. Look out of your window—there are your ruins. Those are the consequences of aggressive war. If you had thrown the Nazis out, say, in 1935, the view from your window would not be marred by rubble, and Germany would be a highly respected country in world politics and trade."

"Maybe that's true," said Hirth.

"Well, Heinrich, supposing some criminal were to take over your government again and another Goebbels were about to pull the wool over the eyes of the people, would you again obey the authority of the state?"

"I'm afraid I'm going to disappoint you", he answered. "I'm not a fighter by nature. My family are very dear to me. I don't like to suffer,—I haven't the strength for it. I'm not the type for revolts, I'm afraid. If I'd be subjected to pressure, I'd probably compromise."

"Well, you're not disappointing me as much as your own country. What do you think will happen to Germany?"

"That's up to the Allies now," he answered. "We've tried and we've lost. I hope you'll let us live, otherwise I have no ambitions for my country."

That ended our discussion on principles and history. I offered him a cigarette, and for a while we smoked in silence. I thought perhaps I had driven the argument too far into the hypothetical. But I had a desire for clarity, not for polite conversation. He evidently had the same impression,—he looked like a whipped school boy.

"Don't get a wrong impression," he said. "I'm not defending what Nazism has done. That's quite beyond anyone's defense. I just want you to understand that a little man like myself had no opportunity to disapprove. I felt that these excesses were temporary war-time affairs. Had we won the war, I'm sure they would have ceased immediately."

This was clear enough. There was no point in pressing him further.

"Did you have to apply Nazi legislation in your work as a judge?" I asked.

"You mean racial laws and that kind of thing? No. I dealt with civil suits, divorces, rent disputes and the like. It was always my aim to have the parties come to an agreement by themselves. I was quite successful, especially in divorce cases. That's what I wanted to be as a judge, a friendly mediator. I think, if I had been forced to apply the Nazi racial and treason laws, I would have refused. But that situation never arose."

"What are you going to do if you can't get your position back at the courts?"

"I wish I knew," he answered. "Law is the only field for which I'm qualified. And I don't see why the judges who were now appointed by your Military Government are one iota better than I. Show me one decision handed down by any of them between 1933 and 1945 that proves they were anti-Nazis. If they hadn't enforced the Nazi law, they would not be here today to accept the new positions."

I realized that in Hirth's mind, the Americans were responsible for the loss of his home and possessions, and now his livelihood. It was not very surprising that an American would not be a welcome guest at family Kaffeeklatsch.

"Well, Heinrich," I said, "you'd probably like to rejoin your family, I won't keep you any longer."

We drank up. He accompanied me down to the jeep, through the ruined part of the town. Two men, probably local wine growers, dressed in their work clothes, stared at us. I realized that the meticulously dressed Judge Hirth must have been known in town as a Nazi, and such cordiality with an American undoubtedly seemed strange to the pair.

"Do you ever come to Frankfurt?" I asked Hirth.

"Yes, my parents still live there. As a matter of fact, my wife and I are planning to visit them next week. This town here is utterly dead. My parents wrote that the opera is playing again in Frankfurt, and we're both very fond of opera."

"What are you planning to see?"

"We'd like to see Fidelio. I've asked my parents to buy tickets for us."

I asked him for details, Fidelio being one of my favorites also, and we arranged to meet briefly after the performance so I could make his wife's acquaintance.

We reached the corner on Rhein Strasse where I had parked the jeep, next to a pile of rubble which had once been a house.

"You weren't here when the SS defended Lorch, were you?" I asked.

"No."

"If you'd been around, would you have helped them?"

"Well, if the local commander had ordered me to do so, certainly I would have fought. Orders are orders. After all, you can't be cross at a man for wanting to defend his home against invasion."

"Even if it simply means unnecessary sacrifices to prolong a lost war?"

"A soldier has no right to decide for himself whether a war is lost or not. That's up to his superiors."

We said good-bye, and he walked on into a pleasant, looking large, old, white house with green shutters on the Rhine river. I drove back to Frankfurt, feeling sorry for the people whose job it is to reeducate Germany.

Tickets for the Frankfurt Opera were on sale through our Special Services office. The opera house was destroyed, and performances took place in a modern, marble-lined banquet hall of the stock exchange building. Seats were unnumbered. Fortunately, I arrived in time. When the curtain rose, the ice-cold hall was filled to capacity with a well-dressed, but slightly emaciated crowd of music lovers. In spite of prevailing temperatures, it was a good performance. The audience were generous with their applause, partly because they appreciated the quality with which Beethoven's immortal score was rendered, partly because the exercise revived their blood circulation.

Scenery for the Spanish state prison in which the truth-loving Florestan was incarcerated by his political opponent, Pizarro, was crudely painted on large canvasses. I watched for signs of emotion among the audience, when Leonore, Florestan's devoted wife and liberator, opened the gates for the half-starved prisoners who left the night of their cells in their prison rags for a brief glimpse of the sun. Beethoven's deeply humanitarian soul found full expression in the wonderfully stirring measures sung by the unfortunates. I felt like asking everyone present whether the scene reminded them of anything in particular. Did they hear Florestan's plaint? It was prominently printed in the program notes:

(With apologies for the translation)

"In the spring days of my life,

Happiness has fled me.

I dared to say the truth,

And chains were my reward."

At the end of the performance, I found Heinrich Hirth and his wife waiting in the corridor as arranged. Mrs. Hirth was a short, straw-blonde, insignificant looking woman of about 25. They were enthusiastic about the opera. There were a few things I wanted to know:

"Was Fidelio performed throughout the war?"

"Certainly," Hirth said. "We saw it at least five times in the last five years."

"How did the audience react to the prison scenes?"

"What do you mean? It's … it's great music. Very moving. People are always very impressed."

"By Beethoven's music only? Or also by his ideas on freedom?"

"Why, by his music, of course," Hirth replied. "He used the subject as a vehicle for it. After all, he didn't create these wonderful melodies for propaganda purposes, did he?"

"Beyond the great music,—or through it—didn't you ever feel that there was a parallel to Nazi Germany and its concentration camps?"

Hirth and his wife laughed. "Oh, nonsense. How absurd. Who would ever think of that," Hirth exclaimed. "This opera depicts conditions in Spain hundreds of years ago. The only thing I associated with it some years back were the atrocities committed by the Reds in the Spanish civil war. But after all, that isn't really the subject of the opera, is it? It is the epic of the loving wife,"— and he looked fondly at his own—"who is willing to sacrifice herself for her husband's life and freedom."

Headlights from the few Americans cars outside pointed the way through the rubble-flanked streets. We said good night.

It took me some time until I could bring myself to attend another concert in the banquet hall of the Frankfurt stock exchange.

"Otto Bernhardt joined the class only two years before graduation. Due to his upbringing in a socially prominent home—his father was an industrialist of importance—he created a good first impression. He had manners and self-control. In the long run, however, these pleasant characteristics were found to hide a mysterious reserve Bernhardt maintained toward teachers and fellow students alike. Although he had changed schools frequently, his above average intelligence had helped him attain notable intellectual successes. He was especially gifted in the field of foreign languages, but lacked the energy and the perseverance to make the best of his talents.

There was rarely cause to criticize Bernhardt. His teachers, however, were not pleased with this seeming perfection, because it sprang from his skill in avoiding collisions rather than from sound ethical concepts. I shall never forget his facial expression during lectures. He seemed to wear a mask. His eyes were hardly ever squarely directed at the lecturer. When they were, they seemed to reveal an abyss. He was one of the very few students who never took me into his confidence. I never knew the nature of the mystery he was so determined to suppress."

Erding

December 2, 1945

When I first saw Otto Bernhardt's name on the list of my fellow-students, I had no recollection of him. He was a member of our class only for the last two years of school, and there had been no contact between us that I could remember. Obrecht could find no trace of him at first, but then, with the aid of police registration records, obtained his parents' address in Marburg.

The 60-mile drive gave me another opportunity to experience the grotesque contrast between destroyed city and untouched country. The ruins of the once-great city of Frankfurt suddenly gave way to the unpretentious clustered northern suburbs. Then, for 40 miles, village after village inhabited by entirely normally living farm people. Suddenly, the destroyed town of Giessen brings the reality of Germany back to one's consciousness. Again, it gives way to the pleasant, prosperous-looking farm country along the enchanting Lahn valley.

As I drove along, the gigantic disparity made me wonder whether this exhausted country would be able to rebuild its cities in a hundred years. I have made no study of the objective facts, and strangely enough, the dimensions of the reconstruction task struck me more clearly as I looked at the healthy country side, than while gazing daily over the city's empty shell from the window of my office at headquarters. German cities developed in the course of many centuries. Their growth was correlated to the expanding German economy and the country's prosperity. If these two were among the basic elements of all city building, was there any reason to believe that the cities would be resurrected at all? Then, perhaps, the impoverished city population would improvise some easily constructible, barrack-type, emergency housing among the ruins of their former stately dwellings. The pressure for place to live, no matter how primitive, would make generous large-scale planning an illusion. When the people would begin to realize that their reduced standard of living was there to stay, primitive emergency housing would become a permanent condition.

By contrast, the farm country through which I was driving, faced no such setback. These villages were probably never rich, but the farmer, if his soil was reliable, was immune to the peaks and abysses of prosperity and depression. He lost no property in the bombings, nor did the military impose extensive requisitions on him. While there was some sentiment for land reform, parallel to that in eastern Germany, there was little concern over the agitation, because individual holdings were not excessively large. The farmers' greatest problem was the rising flood of refugees from the provinces of eastern Germany which had become Polish, and from the de-Germanized Sudeten country. Within a few months, the population of many a Landkreis (rural district) would double. The government would undoubtedly force the farmer to give up some of his standards—his extra rooms, furniture, clothing, chinaware,—because he would not surrender them voluntarily. The line of his charity was sharply drawn. He never had much use for city people or refugees. Much less so now, as long as the cities did not produce the goods he needed,—the shoes, the agricultural machinery, the furniture,—in return for the food he grew. They only offered him money. That was just so much paper. Let the pigs have the milk then.

This farmer knew that he was the kingpin in what remained of the German economy. His mood was not that of hopelessness which pervaded the city. He did not play with suicide ideas. On the contrary, he continued to build. To judge by appearance only, the rate of building in the villages and small towns was many times that of the cities. Fresh patches on houses indicated where a bomb or artillery fragment had struck a few months before, and new buildings, not unusually luxurious or modern, but sturdy and practical, sprang up here and there. The villagers cited two reasons for their activity: They were closer to basic building materials—stone and timber—and had saved some industrial materials through the collapse. More important, every one of them was himself a building craftsman. These impractical city dwellers had to call in a specialist every time they had to have a nail driven in the wall. In the country, every hand knew its way with mortar and saw.

At Potsdam in August, 1945, the Allies had decreed an essentially agrarian economy for Germany. A closer look at city and country was convincing enough that even without such an expressed policy, Germany's farmers, initially at least, would hold the trump cards in the country's development. No matter what happens to eastern refugees, city people, and bomb victims, whether they live or die, starve, freeze or take cyanide, work or loaf, the farm country would thrive. It may lack consumer goods, but it still has a fair reserve from former years. It may lack agricultural machinery and fuel, but it will receive a considerable labor reserve in the form of refugees. The more all of Germany depends on the farmer, the more he can expect to have things his own way. Germany's eight or ten million farm population will make their influence felt. They may be the country's healthiest group, but they have never been accused of being among its progressive thinkers.

I reached Marburg. It has not suffered a great deal from air raids. As a result, air raid victims from other cities have greatly increased its population. I drove through the narrow streets of the inner town at a walk. The sidewalks were overflowing with people who carried bundles, or pushed baby carriages loaded with household goods and an occasional baby. Gossiping women stood in groups in the middle of the street, resentful of traffic.

In one such group which scattered about one foot ahead of the bumper, I found a woman who directed me to Dr. Bernhardt's house. I found it in the outskirts, on a hill overlooking Marburg. It was a modern villa, probably no more than 10 years old, just outside a barbed-wire fence which surrounded a block of requisitioned houses.

A young, fair-haired, buxom woman answered the bell. I asked for Otto Bernhardt. She paled.

"Otto is dead," she said. "I am his sister."

I explained how I knew Otto and she asked me inside.

Dr. Bernhardt and his wife were sitting in the living room. He excused himself for continuing to drink his coffee before it became cold. Mrs. Bernhardt's lips thinned and her eyes moistened, when her daughter told her why I had come.

Otto's father was an impressive personality. He wore a dark, well-pressed business suit, and pearl-headed pin on his tie. He had a Van Dyke beard, and steady, penetrating eyes. Three saber cuts on his left cheek sternly exhibited the fact that as a German student he had belonged to a dueling fraternity. He alone was having his afternoon coffee. The table was set only for him. Mrs. Bernhardt, a grey-haired, haggard woman with bitterness written in her eyes and around the mouth, was keeping him company,—knitting. Otto's sister left us. She said she was a gymnastics teacher, and some children were waiting for her in the next room for their gym lesson.

The large room was elegantly furnished with heavy pieces in good taste. Copies of classical paintings in rich frames adorned the walls. Before a window stood an iron stove, its pipe sticking out through one of the glass panes. It provided the only touch of a coal-less winter in these surroundings of wealth and comfort. A wood fire was burning.

I found Mr. and Mrs. Bernhardt reluctant to speak about their son. They first told me about the misfortunes of the rest of their family. Otto had two sisters, both married. Neither husband had been heard from since April. One was probably a prisoner of the Red Army, the other of the British. Both families had been bombed out and were now living with the Bernhardt's. The house—five rooms—was thus shared by four adults and five children. The German housing authorities had just advised them that in the near future they would have to let one room to an eastern refugee family.

Misfortunes are relative, and I may have encouraged them by mentioning the much less satisfactory living conditions in Frankfurt, where on the average 2 ½ persons share a room in buildings which have remained standing, although more than half of the rooms still needed essential repairs. Their house, at least, had a roof, good glass windows, and fitting doors.

"We appreciate that," said Dr. Bernhardt, "but you can't really enjoy living even in our reduced circumstances, as long as life is so insecure. The Americans have requisitioned this house once, and there are rumors that we may have to evacuate it again. I wouldn't know where to turn. And when we moved in again after your troops left two months ago, we hardly recognized our house. Soldiers are soldiers, I know, and I hardly expected anything else. But what really incensed us is that my wife's fur coat and the children's winter things disappeared. The soldiers permitted German women into the house, and I'm sure these girls stole our things."

Dr. Bernhardt apologized that he could offer me no wine. The soldiers had left him none, he said pointedly. Nor did he dare share his coffee with me,—he felt certain that no American would touch the brew he was reduced to drinking. All he could offer me, he said, was a cigarette.

I said: "Won't you smoke mine?" before I understood his diplomatic sleight-of-hand.

"If you insist," he replied. His hand trembled as he lit the cigarette.

I tried to inquire about Otto again.

"Our poor boy was very brave," Dr. Bernhardt said. There was detachment in his voice rather than grief. His wife stared down at her knitting with reddened eyes. "He was very ill," Otto's father continued, "even when you knew him. By the way here is his picture. It was taken a year before his death."

He rose, took a small framed photo from the desk and gave it to me. Until now, Otto Bernhardt had been no more than a name on my list. Now I remembered him. A serious, gaunt face with straight, dark hair. An intense stare, apparent even in a mediocre photograph. That he had been ill was entirely new to me. Perhaps some of his closer friends knew about it.

Dr. Bernhardt tried to circumscribe Otto's illness. Finally, he mentioned it by name:—epilepsy.

"For Otto's sake, we tried to keep his disease a secret from everybody. That's why he changed school so often. Once an attack had betrayed him to his school mates, he would not set foot in the building again."

Otto's father called him a victim of the first world war. He had contracted meningitis when he was a boy of three, in 1916. The family believed, or wanted outsiders to believe, that Otto's epilepsy was a consequence of his childhood disease.

I asked Dr. Bernhardt what Otto had done after we graduated.

"You'll probably remember," he answered, "that Otto had a definite talent for modern languages. He knew French and English quite well—we had always taken him along on our trips abroad. I sent him to the University of Lausanne in Switzerland. Unfortunately, his stay there was again cut short by one of his attacks. So we decided to let him study at the interpreters institute in Heidelberg. He studied French and English for two years, and I could then place him in the foreign department of I.G. Farben. I was a director of I.G. Farben myself, you know."

The manner of Dr. Bernhardt's description of his son's career indicated that Otto himself had little say in the matter. But even Dr. Bernhardt's directorial influence had not sufficed to maintain Otto's position at I.G. Farben when his fits increased in frequency and violence. Slight disagreements would cause him to react violently, and his superiors felt they could not employ him under the circumstances, Dr. Bernhardt explained.

"We thought that the quiet life at a university would improve his condition. This time we sent him to the University of Cologne. 1938, wasn't it, mother?" he asked his wife. Mrs. Bernhardt nodded.

"The army exempted him, of course. But at the university he had to be a member of one of the Nazi organizations. Otherwise he would have had difficulties. He picked the NSKK, the Nazi motor corps. They held political indoctrination meetings and drilled a little, but otherwise they weren't much of a bother. During the war, though, they had to do a lot of emergency driving. Otto helped out wherever duty called him. One day in 1941, he was called out for emergency work after one of the early air raids on Cologne. There was a lot of excitement, of course, and it affected Otto again. He had a disagreement with his superior. Something very trivial—which way to drive out of the danger area in the city. Well, in the course of the argument, Otto hit his superior with a small fire extinguisher. The man spent several weeks in the hospital."

Dr. Bernhardt said that the Gestapo took charge of the incident. Otto was accused of attempted political assassination.

"As soon as I heard of it," Dr. Bernhardt continued, "I took the next plane down to Cologne. I talked to the Gestapo and made it clear to them that Otto was not responsible for himself in moments of excitement. You know what they did? They ordered a medical examination of my whole family to determine whether Otto's epilepsy was hereditary. I knew the doctors would never make such a decision, of course. But had the Gestapo been able to prove it, Otto would have been sterilized."

Dr. Bernhardt lit another cigarette nervously. His wife had hardly said a word since I had come in. She seemed accustomed to having her husband speak for the family.

"Then the Gestapo ordered Otto placed in an insane asylum. He spent a year there, and it was terribly difficult to obtain his release. It was one of the institutions where the number of severe cases dropped rapidly, and you can imagine what anguish we went through."

All during his account of Otto's unhappy life, Dr. Bernhardt had used circumscriptive language,—probably to spare his wife's emotions. Epileptic fits became "attacks", and a Nazi extermination plant an "institution where the number of severe cases dropped rapidly."

"Finally, I managed to have Otto transferred to a private institution. The Gestapo made me responsible for keeping him out of circulation. He was happier there, but still,—it must have been an appalling life for him. He was surrounded by mentally unbalanced people, although, except for his occasional attacks, he was perfectly normal. Then, just about a year and a half ago, the doctors decided that he had improved to such an extent that he could be released. We had him home for a few months. It was a happy interlude. Last summer he returned to Cologne. He wanted to be active, and without my knowledge, a family friend who owns a building concern gave him a job as a messenger. He knew Otto's story and believed that in an occupation which carried no responsibility Otto would be all right. Then, on the 21st of November, 1944, Otto died."

When Dr. Bernhardt mentioned no cause, I wondered whether Otto had perished in an air raid.

"No," he said. I inquired after the cause. There was a moment's silence, then Dr. Bernhardt turned to his wife:

"I really see no reason for hiding it." Then he said:

"Otto killed himself. He had an attack after another flare-up with his new superior, and our friend had to dismiss him. That evening Otto went to his room and took a whole flask of sleeping tablets. He was unconscious for three days, then he died. ... My wife and I have come to feel that it was probably best that way. Otto had led an inhumanly unhappy life."

The family did not hear about Otto's death until the middle of January. Postal facilities with the Cologne area had been completely disorganized by air attacks. The message they then received only mentioned Otto's death. Not until April, five months later, did they obtain the full story. I expressed my sympathy.

After a while Mrs. Bernhardt asked what I had found out about the rest of the class. Then Dr. Bernhardt turned the subject to present political affairs. His voice quickened, and his stern expression became livelier. It was a more pressing topic to him than the story of his late son.

"It's not every day that I have a chance to talk to an American," he said. "Perhaps you can explain a few things to me. There is much that I fail to understand. Years ago, I used to be quite active in politics. But what goes on today is simply more than I can swallow."

He said that he had been an officer in the first war, and had become a democrat afterwards. He was the head of the Democratic Party in the small Rhenish town in which he then lived and worked. This party, which was flanked during the Weimar Republic by the great workers' Social-Democratic Party on the left, and the powerful Catholic Center Party on the right, was an association of politically powerless middle-class idealists who looked to the Anglo-Saxon democracies for leadership. That they found little encouragement was Dr. Bernhardt's chief complaint.

"Why didn't Britain and the United States help the Republic instead of Hitler?" he wanted to know. "Why did they make the concession of cancelling reparations to the smooth anti-democrat Von Papen, rather than to the democratic government which preceded him? Why did they consider revising the Versailles treaty when Hitler demanded it with a mailed fist, after stubbornly refusing to change as much as a comma to the Weimar Republic which begged on its knees?"

There are few defenders of the Versailles Treaty today. Opinions are divided between those who consider it too harsh, and those who feel it was too soft. During the past 10 years, the weight of world opinion has shifted to the latter view. However, during those same ten years, a normally well-informed man like Dr. Bernhardt was cut off from the development of world opinion.

German moderate foreign policy had always stressed that Versailles had caused a strengthening of reactionary and revanche ideas inside Germany, while discrediting a regime which wanted to cooperate with League of Nations. Undoubtedly, these views gained throughout the world in the late twenties. They brought about a conversion of public opinion favorable to Germany. But this conversion should have come earlier or never. As it was, Hitler reaped the fruits of the prestige the Republic had been able to rebuild abroad in the

14 years of its existence. He obtained the concessions from the victors of the first world war which, granted the Republic a few years earlier, might have enabled it to live.

Historically accurate or not, this line of thought continues to be the apology of those who, like Dr. Bernhardt, permitted power to slip into Hitler's hands when they saw no "legal" means of keeping it from him, and could not muster the courage to prevent the disaster by other means. In recapitulating this experience of the German Republic now, Dr. Bernhardt meant to draw a parallel to the present situation.

"Don't strike us down too hard," he said.

He thought the world had made a mistake in not giving Germany a chance after the last war, and was about to commit the same error again. He was afraid the policy might again lead to war. He thought he had done his duty after the first war by working for international cooperation and a peaceful, if limited, German development, and he would like to do so again. But he felt himself hamstrung by the distrust shown Germany by the outside world.

In even making the point, he showed that he had no conception of the depth and extent of this distrust. He considered it unjustified. The Nazis were responsible for the war, not the Germans. And he made the world equally responsible, along with the Germans, for permitting the Nazis to seize power to begin with.

There remained a question which I had asked many Germans:

"You say, Dr. Bernhardt, that the Nazis were responsible for the war, not the Germans. In what manner did you, as an opponent of your government's war policy, express this opposition?"

"Well, young man," said Dr. Bernhardt, "there's only one answer. The British gave it long ago as the acid test of a man's patriotism: 'Right or wrong, my country.' Once we were at war, I had no choice but to fight for Germany to the best of my ability."

Allowing for variations, Dr. Bernhardt's answer was identical with that I had received to the same question from many Germans, especially of middle class or military background. It meant an impasse in our discussion, as it implied an impasse in the task of "reeducation." The term "nationalism" may sum it up most easily, but not at all adequately. As an irrational factor in German affairs, it continues to confuse issues and people. Omitting it from our uncomplicated and human ways of thought, many of us have come to consider all anti-Nazis our friends. In truth, the bulk of German anti-Nazis, so it would seem, were Germans first, and anti-Nazis second. And even those who prayed for an Allied victory must now oppose the victors' policy for an emasculated Germany, or lose their German soul. In the last analysis, a void of true ideals and motives, and the convenience of following the herd, are hidden by the absolute and final statement: "After all, I am a German." And the world's "So what?" still remains unanswered.

When I failed to reply, Dr. Bernhardt probably realized that his patriotic statement had erected a wall between us. He tried to smile and said:

"Nevertheless, let us hope there will not be another war. All now depends on your relations to Russia."

With that I agreed. I asked him how he felt these relations were developing.

"I hope you understand each other well," he said. "War between the United States and Britain on one side, and Russia on the other, would mean disaster for Germany. I'm afraid there are Germans today who are blind enough to believe that through such a war Germany could rise again. I think that is utopian."

Why of all adjectives he picked this one to describe the possibility of another war, I do not know.

As everywhere else, the rumor factory was busily at work in Marburg. Dr. Bernhardt said people here had their own interpretation for the coal trucks racing through town daily from the Ruhr toward the east and south. They said the coal was only a top layer, covering atom bombs.

I laughed.

Mrs. Bernhardt, too, thought this was funny.

"That's silly, isn't it?" she said. "The Americans would never take their atom bombs so close to the front. They'll fly them into Russian territory from air fields further back, don't you think?"

If her remark was not such a grim illustration of the average German's state of mind, I would offer it to Mr. Webster, the cartoonist, for his series "And nothing can be done about it."

I prepared to leave. Dr. Bernhardt picked up the pack of cigarettes which I had meant to leave behind.

"Aren't you forgetting your cigarettes?" he said. "As a matter of fact, forgive me for saying … but I might as well admit … I am a chain smoker and without cigarettes my nervous system comes close to collapse. Would you sell me your cigarettes? I'll pay you any price. When I can't find any in the black market I go out in the street to look for the ends your soldiers throw away. It is a very humiliating experience. But I simply need them. So, — if you could help me out …?"

I gave him the few cigarettes I had with me, and he thanked me profusely. His wife had tears in her eyes again, and I could think of several motives.

"Herbert Netzer is the son of a smart, mature, adaptable father who was saved by his diplomatic intelligence and conciliatory ways from committing himself in any direction. Herbert was a gifted observer, and an easy imitator. Under his father's influence he could not have developed a strong character, even if he had been hereditarily equipped for it. In spite of his amiable personality, I have always considered him heartless. Whenever his decisions were morally good, they coincided with his advantage: "Good is what serves my purpose." He played with life, hardly restraining his instincts, but his remarkable intelligence prevented serious clashes.

He played with friendships as with life, and friends soon realized him to be a bluffer, unwilling to bring real sacrifices. His incredibly swift physical reactions are matched by his mental ability. In the field of ethics, the latter makes him an amoral personality, beyond good and evil."

Erding

December 8, 1945

It seems that my ex-class mates scattered in a semi-circle north of Frankfurt, not two in the same place. The Hessian town of Schotten was the next goal. Herbert Netzer was supposed to have his home there, according to Obrecht's information.

I reached the old, unspectacular, small town after an hour and a half's fast jeep drive through rolling farm country and wooded hills. Netzer's address was a small hotel, the Hessische Hof, in the center of town, reached over cobble-stoned streets. It had a blue stucco facade, with its name in heavy black lettering. Small windows in thick walls indicated that winters were cold in this area. I drove the jeep through the wide, wooden gate into a yard.

By a barn in a corner, a man, surrounded by children, was sawing wood. When he looked up at the jeep, I recognized my school chum Herbert Netzer. For a few seconds, he squinted in my direction, then continued to saw.

The children were now surrounding the jeep, demanding chewing gum. Then they trailed me over to Herbert's corner. He looked up again.

"Don't I know you?" he said in English.

"Wouldn't surprise me," I said.

He recognized me.

"How in hell did you ever find me out here?" he wondered.

With his shirt sleeves rolled up, his face flushed, blond hair hanging down over his forehead, Herbert looked like an advertisement for the Nazi Labor Service. He was tall, bony, decidedly good-looking in a Nordic way. His hair was receding in one corner, adding a touch of intellectuality to the general impression. The Jewish grand- or great-grandmother I remembered to have been among his ancestors had not visibly contributed to his Teutonic appearance.

If I had been sawing wood, and he had suddenly stood before me, I doubt whether I would have recognized him as easily. He had changed a great deal—to his advantage. The receding hair over his right temple—that was it. In school days he had been a scrapper, quite brutal and inconsiderate at times, an excellent athlete, with a tendency to employ his intellect to think up more and better ways of getting into hot water. It had usually taken the intervention of his father, headmaster at another Frankfurt school, to get him out. On my way up to see him, I was quite certain I'd find an embittered deactivated officer, rather than the friendly, alert intellectual who was now shaking my hand.

Netzer still seemed impulsive enough. His low-voiced rapid-fire talk struck a familiar note, bridging 15 years. Sawing wood was apparently his present way of letting off steam,—at the same time a highly useful activity.

"Glad the engine for the power saw is out of gas," he said. "Gives a man some exercise."

He picked up half a dozen blocks of wood like so many match sticks and walked ahead into the hotel. His room was on the second floor, reached through a low-ceilinged corridor and a staircase embellished with pictures of the war of 1870. A life-size portrait of Bismarck covered half a wall on the landing.

"Terribly hot in here," he yelled as he opened the door to his room. He dashed across it and tore the window open. Then he introduced his family— his wife, his three-year old son Hans, and his father. They were sitting by a small table, having their afternoon coffee—milk for junior.

The room was hardly wider than a clothes closet, and about 20 feet long. There was a kitchen sink by the window. The place looked like a kitchen remade into living quarters.

His wife was lovely. She was almost as blonde as Herbert. With her white, fitting sports sweater and her tastefully applied make-up, she might have come straight from an American college campus. Netzer, obviously used to reading the minds of people who contemplated his wife's looks, said: "Cute, isn't she?" She blushed modestly.

That Netzer junior should have turned out to be the prize-winning type of a boy was only natural.

"Wipe your mouth and take a bow to the American", his father ordered him. Junior slid off his chair and did as he was told. Then, to make more room, he climbed on his mother's lap.

Herbert's father sat in the only available easy chair by a large radio set, coffee cup in hand. I had known him slightly years ago, and he seemed not very much older. He was a tall, heavy-set man, almost bald, more the type of a business executive than that of a professor.

"Have a cigarette," Herbert said pulling out a pack of Chesterfields. "Go ahead," he urged, "I have plenty of them." I knew he meant it.

"And where've you been since we graduated?" he asked. "Last I knew you were going to work for the League of Nations. Oh boy, that was a hot one."

He was right—that had been my favorite school boy dream. He put me through a blitz cross-examination on the intervening years. I knew him well enough to realize that if I wanted him to talk about his own story, I had to submit to this first.

His wife took two more cups and saucers from the closets and poured us coffee. It was good, black American coffee, and there were cream and sugar to go with it.

"This is only for Saturdays and Sundays," Herbert said. "I know some of your officers here in town. Nice bunch of boys. When I'm out, they come to visit my wife and the boy. Your soldiers really like children, don't they? Hans here gets more chocolate than he can eat. Would you like to meet these friends of ours? They'll be up for bridge later in the afternoon. Regular Saturday event, you know. When they lose, they pay off with luxuries like coffee that are hard for me to get. As a matter of fact, they do, even if they win. Swell bunch."

"Do you know English, too?" I asked Herbert's wife.

"Oh yes," she said. "I spent a year in the United States just before the war. At college. I had a grand time. I returned home to Berlin in the fall of 1939, just before we defeated Poland."

"Were the students nasty to you because you were German?" I asked.

"Oh no," she said. "There were some of course, especially after the Munich conference. But not my friends. They shared my opinions about the British and their imperialism which was choking Germany. I hope they haven't changed after you entered the war. I've heard from them again recently through these officers here, but they wrote nothing about politics. It's wonderful that the war is over, and we can be friends again, isn't it? I even tried to maintain my friendships to Americans during the war."

I asked her how she had done that, and she reached for a silver tray on a shelf above the table. She handed it to me. There was an engraved English inscription: "Best wishes for the happiness of Herbert and Louise Netzer", followed by about a dozen names of American and British officers, and the dateline "Oberursel, April 23, 1942."

"This was my wedding present," she said. I worked at a prisoner camp for English and American fliers."

This was quite a discovery. Located at Oberursel during the war was Dulag Luft, the Nazis' interrogation camp for Allied fliers shot down over western Europe. A British court martial had just sentenced the German commanding officer of the camp and one of his interrogators to several years in prison for mistreatment of Allied personnel. But cruelty was not the only method used by the Germans to extract military information from our prisoners. Kindness was sometimes found to work better. To judge by Mrs. Netzer's silver tray, that's where she fitted in.

"What did your work at Oberursel consist of?" I asked.

"I did some office work. Filing cards and such awful stuff."

"What was on those cards?"

"Oh, you know, — all kinds of information like your planes and units and crews and so on. But I liked my other assignment much better—to mix with the prisoners and see that they had all they needed. I think they liked me too. Wonderful bunch of boys, your fliers. I wish I could meet some of them again— at their homes. They told me all about their homes and their families. They were so homesick. And it's the same with these new friends of ours who'll be here for a bridge game in a while. They're homesick. That's why they like to come here, they say,—we know English, and they can talk to us about home. I only hope these friendships will last."

From the free and friendly manner with which she described her peace and war-time achievements, it was clear that she expected nothing but understanding and approval. Honi soit qui mal y pense.

I asked Herbert whether his experiences had been as interesting. He gave his enthusiastic wife a not too friendly look and said with an undertone of sarcasm that in some ways they had. Then he began to talk about himself. It was rather difficult to piece his story together because of the bursts of eloquence with which he told it, and the indefinite allusions he sometimes substituted for straight facts.

Herbert Netzer was an engineer. After our graduation, he studied at Frankfurt University, and later at a technical school in Darmstadt, south of Frankfurt. Before I had a chance to ask him about it, he said that he never joined the party, only a special compulsory SA student formation. And, he said, his membership in it lapsed as soon as he left school.

Herbert presented his nearly spotless non-Nazi record rather proudly. "I had the Gestapo on my neck twice," he said.

"Do you remember Paul Rossert?"

"Of course," I said. Rossert was one of our class mates, a rather close friend of Herbert's during the last years of school. Obrecht had so far failed to find any trace of him or his family in Frankfurt. I was glad to hear Herbert mention his name.

"Well, Paul turned Communist," Herbert said, "and when the Nazis came he had trouble at the university. By the way, I don't know what happened to him. He was active in the underground, and they put him in a concentration camp in 1939. He kept in touch with his mother until 1942. From then on I don't know. I tried to find his mother in Frankfurt, but no success. His parents were divorced,—you knew that, didn't you?"

I told Herbert that I was trying hard to find Paul, his father or his mother, and that Dr. Erding had promised to look for Professor Rossert's address. Herbert went on:

"Paul and I remained good friends until the war. That is, I didn't like his wife very much, and we saw less of each other after he was married. His wife was a Communist organizer and really took him in tow. It's never good when a wife is a man's intellectual superior, is it darling?" He looked at his wife with a grin.

"Yes, dear Herbert," she said without looking up.

Herbert turned back toward me. "They engaged in underground work against the Nazis. Leaflets, chain letters and so on. Perhaps even intelligence work for the Russians, I don't know. But until 1936, I was quite well informed. In that year, the Gestapo tracked a connection with the Spanish Republicans to our group. We were supposed to have smuggled arms to them through France. They interrogated all of us, but, of course, they couldn't get anything out of me! So that time Paul got away. I remained under Gestapo surveillance. I'm sure of that. My letters were always opened, and my movements were watched. In 1937 they were mad at me again. You know I was born in Alsace? I had dual citizenship, both French and German. The French called me up for a year's military training in 1937. I wouldn't have minded going, but the police refused me an exit visa."

Herbert's difficulties with the Gestapo apparently ceased when he obtained his engineering degree. Siemens, the large German electrical concern, hired him immediately, he said, and work there was so fascinating that he lost all interest in political affairs. His specialty were electric steering devices for unmanned aircraft.

When war came, Herbert was drafted. "I didn't mind it, but I thought my work had been pretty important. Hitler didn't think so. 'I don't need engineers,' he said, 'I need soldiers.' So for six months, I scrubbed latrines. Then Hitler changed his mind, and said that the genius of German engineers would win the war for the fatherland. I was put back at the drawing board. Wasn't so easy after six months of latrines."

I said that latrines were an essential factor in the American army too, and he shouldn't feel too bitter about it. Yes, he replied, but in those six months he could have done much valuable work.

"What did you work on?"

"The V-1. I contributed to the steering mechanism. Later I worked on our gliding bombs, aircraft released and rocket fired. It was exciting work."

Herbert's research was supervised by the German Air Force, and he rose to such responsibilities, he said, that he took part in conferences with General Milch, and once with Goering in person.

"Don't think for a minute that we intended to use the V-1s with the explosive charge you know. It was planned to carry atomic bombs. Our atomic development just didn't keep the pace. Probably would have taken us another eight years. Meanwhile you discovered the bomb, and the Russians probably are close to it, too. You know, I had a hunch about that. I was pessimistic from the beginning. I made several bets between 1939 and 1941 that we'd lose the war. At that time, I was given odds. Just cashed in on them last week."

I tried to bring the facets of Herbert's attitude to one denominator, and I told him I was baffled. He was an anti-Nazi from the beginning, with Communist underground contacts. He considered himself a near-victim of Gestapo persecution. The war, he thought, could not be won. Then he served the war machine as an engineer on V-weapons, deriving great satisfaction from his work.

"What's illogical about that?" he asked. "Once we were at war, what else could I have done? I'm a German,—we were fighting for our existence. Had I worked against the war effort, or even if I had remained passive, I would have become a traitor."

"If that was the general conception," I said, "then all Hitler had to do to get every German's support,—Nazi, indifferent, and anti-Nazi,—was to plunge into war."

"I suppose it worked that way," Netzer answered. "Once we were at war, it became perfectly clear that would all hang—together. Your bombs made no distinction between Nazis, indifferent, and anti-Nazis. And we knew damn well that if we lost, all of Germany would be treated as she probably deserved—we could expect no special exemptions. That part of it has certainly come true."

"How would anti-Nazis have fared if Germany had won?"

"Terribly. We could have had to shine Nazi boots for the rest of our lives."

"Then why didn't you fight against the Nazis instead of for them?"

"I didn't fight for them. I fought with Germany. I could never have fought on the other side. I had to do my duty."

I had asked my pet question, and received the expected answer. There are, however, shades of stubbornness in German nationalism. I asked him whether in his opinion the German generals and conservatives who attempted to kill Hitler in July 1944 were traitors or patriots.

"That's a difficult question. But I think they were patriots. They were fully informed on our desperate situation, and wanted to bring the war to a close."

"And why should a German be considered a traitor if he acted against war from the beginning?"

"Because he was not informed. We may have been able to win!"

Herbert Netzer's father had listened to us closely, and with obviously growing impatience. He had made a few gestures as though he wanted to interrupt, but his son's determined conversational manner was not easily stopped.

"You're both too young and too ignorant of history," he now said. "The difference between treason and patriotism is sometimes hard to detect, at times even non-existent. And it isn't determined by pure ethics any more than by blind nationalism. We Germans are a nation whose conduct developed from innumerable historical factors. I mean the conduct of the people as a whole, not of the individual. But for the people as a whole, as for all nations, the primary urge is that of survival, of relative material improvement and well-being. That's what Hitler assured the people, and they followed him. Even into war. At that time the people were ready to crucify any man who dared obstruct the nation's hopes and aspirations. I was against war. The Nazis threw me out of office in 1938, because I refused to teach history their way. Had I gone further in my opposition, I would have become a traitor. There were a hundred justifications for opposition. But the people had been talked into believing that the war was in their interest. And it is their common, average view which makes a man a sinner or a saint. That view can be corrected only by one thing—military defeat. In 1944, the war was obviously lost, and the people were anxious to get out of it. Therefore, the generals who revolted against Hitler became national heroes. The people's well-being, instead of war, now demanded peace. I'm afraid a nation's fight for survival can't be measured in terms of logic and ethics."

I agreed with Professor Netzer that I was too ignorant of history to present the case for ethics in international affairs more convincingly. However, if he applied his empiric views to Germany's present position, he would have no cause for complaint.

"As a historian—no," he said. "Our bid for the famous place in the sun was turned back by a powerful combination of countries, and vae victis applies to us as it has always applied to the defeated. But as a German, and as a man who has opposed Nazism and its abolition of ethics, my hope now rests in the progressive views of international life for which your country has ostensibly gone to war. But I haven't much hope. I see no evidence yet that you have freed the world from fear and want. Instead, the victors are scrambling for position for the next conflict. If it should come, then Germany's contribution may tip the scales for Christian civilization, and we may yet redeem ourselves."

Professor Netzer put his empty coffee cup away and walked over to the door where his overcoat was hanging. He pulled a batch of papers from a pocket.

"This is something I'd like you to read. I have a friend who is an industrialist. He came to me one day and told me he had excellent connections to people high up in the victorious governments. Those people were greatly interested in knowing how a thinking anti-Nazi German looked at the present situation, and at occupational policies. He asked me to write an essay on my views. I had it ready for him when he returned, but then he told me that the higher-ups he knew were Frenchmen. Well, I didn't want him to take the essay as it was, because I had been under the impression that he was in touch with Americans. I saw no reason for telling the French what we criticize in American Military Government. So I revised it for French consumption. This is a copy of the paper I turned over to him. If you'd like to read it, I think you'd understand us better."

He offered me his easy chair and began to play with his grandson. I read the document through hastily, and then asked him whether he would permit me to take it along. He agreed, and a translation of it follows:

"It is a beautiful thought that there are men outside our boundaries who wish to know how the great present-day experiences are mirrored in the mind of a thinking German,—one who wishes to understand events and their long-range continuity quietly and objectively.

The author believes that the great events of human development cannot be understood from a materialistic point of view. Rather, they are the outcome of factors which are determined by a spiritual principle, even if their connection is often hard to recognize. Contemporaries see only a moving, rapidly changing surface. But underneath, hidden by it, runs a great and steady tide which can only be accelerated or retarded by events on the surface, but never changed in its direction.

To understand the events of today, we must briefly survey the beginnings of the development we are witnessing.

We are faced with a deep hiatus in human evolution. None in the history of European culture has equaled it since the downfall of the Ancient World with its fixed spiritual, political, and economic order. Three centuries later a new form of organized life was founded. The new Empire rose from the fusion of the Germanic nations with the Ancient World, under the influence of Christianity. It was not a state, but the state of the occident. As the Holy Roman Empire it existed for a thousand years. For half that period, it determined the form of the occidental world.

Europe then was largely a cultural unit. The knights and the clergy were supranational in their character. The crusades were the strongest expression of this community.

The Empire fell when its spiritual content and mission were lost. Faith vanished, and man, in the Renaissance, sought the law of the world in himself.

In this period, a series of national states sprang up around Germany. In the 17th century, France took a leading position among them. The old European unity was torn asunder. Germany did not become a national state, but remained split into numerous territories which, individually, could ally themselves with foreign powers against the impotent German Empire.

At the beginning of the 16th century, Germany was a flowering garden with queen-like cities. For a second time, the German spirit entered the world with a mission from God—Luther's reformation. As a result, while other nations expanded and built up overseas empires, Germany was locked in a life-and-death struggle which lasted thirty years. At its end, Germany was a desert, with all its cultural life at an end, and half of its population dead.

The survivors of this catastrophe which so closely resembled Germany's present straits, took 200 years to overcome its consequences.

Meanwhile, Germany presented the world with a third spiritual empire: the rule of German idealism, climaxed by the names of Lessing, Herder, Goethe, Schiller, Kant, and Hegel. The old, cultural ties of the middle ages with France seemed to reform. But these spiritual beginnings broke in the face of hard material discrepancies.

The spirit needs a body on earth. Even the "nation of poets and thinkers," as Germany was called in sarcastic appreciation, needed one. Under immense difficulties, the Prussian state rose to the leadership of the new Germany. Under Bismarck's wise and moderate guidance, it experienced a long and prosperous period of peace. Material developments seemed to promise unlimited progress. A shallow, spiritually unfounded optimism made the country overlook that this period of human history was in truth closing.

However, modern technology, coupled with liberal forms of life, had enabled the population of Europe to rise from 180 million in 1800 to 460 million in 1914.

This rise created entirely new conditions. The population of Germany rose from 41 million in 1871 to nearly 70 million in 1914.

In 1871, Bismarck could consider a Germany of 41 million people a saturated national unit. But how could the same soil, much of it so poor, feed nearly twice this number? Participation in world trade furnished the only possible answer.

German industrial quality and commercial enterprise made this a practical method of importing needed foodstuffs and raw materials from abroad. This was, however, a dangerous position. Competitors who had command of the high seas were able at any time to interrupt the flow of vital German imports by force of arms.

Germany's central position made her vulnerable to encirclement. A statesman told Bismarck: "Vous avez le cauchemar des coalitions." The German chancellor indeed suffered from this nightmare. The Franco-Russian Alliance became a deathly danger, as soon as the British Empire joined it. Meanwhile, as the volume of German trade approached that of the British, the wish to eliminate the bothersome competitor by a warlike blow became increasingly evident in England. Not Germany made the First World War, "Made in Germany" did.

As William II had accurately foreseen, Germany had to bow to encirclement and blockade, when it was unable to win the war quickly. The blockade broke Germany materially and spiritually. Only the Almighty knows how many millions of Germans succumbed to it.

When the war was over, it became clear that the Allies only had an annihilation program in store for Germany, not a constructive plan. Allied unity consisted of the premise that Wilson's promises which caused Germany to lay down its arms, should not be kept.

This fact has prolonged the second World War unnecessarily by some nine months, causing the death of many German and Allied civilians and soldiers. The German people lacked all faith in the assurances given to effect Germany's capitulation.

The first World War was led by the Allies in order to create a democratic Germany. Germany was never as ready and willing to accept democratic thought as in 1918. Elections to the National Assembly resulted in a surprising victory of the democratic parties.

This would have been the moment for the victors to support the Weimar Republic in its difficult beginnings, as Bismarck had supported the young French Third Republic after 1871.

Unfortunately, this did not take place. Excluded from the League of Nations, the German democratic government suffered one defeat after another abroad until the German people regarded it as nothing but representatives of the Reparations

Commission. From year to year it lost more moral credit among the people. The radical parties gained rapidly.

Germany's economic position became unbearable. Enormous reparations could be paid only in the form of exports. Headed by the United States, Allied countries closed their doors to German exports by high tariffs. When "dumping" failed, German merchandise remained unsaleable. Factories closed down. 14 million Germans were either unemployed, or working part time only. Again, the country experienced unspeakable misery. For a second time the weakness of Germany's position became evident. The countries from which Germany had imported food destroyed their products, while Germany starved.

German democracy weakened increasingly. More and more voters believed that unconditional union with Russia offered a way out. The general mood of desperation engendered the belief that only a dictatorship was capable of dealing with Germany's extreme need.

This wave of desperation carried Hitler into power. He would never have attained his aims, had the victors given German democracy even the slightest assistance. The proof seemed furnished that in a desperate situation, a democracy is helpless.

Hitler possessed the suggestive powers to make this impoverished nation believe he would save it. He became chancellor by democratic means, through the ballot. When he reached the top, he kicked over the ladder which had carried him, and erected a dictatorship. The workers, who had fought him most bitterly, became his staunchest adherents. Hitler not only overcame unemployment, but also fulfilled so many radical demands of the workers that his system was justly called National-Bolshevism.

The economy was revived by a state which became the sole contractor. The method of curing unemployment by making the wheels of the armament industry turn has since been copied elsewhere.

Hitler won the workers and a large part of the peasantry by providing work and favorable living conditions.

Other parts of the people had to concede Hitler's great successes in the field of foreign policy. Demands were realized which every German considered justified by Divine and human law, especially the unity of people and nation.

The year 1938 marked Hitler's zenith. Leading statesmen mastered a situation which was more complicated than that of 1914 after the assassination at Sarajevo, without recourse to arms. A new epoch in world history seemed to begin. The initiative of responsible statesmen succeeded where cabinets and parliaments had failed: To eliminate war as a means to solve international problems. We should bow in homage to the memory of Chamberlain.

Much remained to separate the thinking German from Hitler: His utilitarian morals proclaiming that which served the German people as the only measure of all values; the materialism of his racial theories; his contempt for our religious life; Gestapo pressure. But Hitler had achieved something which earned him many adherents among his former opponents in the educated classes: The German people had finally won the right with which God has endowed all nations, to fashion their own lives in their own country without having to see millions of their brothers suffer the ignominy of second-class citizenship in bordering countries. Had Hitler been satisfied with this success, he may have been able to stabilize his position.

However, after the Munich conference, both his external and internal policies abandoned all ethical foundations. Germans who based their lives on ethical concepts, their disapproval stifled, were increasingly horrified.

Quietly, in the darkness of night, Hitler's regiments went to war followed by tear-filled eyes. How different a scene from the enthusiastic farewell to our troops in 1914, when the German people felt—rightly or wrongly—that they were engaged in a holy war for the defense of their country.

Those who lived in England or the United States cannot imagine the wartime suffering and dangers endured by those of us who rejected Hitler's policies. The survivors hardly understand yet how they escaped the double danger of Gestapo and death from the air.

We know one thing: Germany's cities are in ruin, and with them the cultural shrines which belonged to humanity as well as to Germany. The German too, body and mind, was severely hurt. Twelve years of a bloody terror have broken his spine.

The bulk of our people are too tired and too ill physically and mentally to have a clear understanding of anything beyond the most primitive animalistic needs. An enormously complicated civilization was largely reduced to forms of life common to the stone age.

We realize that the crisis has not yet reached its nadir. The coming winter will kill millions of Germans through hunger and cold. The Nazi gas chambers were a relatively humane procedure. When the gas works of a town in western Germany resumed production recently, several hundred persons on the first day ended their lives voluntarily.

But this is only the beginning.

Several months ago, Churchill warned the world of the roots of future wars which he saw in the decision to take one quarter of Germany's arable land away from us. The importance of the food problem for Germany was stressed above.

Hitler's aim to gain the Ukraine as a breadbasket for our people was an outgrowth of these considerations. In this sense, his war against Russia was a war for food. Now, Germany's eastern agricultural areas are being taken away. The dangerously overpopulated areas in the west are not only to feed themselves, but are also to receive millions of Germans driven from their homes in the east. A drastic simile may explain the situation:

A number of men are crowded into a narrow cage. They can more or less support themselves by making things with their hands. They sell these through the bars in return for bread to those outside. One day, this trade ends,—for some reason it becomes impossible. The poor inmates see starvation before them, and revolt against their keepers. They attempt to break the bars and escape. They are, however, overcome. As a penalty, more men are cramped into the cage. Then they are told to behave themselves. Is this picture sufficiently clear?

It is said that the German people must feed itself out of its own soil. This rather reminds of the ancient custom applied when a man was condemned to death by starvation. Before he was immured, he was given a loaf of bread and a jug of water. If he died just the same, one's conscience was appeased.

To banish the threat of starvation which has been hanging over Germany since 1871, is the task of today, the only one that matters, overshadowing all else. Would it not be more merciful to ship, say, a minimum of 10 million young Germans with their wives to under-populated areas overseas, giving them an opportunity to settle? German prisoners of war have longingly glanced over the beautiful vastness of Canada. Would not these people become the most loyal citizens of a state which would save and guarantee their lives? When will the world understand that it was not the urge to rule the world which pressed arms into the hands of the German people as such (as distinct from their government), but the fear of hunger? Germans know today that their history as an independent great power is finished. They don't care which flag waves over their heads, as long as it protects them.

This mood is intensified by the social upheaval which has taken place and is taking place in Germany. A large proportion of the people have lost all their belongings. Out of their ruined houses, they saved nothing but their naked bodies. Others lost their livelihood and lack the means even to purchase their sparse food ration. Added to them are the millions who were driven from their homes. Never in the course of history has such an immense uprooting taken place in so short a time.

Those who are faced by destitution can only hope to improve their lot by taking something from others. The Marxist factory worker who anticipated a world revolution, became a conservative small bourgeois, bent on preserving his property, the moment he owned a small house with a little garden. Conversely, all those will become Communists who believe that their lot can be improved only under this system.

Free elections in Germany today would result in an overwhelming Communist victory. Germans would not be surprised if the dictatorship of one party were to be replaced by that of another. Our young generation is especially vulnerable. Certain mechanical mental processes were hammered into it. They never knew anything except the rule of a political party, representing a definite and exclusive philosophy. For them, the word "democracy" is an empty sound without meaning and propagandistic attraction. A Communist government, once selected, would immediately apply for acceptance into the Soviet Union.

The French elections are of greatest interest in this connection. The Communists now are the strongest single political party in France. Are the French taking the same road by political instinct, as the Germans due to their hopeless mass misery? Clerical opposition in Spain may be short-lived, and France may go the way of Hitler and Mussolini. Then Communism would be the common form of life from the Pacific to Gibraltar. The fatal rift of Charlemagne's Empire would be sealed. England would become an advance bastion of the United States, facing an immense continental block with the most powerful war potential the world has ever seen.

The problem remains whether there is not another grouping of great nations which Germany may join.

The answer is in the affirmative. Germany could turn west. As England once offered France membership in the British Commonwealth of Nations, so Germany could enter the Anglo-American group, as a federated state, or as a territory. The name does not matter.

There is an opportunity to bring this solution about. While the democratic ideal in Germany does not possess the same power of attraction as bolshevism,— there should be no doubt about this,—the western powers possess a highly developed economic system. They are able in a relatively short time to repair the immense war damages in Central Europe at least to such an extent that for the German masses, life would again be worth living.

But in that case Germans should not be told: You must help yourselves, we can do nothing for you. Instead, the aim should be clearly announced: There will be difficulties, but you will ultimately belong as free and equal members to a powerful empire.

The future borders of Asia and of Bolshevism would lie along the Oder and the Elbe.

There is no third solution of a permanent character. The future Germany can develop only within the framework of a larger whole. It can either adhere to the great eastern realm, or to the Anglo-Saxon, Western European association of nations.

Germany lies between two magnetic poles. None but the ignorant and the foolish can deny that these two cores of power embody mutually exclusive contrasts—the democratic-individualistic-capitalist Anglo Saxon world, vs. the autocratic-collectivist-communist world. There is no doubt that some day, sooner or later, the question of a final decision between Moscow and Washington will arise.

Germany lies prostrate today, fever-ridden. But it is possible that its decision on which side to commit its last reserves will tip the scales of east vs. west. For a fourth time, then, Germany would fulfill its spiritual mission.

It is by accident that I came across the following passage in an otherwise inconsequential American mystery novel: "You can't punish any human being by putting him in an intolerable situation, unless you are prepared to take the consequences. That's not an easy thing for any person to understand, but it's important. It's the reason we'll go on having wars for several centuries to come; the victors can never remember that simple fact when the time comes to write a peace treaty."

Has the "simple fact" penetrated the minds of the statesmen who are faced with the gigantic task of reshaping the world?

Our globe is shrinking rapidly. Ultimately, it will be ruled by one government—unless its inhabitants are annihilated by the newly discovered atomic powers.

We do not know, and our poor human brains cannot know:—perhaps it is the will of God Almighty to have humanity destroy itself because it failed to live according to His laws."

While I was reading, Professor Netzer, with his grandson on his lap, played with the radio. He found some American jazz at first, which obviously none of them liked to listen to. It was a station of the American Forces Network with the hottest jive in their record library. The professor looked over toward me for signs of approval. I said if he would rather listen to something else, it would be all right with me. He shook his head slowly indicating his lack of comprehension of Americans generally and their music in particular, and dialed on.

Next he hit a German station which was broadcasting a description of the Nuremberg trial. Herbert objected loudly: "Turn that nonsense off!" The professor found a station of the BBC which was broadcasting light music. "There's a good station for you," he said. Herbert's wife cleaned the dishes from the table. Herbert busied himself with the plug of a desk lamp which was out of order. I read on in amazement at the mixture of truth, half-truth, and outright falsehood which Professor Netzer, in his opening paragraph, had described as the product of quiet and objective long-range thinking.

When I finished, I realized that to answer him I would have to raise a dozen different points on which I could never come to agreement with him. What struck me as most vicious, was his Leitmotiv of the German "mission" in the world, with the implication that if it could not be fulfilled, the world might as well be atomized.

A few days before, I had received Dr. Erding's excellent character sketches of my fellow students through the mail. I happened to have them with me. The sketch of Wilhelm Recht was the one which came to my mind while I read Professor Netzer's paper.

I thanked the professor for the loan of the document and agreed with him that it had improved my understanding of him: "Now to make this understanding more mutual, let me read to you a characterization of the Germany I see described in your document. This was written to apply to one man only, and I'm not usually inclined to generalize. But with some minor corrections, I find the parallel very striking indeed."

Then I read the sketch on Recht in this form:

"Born late into the family of nations, Germany showed traits of senility even while she was still young. She was surly and ill at ease, always suspicious of her surroundings, which she thought, infamously opposed her every step. She used her better-than-average intelligence to defeat this imaginary opposition by indirect, deviously clever means. Without a sense of humor, she lacked the playful freshness and unconcern of the healthy young nation. She was reliable and conscientious, but stubbornly opinionated and hard to convince. Her actions were always carefully calculated, never impulsive. . . ."

Professor Netzer listened to this with a caustic smile. In the interest of continued conversation, I thought I had better spare him the last sentence of the converted character sketch which would have read: "Germany is an egoistic, asocial country which, with excessive prudence, intends to save and secure her own position."

"That shows you how hard it is to be objective," Professor Netzer said. "I can well imagine that this is what we look like from the outside. I assure you I have no illusions about the present state of German prestige abroad. Perhaps I shouldn't have turned this document over to my friend with the French connections."

"One thing your French readers will like least," I said, "is that you call them 'ignorant and foolish'. Most people outside Germany believe rather strongly that 'mutually exclusive contrasts' as you called them, between east and west, can very well be bridged. Then there is another point on which you won't be very convincing, and that is your estimate of Communist strength in Germany. Did you write this before or after the elections in Austria?"

These elections at which the Communist party had been decisively defeated, had taken place a few weeks earlier.

"Before the Austrian elections," Professor Netzer answered. "But I think it's only a temporary defeat. And the Socialists are certainly gaining. In the last analysis that's one and the same thing. Otherwise they wouldn't have been talking about merging the two parties ever since the end of the war."

"I'm afraid this is another thought your French readers won't appreciate," I said. "Firstly, because they are apt to be Socialists themselves, and secondly because the Socialists have so far refused to merge with the Communists. This for a reason with which you should sympathize: The Socialists have declined to accept the Communists' eastern orientation."

"A Socialist dictatorship is as obnoxious to me as a Communist one," the professor said. I let the matter rest with some regret. His mountainous prejudices had undoubtedly a great deal to do with his age and occupation. At the same time, a measure of European sentiment spoke from his document. Due either to his stubbornness or our inadequate information services, he had found no intellectual contact with modern European trends,—trends which were almost exclusively represented by western European social democracy, under the leadership of British labor.

I asked Professor Netzer which ideas he had deleted from the document when he found it intended for French rather than American readers.

"Primarily what I think about our present political life," he answered. "Herbert and I have attended several political meetings together, not just one party, but of all parties. We were utterly disgusted. Not a constructive thought in any of their programs. This is what they consist of: Remove the Nazis from office; denounce those former Nazis who haven't been removed from office yet; expropriate the Nazis; and so on. I see only a repetition of our sordid political life before 1933, and with less meaning. Of course, there can be no meaning, because we have no freedom of action. The country is split in five, and we can't say 'bah' without filling in a Fragebogen and obtaining permission. However we may have disliked it, the Nazis at least had a political and economic program. But our new parties? What can they work for? German unity? That's up to the occupying powers. Improving Germany's ability to export? The Allies are determining our industrial capacity. Reorganizing our finances? Our currency is being inflated further with occupation money. Building houses? Building materials are requisitioned. Don't misunderstand me—the Allies have a perfect right to settle our fate as they wish. We have lost the war. But they should recognize that democracy cannot grow under such conditions. Our political life is nothing but a scramble for the jobs vacated by Nazis. But the people know where real political power actually lies. This pretense of democratic freedom on the American model is a disgrace, and no decent German will have anything to do with it."

I objected that I knew many of the people now active in political life as highly respectable Germans and uncompromising democrats. Herbert took up his father's argument with bitter sarcasm:

"There are only two kinds of Germans today," he said. "Those who realize how hopeless the whole situation is, and those who are going to find out very soon. I'm an engineer. I calculate things in figures and without emotion. I can't be fooled."

Herbert's claim to sober thought paralleled his father's claim to objectivity. What were his personal motives for this hopelessness? He lost his belongings in the bombing of Frankfurt—so did many others. But here, with American friends to help him over some of the worst shortages, he seemed relatively well off. The boy had milk to drink, and the whole family looked healthy and well-fed.

I asked Herbert what he was doing now.

"We had a small test lab for our steering devices near here," he said, "which I now own. Some of the all-purpose machinery is in pretty good condition. Fifteen of my former colleagues work with me, and we repair dairy and agricultural machines for the farmers. That's about the best thing you can do these days, because they pay you in food."

When I remarked that he should realize how lucky he was with this access to food, he objected that a man did not have to suffer starvation in person to see what goes on around him. He repeated the often-heard argument that Germany would not be permitted access to world markets, would not be able to export in sufficient quantities to cover its needs of raw materials and food. "Besides," he said, "we'll have to feed ten million Germans the Poles and Czechs are expelling from the east. That just won't be possible. We have neither the necessary food production, nor the chance to import. And if I look further ahead, I see the dilemma of our international position, between the two worlds on whose collaboration the peace of the world depends. If Washington and Moscow understand each other, they'll agree to keep Germany powerless, impotent, and off the world's markets. If they decide to fight it out, they'll do so in Germany. Just where do you see any hope for us? Don't you think we might as well face it? All right—we are guilty of starting the war. We hear that all day long in your press and radio,—nothing but guilt, guilt, guilt. And we're being punished. I was an anti-Nazi, but I understand I have to suffer with the rest. Why don't you drop some atom bombs on us and finish the business? Would be so much more merciful than extermination by starvation and disease. The bomb is our only hope—we wouldn't hear the bang!"

Herbert Netzer, the cool and calculating engineer, had become quite emotional. But he insisted he had not over-dramatized the case.

In reply I could only point to the positive provisions of the Potsdam agreement, and to economic post-war beginnings: The slow resumption of inter-zonal business; the setting up of export and import machinery; American food imports into Germany—so far without compensation; the slow revival of the European economy as a whole; and above all the American's natural aversion to seeing anyone starve, even a German. But so far starvation conditions had not yet arisen, at least not in the American zone, although a severe cut in the customary standard of living had inevitably taken place.

I also repeated a point to him which a friend had made who had lived in Russia during the twenties. He had compared the plight of Russia then to Germany's today. The Russian economic policy had consciously neglected to supply the population with consumer goods and even food, and strained every nerve to equip the country with capital goods. If they wanted to overcome the consequences of the war, Germans would have to bring similar sacrifices.

Netzer was not willing to accept the analogy.

"That doesn't work in western Europe," he said. "Our standard of living was too high for it. I'm afraid we'll take another way out before we permit ourselves to be reduced to Russian standards. Unfortunately, I can offer you the proof for this contention. Just a few days ago, we had the news that my sister, her husband and their two children had committed suicide by taking cyanide."

I had known the girl as a child. It was a tragic argument, even if it was a personal one. Professor Netzer sat slumped on his chair, staring into space, and holding his grandson closely, as though to protect him.

"They weren't Nazis," Herbert continued. "Her husband taught chemistry at Jena university. After they had a look at his record, the Soviet Military Government promised to let him teach again as soon as the university reopened. That's what a letter from them said in August. After that, something must have happened. They smuggled two more letters to us. In one my sister said that their home had been looted, and then that her husband may not be permitted to teach after all. Whatever the story behind it—they gave up. A last and very desperate letter arrived, and now this news. You see, they preferred not to live to sinking further. I fear that many Germans will choose suicide rather than increasing bolshevization."

For himself, Herbert said, he was glad to have his small plant, and enough to eat for the time being. But he was looking for a chance to leave Germany.

"My wife would like to go to America because she has her friends there. But I think Brazil would be a better choice. Too bad—in this rotten village here I can't find a teacher of Portuguese."

I started to leave. Herbert's wife asked whether I wouldn't wait for the American officers she expected, but I regretted that I couldn't stay. It had occurred to me that it would be interesting to present Professor Netzer's document to Dr. Erding for his reaction. His home in Grünberg was not too far from Schotten, and I could still spend an hour or so with him before returning to Frankfurt.

Professor Netzer apparently had been brooding about his document. "You don't think I should have turned it over to the French?" he asked.

"Well, no." I said. "They'll probably find it interesting. I only doubt whether it will have the effect you intended it to have."

"Yes," he said, "that worries me now. It's so easy to isolate yourself intellectually when you haven't any access to facts and opinions elsewhere. You can ask Herbert—I curse the German radio and press day and night. They're as bad as the Goebbels product."

I told him that the press was free to write what it wanted, short of inciting to revolt against the occupation powers: But he laughed.

"You ought to know us Germans better. Our journalists won't risk incurring your displeasure, and we'll never believe what they say. They are too used to Goebbels' whip, and we are too used to reading between lines. If you'd reprint the Bible in the papers tomorrow, we'd probably consider it propaganda. No, it'll take us years to rebuild a respectable press—not to speak of intellectually qualified readers."

Herbert and his son Hans accompanied me downstairs to the jeep. We put Hans on the radiator for the ride through the courtyard and out the gate. He sat proudly erect and happy. I saw no reason why, if his parents really took him overseas, he should ever be stunted in his mental stature by the fatal "After all, I'm a German."

It was dark when I reached Grünberg and Dr. Erding's house. I found the old language professor sitting in his kitchen in shirt-sleeves and slippers, turning the leaves of an immense dictionary. A copy of TIME was in front of him on the table.

"Oh, I'm so glad you're here," he said. "I always thought I had kept up with the English language pretty well, the American version included, but this magazine you sent me has me baffled. What is 'globaloney'?"

I discouraged Dr. Erding from trying to find TIME and Luce words in the dictionary. He confessed that it had been of no use to him with a considerable list of neo-American vocabulary, including OP Administrator, tycoon, ecdysiast and cinemogul. They took a considerable amount of explaining, because he insisted on linguistic definition and etymological derivations, of which, if I knew them, he took careful notes.

Mrs. Erding was not at home. She had gone to church to practice with the choir for a Christmas program in which she was to sing soprano solo. But she had lit a wood fire in the kitchen stove before leaving, and the room was decidedly cozy.

Dr. Erding seemed incomparably more at ease than the last time I had seen him nearly two months ago. He appeared to have gained some weight.

I produced Professor Netzer's paper and described the circumstances of its origin. As Dr. Erding knew Professor Netzer rather well, I did not name the author.

Dr. Erding said that for some time past he had been trying to commit his own thoughts on paper, and this would make very interesting reading for him.

When he became engrossed in the document, I picked up the copy of TIME. However, he started to comment almost immediately, and I took notes of his reactions as he went along.

"You say this was written by a historian?" he remarked. "Rather a poor one, I'd say. We've been burdened with too many of his kind. 'For a second time, the German spirit entered the world with a mission from God', he says here in connection with the Reformation. Mysticism and history don't belong together. Mysticism is not a science. The man has a short memory:—Most great political crooks are inclined to equip themselves with a mission from God."

"I'm a protestant," he continued, "but if I look at the political results of the Reformation, I'm not so certain about its connection with God. Had it been carried through completely in Germany, it may have been a blessing. But it was only half finished, and thus became a disaster. Luther conferred the powers of the Pope on the multitude of territorial princes. The princes, 'by the Grace of God', had absolute control over body <u>and soul</u> of their subjects. Much of our German psychology of subservience which I see at the core of our miserable national development, goes right back to absolutism and Luther. God may have tolerated the Reformation, the persecution of the peasants, and the horrors of the Thirty Years war, but to ascribe these events to God's <u>will</u> amounts to sacrilege."

He read on. "'Nation of poets and thinkers as Germany was called in sarcastic appreciation.' There was no sarcasm implied at all. When this phrase was coined, it was meant in pure admiration. Your historian should know where the sarcasm originated. It was introduced by the jingoists who placed the soldier above the poet and the thinker, to stimulate the people's imperialistic fervor. Then this: 'Bismarck's wise and moderate guidance' ... Guidance, yes ... wise, perhaps ... but moderate?"

Dr. Erding read for a while, then he smiled. "That the author of this paper does not belong to the younger generation is quite obvious. This is the old-school interpretation of the origin of the first World War. Characteristic for the man. He sees war as the only means to avert a blockade of food and raw materials. That peaceful compromise may have worked better, never occurs to him. 'The wish to eliminate the bothersome competitor' was easily as strong in Germany as it was in England. The noise of rattling sabers and the jabber about our shining armor was considerably louder here than across the channel. Nor is there room in the author's interpretation for the repeated offers from London for an Anglo-German alliance. William II turned it down because it would have limited his ambitions. If the alliance had come about, this history professor would have no cause to complain of the deathly danger presented the Franco-Russian-British alliance. The British would have had no cause to join it."

"I see," Dr. Erding continued, "here come Wilson's Fourteen Points. That Allies did not abide by them is true. But that this fact should have had any influence of the duration of the Second World War, is preposterous. This time the Allies left no doubt that unconditional surrender was Germany's only way out. Nothing was promised. Again this man wants to divert the reader's attention from a purely German responsibility. There are two reasons why the war lasted so long after it was plainly lost: The first is that the regime had cowed the people so completely by the use of lies and terror, that they were no longer capable of independent decisions. More decisive was the second cause: There was no stopping for the Nazi fanatics and their dishonorable generals who were fully conscious of their monumental criminal guilt. To prolong their lives, the whole nation had to be driven to a mendacious heroic doom."

"Yes," Dr. Erding said after reading further, "for once I agree. The victors would have been wise to give the Weimar Republic their full support. But it would be foolish to overlook such milestones as the Dawes Plan, the Locarno

Pact, Germany's admission into the League of Nations, the foreign loans, and the evacuation of the Rhineland by Allied occupation troops. This progress was due to growing insight and good will on the part of Allied statesmen. But our nationalists and militarists in and out of uniform were united in principle and practice to deny and distort every success achieved by the hated Republic. The nationalist press was their tool. With its diligent misinterpretations and calumnies, it had sufficient influence to poison public opinion. This is how our young German democracy slowly withered,—until Hitler tramped it to death with his boots."

It seemed that Dr. Erding's eloquence was stimulated when he realized that I was taking notes. If so, I was satisfied with the effect. His voice was booming as though he was addressing the student body of the Ebert Schule. While he spoke, he dropped Professor Netzer's paper on the table, and paced the kitchen—it allowed him exactly three steps in either direction.

He picked up the paper again. "Well, I'd have to object to nearly every word in here, but let me pick out some essential points. The author's opinions notwithstanding, Hitler's successes in the field of foreign policy did <u>not</u> bring him the support of those among us who regarded law and justice as highest values. These successes were due to the blackmail and lies, and we anticipated an unhappy ending. Only this has to be said: Among the victims of these lies and blackmail methods were statesmen who disposed of sufficient power to call Hitler's bluff early. I think it is true that Germany has to shoulder a collective guilt, but I should like to see it extended to a lesser degree to the nations who buried their heads in the sand while the evil grew. The possession of power carries with it an obligation to use it in time to avert a world catastrophe."

"Let's see how this goes on," Dr. Erding continued, "...'the unity of people and nation, justified by Divine and human law'. Hitler and Goebbels used exactly that language in the rape of Austria and the Sudetenland, and opportunity permitting, they would have used it on the German speaking part of Switzerland. They never applied it to the German parts of South Tyrol which has suffered Italian oppression for decades, because that did not fit into the plans for conquest. That's how seriously they were concerned with Divine and human law."

"Aha ... Munich. 'We should bow in homage to the memory of Chamberlain'. I beg to be excused from the ceremony. The verdict on Munich should be clear by now: The execution of a monstrous crime was postponed, enabling the criminal to redouble his efforts in final preparations."

"Well," Dr. Erding continued, "this is where I begin to agree again. Germany's cities are undoubtedly in ruins, and our people are tired and ill. We are facing an unprecedented economic crisis. Yet, we should be careful in prophesying the death of millions. And to compare this calamity, if it occurs, to the horrors of the gas chambers, presupposes that death from hunger and cold is the result of a preconceived criminal act. That is obvious nonsense. The story about the hundreds of suicides when the gas was turned on in a western German city sounds like part of our rich rumor crop. Your historian should know enough to supply dates and places."

"Oh, … this is bad again," Dr. Erding said. "'Hitler's war against Russia … a war for food.' If war were the only way to feed a nation, then war would be the permanent condition of Europe. Hitler intended to secure food and raw materials for a vastly increased German population, to serve as a base for ultimate world domination. This brings us to the author's drastic picture of the crowded cage. The award of Eastern Germany to the Poles is a catastrophe for us, and I fear for Europe also. The simile of the cage is very impressive. But are there no other possibilities? There are indications that we will not be left to starve after all. At the same time, the great reduction of our living standards will probably lead to an increased death rate, and a lowered birth rate. This may slowly adjust the misproportion of space and people, and allow us a peaceful existence at a moderate standard. We would refuse to favor our generals and industrial potentates with unrestrained procreation. To the contrary, having learned our lesson, we should assume the responsibility of leaving hundreds of thousands unborn, rather than exposing them to lack of food, work and space, and ultimately to the butchery of war. Hitler presented newly-wed couples with a copy of *Mein Kampf*. We would be wise to substitute birth control instructions."

I admitted to Dr. Erding that in a year's close contact with Germans from all walks of life, this was the first time I had heard views of such—almost radical—moderation. He in turn agreed that few Germans were yet ready to accept them.

"Now," I asked, "what do you think of the two magnetic poles, east and west, between which, according to this author, Germany will have to make a choice?"

"I more or less agree with him," Dr. Erding replied. "That's the best part of his memorandum, except for his return to the realm of mysticism. In the long run, we will either have to become a part of the Russian-Communist world, or the Anglo-American block. We seem to hesitate instinctively from embracing the eastern orientation. It would be an act of historic desperation. We consider ourselves a part of the cultural world of the occident. We are tied to it by a thousand ties. Whether we can remain a part of it is up to England and the United States. We don't know yet whether the angel of history will come forth with the flaming arrow, or with a helping hand. But the choice may be as decisive for other nations as for ourselves."

"Don't you believe," I suggested, "that Europe might become a meeting ground of east and west? That it might act as a catalyst in the slow process of adjustment which would fit the world for a single government?"

"I'm afraid I don't," Dr. Erding replied. "Contrasts are too fundamental. It will be one or the other. But perhaps … if you have very wise statesmen … ?"

Dr. Erding handed Professor Netzer's paper back to me. I asked him whether he recalled the character sketch he had written of Wilhelm Recht.

"You mean he wrote this piece?"

"No," I said. "I only wondered whether you saw any parallel between the psychology expressed in this document and Recht's character." I read the character sketch to him.

"Yes," he replied, "there certainly is a parallel. This would make Recht the outstanding representative of our German national character. But it would be true only if we accepted this document as representative of the German view. Fortunately it is not. We have better historians than the man who wrote this, and I sincerely hope we can find more among the younger generation."

Dr. Erding asked me for the news of my class mates I had so far collected. After a short account of each man, he commented: "As far as I can judge, they all developed along the clear lines prescribed by their character. It confirms all my beliefs about environment and education."

It was too late in the evening to spin these out, but before I left to return to Frankfurt, Dr. Erding gave me Professor Rossert's address which he had meanwhile found.

"It's three years old," he said as he took me down the stairs to the jeep, "but he lived in a small town which probably hasn't been damaged in the war. You may still find him there."

"Paul Rossert is a late child of an unhappy marriage. Both parents pampered him, and, unfortunately, played him against each other. His father endowed him with an easy concept of life, and a quest for enjoyment. Paul's character remained caught in the instinctive,—a dangerous lack of development because of his soft, almost feminine nature. Moody and impulsive, he never sought the guilt for failure in himself. He was incapable of energetic and persistent work, unless it furthered his own wishes and ideas. His strongly sensual nature, if his other characteristics extend into the sexual, will make him a slave to a strong-willed woman."

_____

Erding

December 9, 1945

To find Professor Arthur Rossert, father of my school mate Paul Rossert, I drove to Eberbach, a small, old town in the lovely, winding Neckar valley, following up Dr. Erding's lead. I took Hitler's strategic super-highway, the Autobahn, which had served General Patton so well, to Heidelberg, the only survivor among Germany's proud cities. Entirely undamaged, Heidelberg has become the Mecca of German city-dwellers who doubled its normal population. Only the town's bridges fell victim to the Nazi manic for destruction in their final retreat.

The drive up the Neckar valley was rewarding even through the fog and drizzle. The river carves its way through hills topped by medieval fortified villages. The old towns along the banks were lively with people who didn't all seem to belong there—evacuees from the destroyed cities and refugees from the east. Some of the picturesque tourist spots served as billets for small American units stationed there. Power stations along the river were in operation, and through their locks barges passed, loaded mostly with coal. Beached hulls of barges and tugs were reminders of the Nazis' scuttling, or of Allied air superiority—hard to tell which.

In Eberbach, a German policeman helped me find Professor Rossert's house. It was in the town's outskirts, some 50 yards away from a dirt road. It faced the river in the valley below, and a short distance behind it dense pine woods covered the hill.

The house had suffered severe damage from either bombing or fighting. No other building in the vicinity seemed to have been affected. But the damaged part was patched up quite well with a brand-new raw brick wall, and even new glass windows—a rarity in Germany.

I was not quite certain what kind of a professor Paul's father was. I remember him as a well-known photographer in Frankfurt, rather of the old school. Now I realized that his interests encompassed art in general. The garden in front of his house was almost littered with statues from all periods of the art of sculpture. Classic heads stood beside modern nudes and medieval religious statues.

The main entrance was of solid iron, embellished with a wrought iron center panel and door handle. I could not hear whether the bell worked or not, but a huge Alsatian dog behind a ground floor bay window raised such a racket that I would not remain unnoticed, if anyone was at home.

A gray-haired man with heavy glasses, dressed in a sports sweater, opened a second-floor window and wanted to know who was there.

I mentioned my name.

"Who sent you?"

"Nobody. Are you Professor Rossert?"

"Yes."

"I knew your son."

"I'll be down. Just a minute."

He slammed the window shut, and after a while, the iron front-door opened with an oil-hungry creak. The professor, well and comfortably dressed, looked at me curiously. He seemed about 60 or a little older, and hard of hearing. He held his hand to his ear. I told him I was a schoolmate of his son Paul.

"But ... you're still in uniform!" he exclaimed.

He took a closer look.

"Ach so—it's an <u>American</u> uniform. What are you now? Do you know that Paul is dead? We've given up hope."

His eyes filled with tears.

He went ahead upstairs through rooms which were still in a state of chaos from whatever hit this house, into a large, well-furnished living room. It was an artist's idea of a living room all right. A huge couch, covered by an oriental rug, occupied nearly a quarter of the floor. A table was set for four with lovely china for a traditionally German afternoon coffee session—cake plates and coffee cups. There was an antique desk and several very comfortable easy chairs. The large window afforded a splendid view of the river valley.

The walls were hung, frame to frame, with paintings. Mrs. Rossert, a determined-looking woman some 20 years younger than the professor, who joined us in the living room, was the model for two huge canvasses. Not being a judge of art, I could only tell that they were naturalistic studies with great emphasis on detail. Mrs. Rossert's white lace sleeves seemed more life-like than her expression, and dominated one portrait entirely. Another painting in subdued colors showed the professor with his son Paul. The remainder were landscapes.

Professor Rossert was pleased when I complimented him on his work. He explained that the present Mrs. Rossert, his model for the two portraits, was not Paul's mother. His first marriage had ended in divorce.

"I took up painting only in 1931," the professor said. "It had been my life's ambition. Recently I've been doing some work for Americans who are stationed in this vicinity. They seem to be rather fond of charcoal portrait sketches. And we were richly rewarded with some coffee and other such luxuries. That's how we're fortunate enough to be able to offer you a cup." Mrs. Rossert left the room to prepare it.

Professor Rossert had also helped illustrate the regimental history of an engineer unit which had fought its way from North Africa, through Sicily, Italy, Southern France and Germany, to Eberbach. He had a copy of the printed book. One painting, reproduced in full color as frontispiece, showed this route through the various typical landscapes.

The landing beaches of North Africa were in the foreground, German medieval villages far back, and a path led to them over the massive rocks of Mt. Cassino where the unit had apparently done its heaviest fighting.

"They also wanted a picture of one of their men who was killed," the professor said. "They insisted on a portrait of him looking down from the heavens above on his grave at Mt. Cassino. Typically American idea, isn't it? It was difficult to dissuade them. Here is the result."

He leafed through the book. It was a simple sketch of Cassino, with the man's photograph in one lower corner, and a memorial verse in the other.

"I'm very fond of the Americans we've met. Especially the older ones with a little judgment, who've had a career in life, and some experience. I hope the friendships we concluded will last. But I'm afraid they'll forget about us as soon as they leave here. They all talk of nothing but going home."

Photos of Paul were scattered throughout the room.

"Most of them were taken in 1938 and 1939, before they put him in jail," Professor Rossert said. "Do you remember him?"

One photo showed him with a sly look on his face, embracing a nearly life-sized statue of Leda and the swan. Others were portraits, some very well done.

Paul's features had sharpened from boy to man. In early school years he was a slight, unsportive, sickly boy, growing more and more serious as we became older. He was at the receiving end of much hazing. The class bullies considered him a weakling because it was neither in his power, nor apparently his wish, to fight them back. Instead, he formed a close friendship with one of them, Netzer. Thus, he had some measure of protection from the rest.

I don't believe Paul was a very a conscientious student, but he was capable of scholastic spurts which would help him over critical exams. There were some apple-polishing tendencies in him, and the he-man teachers disliked him for this. Dr. Erding probably knew best how to treat him. He discouraged apple-polishing, but in later school years gave Paul an occasional lift in the eyes of the class by crediting him for mature political thought. Paul Rossert had turned out to be a good political debater. He would take his stand, usually violently opposed by our nationalistic history teacher who on one such occasion told the class there should be ways of knocking such shameless un-German attitudes out of this weakling. After school, the class bullies promptly descended upon Paul, who permitted himself to be beaten up without any attempt to defend himself. He said later of the incident that he was too proud to fight these brainless athletes.

Considering Paul a coward, the class majority now turned its prejudices fully against him. The antagonism created by his political opinions grew. He stood to the left of what this middle-class student group was willing to tolerate. I do not believe that at the time Paul had made up his mind whether to be a Socialist or a Communist. He was devouring political literature which turned him violently anti-nationalist. But he was still undecidedly groping his way through the controversy which rent the German working class.

From here on, Paul's father drew the picture for me. With his friend Herbert Netzer, Paul went to the University of Frankfurt to study physics. His professor, a non-Aryan scientist who later migrated to Ankara, pronounced him among the most talented and capable in a group of 80. In 1931 or 1932, Paul formed a friendship with a Frankfurt girl who influenced him further in the direction of communism. Professor Rossert said that he had many debates with his son on the subject, but that he could never shake Paul's opinions from then on.

"After all," the professor said, "we are not members of the working class. We had no real first-hand knowledge of the conditions for the workers. I told Paul to stay with his own crowd. But he wouldn't listen."

Paul's friendship with the girl broke up, and shortly afterward he fell in love with another student at the university, daughter of a Freiburg professor, who was four years his senior. Her name was Ilse Renner, and her field of study was education. She was an active worker for the Communist party. After 1933 her political work became illegal, but she continued it with increased vigor. Professor Rossert said that under her guidance, and through a cousin who migrated to France to direct Communist underground work among German students from there, Paul began to participate in organized anti-Nazi activities.

Professor Rossert was not certain what Paul's motives were. He felt that there was an element of conviction and idealism in Paul's attitude. But decisive, he thought, was Paul's opinion after 1933 that no one except the Communists was actually fighting the Nazis. The Social-Democrats had given in without a struggle, and the bourgeois parties opposed to Nazism never seemed to give a thought to the possibility of fighting it. The professor and Paul went to many

Nazi party rallies together in the early Nazi years. They wanted to have full information. They never differed on the character and implications of the evil thing that paraded before them. Paul's reaction was to fight it, the professor's was to stay out of its path. Neither, in hours and days of debate, managed to convince the other.

Paul's first brush with the authorities came in 1933, a few months after the Nazis had seized power. The University Senate was engaged in eliminating politically undesirable students from the institution. Paul was called before it on three charges, his father said. He was accused of being a member of the now illegal Kostufra—a Communist student group. Paul was able to deny this because he had held membership in it and in the Communist party under a false name. Secondly, he was charged with having encouraged his comrades to turn a firehose on a band of SA brown shirts who invaded the university grounds one day in order to beat up Jewish students. Paul told the Senate he had only been a bystander in the affair. The third count was that he had spread the "rumor" that Goering had set the Reichstag building on fire, not the Communists. This, Paul said, he had merely repeated after reading it in a French newspaper. The University Senate acquitted him. Ilse Renner also was able to continue her education studies at the university.

From that time on, however, Paul was under Gestapo surveillance. To avoid surprise in a house search which was to be expected, Paul stored a number of books on socialism and communism with a friend who had a "clean" political slate. They were theoretical books—Marx, Lenin, Trotsky, Engels,— but if they had been found at Paul's home, it would have been embarrassing. One day in 1937, Paul's friend moved to Berlin and wrote a note to Paul that he could no longer store the books for him. This letter was intercepted by the Gestapo, and Paul's friend was questioned. At the same time, the Gestapo had observed two French students whom they suspected of Communist activities enter and leave Paul's house. Paul and Ilse were arrested and charged with high treason before the People's Court in Kassel.

"Only a few months ago Ilse told me that these two students were members of the underground who smuggled subversive leaflets to Paul," Professor Rossert said. "They, too, were arrested and tried. The Gestapo had, however, insufficient evidence to satisfy the court, and the two Frenchmen were acquitted. They admitted nothing in nearly five months of questioning. Since the case against Paul and Ilse rested almost entirely on the same evidence, they too were acquitted. I had hired a very courageous lawyer for them who also managed to place the incident of the Communist books in an innocent light. After six months in prison while the investigation was under way, Paul and Ilse were freed again."

Judges and witnesses had used disparaging language about Paul's "mistress" under whose influence he was supposedly acting. With the professor's financial help, Paul and Ilse were married, although both were still students, and would not be earning a living for several years.

The trial, even though its outcome was favorable, did not help Paul's standing at the university. When the time came a year later for him to write his doctor's thesis, no professor could be found to assign one to him. Officially, the faculty used all kinds of excuses—lack of time, too many students, no suitable subject—to bar Paul's way.

A few months ago, Professor Rossert addressed a memorandum on his son's experiences to the de-denazified University of Frankfurt.

"Do you think I'm wrong if I want to prevent these so-called educators from teaching again?" he said. "If this memorandum won't do it, I'll go down to their first lecture, and before they can start, I'll ask their students whether they want to listen to these brutes. I'll tell them the story of my son."

The memorandum gave an account of a visit by Professor Rossert to one of Paul's professors. Rossert wanted to know why his son could not be assigned a doctor's thesis. This is a partial translation:

> "Professor R. told me my son Paul had often appeared late at the physics institute. Instead of arriving at 8 a.m., he had come at five or ten minutes past eight. (In truth, it was a practice at German universities that students could arrange their own working hours at the labs.) Paul Rossert had also made inaccurate physical measurements. (This was due to the fact that he had contracted mercury poisoning because of unsatisfactory lab conditions.) Professor R. had also found out that Paul had not altered his radical leftist sympathies for which he had once been arraigned by the University Senate. (He had been acquitted.) Professor R. advised me to send my son into the labor service, or even better, into the army, to prove his national reliability.
>
> A few days later, a fellow student of my son, Herbert Netzer, was given the mission of informing him that there would be no point in continuing his attempts to obtain an assignment for a doctor's thesis at the University of Frankfurt. Netzer was under orders not to reveal the origin of this mission. My

son's political attitude was given as the reason for the refusal."

Netzer, when I saw him, had not mentioned a word of this incident. I asked Professor Rossert about the story of the arms smuggle to Spain Netzer had mentioned. There was nothing to it. Netzer had had no share in Paul's political activities, Professor Rossert said. He may have been under Gestapo surveillance for a while because he was known as one of Paul's friends. I now gained the impression that Netzer, in talking to me, had tried to use his former friendship with Paul to underline his own anti-Nazism. Another common procedure in Germany today.

Mrs. Rossert returned from her kitchen with a pot of steaming coffee on a tray. There were also all the other luxuries Germans usually don't have: sugar, milk, cake. She invited us to sit at the table.

Professor Rossert put the copy of the memorandum away.

"Even in 1938, I tried to talk Paul out of his Communist underground work. But these professors put Paul on the wrong track for good," he said bitterly. "Had Paul made his doctor, his work might have absorbed him and kept him out of trouble."

Mrs. Rossert was cutting the cake. She shook her head. "You know that isn't so," she said in a kind and firm voice. "You are trying to fix the blame for Paul's tragedy. Don't you agree that Paul's first allegiance was to his convictions? Nothing would have deterred him. He had to go his way."

It was clear that in his grief, Paul's father looked for the guilty— not excluding himself. This was apparently not the first time he had been admonished by his wife.

"I don't know," he said. "Why couldn't that boy have thought of himself and his own life just a little? I have no other children."

He was close to tears again.

Actually, the Rosserts had expected other guests. Fortunately, they were late.

It was certain that the good things on the table were not in plentiful supply in the house. It was the housewife's pride, though, to be able to offer them. The trick of the polite guest was to appear to be digging in violently, while actually measuring the sugar in grains, and the milk in drops. The cake was excellent, and a little harder to resist.

For a while we tried to talk about neutral subjects—the weather, life in the Neckar valley and the large cities, my experiences in the war. But Professor Rossert very quickly resumed his account of Paul's life. He realized it was what I had come to hear, and he seemed to welcome this opportunity to speak of his son.

When Paul was refused a doctor's thesis, his stay at the University of Frankfurt came to an end. He and his wife moved to Giessen, and Professor Rossert praised the faculty there for their helpfulness.

"I went to Giessen often," he said. "Paul's professor told me he was doing well on the complicated physics thesis which had been assigned to him. I hoped the transfer to Giessen and his work on the thesis would turn Paul's mind away from his political activities,—but no. He headed an underground cell of five. I once walked in on them while they were meeting in Paul's room. I disliked all of them. One was a gardener's assistant, and two others had been imprisoned at a reform school. Then there was an unemployed law clerk who needed financial help all the time. Paul gave him money regularly."

"Wasn't that the Gestapo informer?" Mrs. Rossert asked.

"Yes," her husband answered. "Many of these things I only found out when Ilse told us recently. She said this law clerk had been keeping the Gestapo informed on everything they did. After their trial before the People's Court in Kassel in 1937, their contacts with the communist organization abroad were cut off. Otherwise, Ilse told me, they would have been warned about the man. When I pleaded with Paul after the cell meeting I had accidentally crashed to stop this work, he told me not to worry. He could trust every man in his group. He said he was willing to risk his life, but not carelessly and senselessly. Had he known who this law clerk really was, perhaps he would have followed my advice. Instead, his cell did such tricks as dropping Communist leaflets in public places in Frankfurt the night before Hitler's birthday in 1938."

I asked the professor whether he remembered the contents of the leaflet.

"I think I do," he replied. "It was about a month after the Nazis took Austria. The plebiscite in which the usual 99% voted for incorporation into the Reich had just taken place. It was 99.08% to be exact. The leaflet was written in the form of an open letter to Hitler and asked what had happened to the many thousands of Austrian Communists who had voted against incorporation. It revealed how many persons had been shot in Vienna alone during the first three days of Nazi occupation, and how many thousands more had been shot, imprisoned and sent to concentration camps in the first two weeks. The leaflet attacked Dr. Ley and his 'Strength Through Joy' ships which were intended to become troop transports and airplane carriers in the coming war. It contrasted the cost of these ships with the amount spent on workers' houses. There were other points about exports of war equipment to Japan for use in its imperialistic war against the people of China, and so on. You've seen pamphlets like this,—written for popular reading and for effect among the less educated. Paul used the radio to get news for it. Ilse told me recently that this leaflet was intended to be the first in a series they wanted to bring out once a month. They planned to expose the most dangerous Nazi swindles. But it remained the only one. The Gestapo immediately arrested the owner of the shop where the leaflet had been printed and Paul decided the work was too dangerous after all. He and Ilse and their underground cell were left alone by the Gestapo for the time being."

Professor Rossert asked his wife for another cup of coffee, then he continued:

"Almost a year later, in the spring of 1939, the professor under whom Paul was working at Giessen, was transferred to Berlin. Paul and Ilse followed him. They broke up their underground cell, and Paul told the law clerk he could no longer support him. Now this unspeakable individual, who had been working for the Gestapo all along, revealed the full beauty of his character. He began to blackmail Paul. If the payments would not continue, he said, Paul should not count on studying in Berlin. And there were some people in Frankfurt who would be greatly interested in knowing who wrote the Hitler birthday leaflets the year before. I gave Paul the money to pay him off … After this menace seemed to have passed, Paul took the exams for his doctor's degree. He passed the written, but failed in the oral examination. The professor asked a first question which Paul could not answer, and then simply sat staring at Paul for 10 minutes. Then he declared that Paul had failed."

We had emptied our cups, and I brought out some cigarettes. Professor Rossert declined because, he said, the doctor had forbidden him to smoke, but Mrs. Rossert was glad to accept. He went on:

"Ten days before the war broke out, Paul and Ilse were arrested again. They were held in prison without trial for a year. In August 1940, their case came before the People's Court in Berlin. The charge was high treason, and the law clerk appeared as state witness. The jury was composed of Nazi laymen and two officers, one army, and one from the air force. The judge had a reputation for disliking to close a session without one or more death sentences. After the trial, the air force officer told me that Paul's life had not hung by a thread, but by a hair. He was saved by his lawyer—the best I could find—who argued that Paul's wife was the real activist and was responsible for Paul's erring ways. The prosecutor demanded the death penalty for Paul, and 15 years of penal servitude for Ilse. The court sentenced both to penal servitude for life. The law clerk was given 15 years in prison, but I'm sure he never served a day of it."

"Were these terrible sentences given just for the leaflets they distributed on Hitler's birthday?" I asked.

"No," the professor replied, "that was only one piece of evidence. More damaging was a diary this law clerk had kept. He had taken down scraps of conversation at the meetings of Paul's cell. The chief charge became that of 'preparing an attempt upon the life of a member of the Reich government.' The law clerk gave evidence that at a cell meeting someone had asked Paul for the surest way to kill Hitler. Paul was supposed to have answered that a bottle of hydrocyanic acid, slightly nicked so it would certainly break, to be thrown at Hitler's feet, would do the job best. There were scraps of conversation recorded in the diary about hydrocyanic acid, soda water bottles, and a glazier's diamond. The prosecutor made a murder plot out of it ..."

Mrs. Rossert interrupted. "Why don't you show the lieutenant Ilse's letter?" she asked.

"I was just about to do that," the professor said and took some papers from the desk. "As all our family and friends were entirely in the dark about what happened, Paul's wife a few weeks ago wrote an account of the developments from the trial on. I copied it and sent it to our friends. I'd like you to read it. She knows much more about this tragedy than I do."

While Paul's father looked for other papers and letters he wanted to show me, and Mrs. Rossert reset the table for the guests she was expecting, I read this dramatic account of the last six years of Paul's life:

"... Paul was much too good a physicist to conceive the childish plot for which we were convicted. We talked in our circle about hydrocyanic acid, but only in connection with an accident which had taken place at Giessen university. Paul explained that it was possible to kill a man with it without drawing the slightest attention, by squirting a few drops on the man's collar. After a few minutes, any doctor would pronounce him dead of heart failure. We also spoke of bottles—we intended to fill one with illuminating gas, take it out of town and fill small children's balloons with it when the wind was right, for the distribution of anti-Nazi leaflets. Paul also owned a glazier's diamond which he used to cut his photographic plates. Out of this stew of details, the Gestapo concocted Paul's alleged plot to kill Hitler. It is true that we discussed the practical possibilities of killing him between the two of us, but the subject was never mentioned in our *underground group. For that matter, we were bound by party discipline which condemns individual acts of terror.*

While the trial was under way, and prosecutor, judge, and Gestapo witnesses gave evidence of their thirst for our blood, if not of our 'guilt', Paul and I fully expected to be executed. We knew the horror of feeling cold steel in the back of our necks. Then sentence was passed. Paul and I saw each other for the last time. We were left alone for a few minutes in a prison van. We were unspeakably happy. We would live. We would be liberated, and our work would continue in a new, free world. Paul thought the war would last five years more. I thought it would only be four. He was right.

Paul served at hard labor in the prisons of Brandenburg, Hameln, and Celle. In two years at Brandenburg he witnessed more than 1,000 executions from his cell window—more than one a day. In the fall of 1944, he was transferred to the concentration camp Neuengamme, near Hamburg.

I was sent to the women's penitentiary at Cottbus, Germany's most humane institution of this type. I had the good luck of remaining there until January 1945. Then I was taken to the penitentiary at Waldheim near Chemnitz, where severe forms of punishment and torture were practiced. There the Red Army liberated me on May 7, 1945.

All the years in prison, Paul and I concentrated our every effort on remaining mentally elastic and sensitive. He had to remember how to think, because we would have to continue our work after our liberation. After six months, we were allowed to write two letters of two pages of 15 lines each, every six weeks. Later this was reduced to half a sheet of paper every four months. Paul wrote two letters to me for every one he sent his family. We always tried to discuss some problem of philosophy or history with each other in cable style.

In a way, we were perhaps better informed than people outside. We were not continuously hammered by Nazi propaganda, and thus could think more clearly and read better between the lines. We never hid the opinion from our gaolers that we would leave the prison as free people. The sentence 'for life' sounded harsh, but we knew it would become true only, if the Nazi bandits killed us at the last minute. We even developed a code for our letters which eluded the censor's vigilance. We arranged an exact plan for meeting after our liberation. Hamburg was to be our place of reunion. Unfortunately, Paul's letters were lost at Waldheim on the day the Red Army broke down our prison gates.

Fifty of us made our way from Waldheim to Hamburg last May. We were welcomed everywhere, and well fed. Dreadful news was awaiting me at the emergency organization of former concentration camp inmates in Hamburg.

I spoke to one of Paul's comrades who had been a camp clerk at Neuengamme concentration camp. After the liberation of Buchenwald by American troops, Himmler sent a secret order to Neuengamme that no political prisoners were to fall alive into Allied hands. The camp clerk intercepted the order and it became the signal among inmates for a desperate plot to seize power from the SS. Shortly before the mutiny was scheduled to take place, the camp was dissolved because Allied troops were approaching. Beginning April 20, prisoners were transported in small groups to Neustadt near Lübeck. They were to be taken to the island of Fehmarn for extermination.

Neuengamme had 19,000 inmates. 11,000 of them were crammed on board the Deutschland, the Cap Arcona, and the Thielbeck in the harbor of Neustadt on May 2. Paul was seen by several survivors on the Thielbeck, smallest of the ships, which carried only about 600 prisoners. On all three, prisoners had agreed to attempt a simultaneous mutiny at 3:30 in the afternoon.

The ships were about four miles at sea, when the SS fell out among themselves. One faction wanted to scuttle the ships without further delay leaving the prisoners to drown, and themselves return ashore in life boats. The other faction wanted to continue the run to Fehmarn. At 2 p.m., while they were arguing, enemy planes arrived at the scene and signaled the ship to hoist the surrender flag and return to port. The SS crews replied with anti-aircraft fire from all three ships. Thereupon the ships were bombed. The Thielbeck sank rapidly. Only prisoners crowded on deck had a chance to reach life boats. They tried to make land. Meanwhile armored British spearheads had reached the beach and, believing themselves to be confronted with a Nazi attempt to land reinforcements, fired on the boats. Only 22 prisoners survived this dual catastrophe. Paul was not among them.

The Deutschland and Cap Arcona remained adrift and burning for several hours. The SS crews took to the life boats. From there they fired at swimming survivors who attempted to board the boats. Those who tried to hold on were hit on the hands. Many stripped off their prison uniforms and called out that they were crew members. They were saved. Of the 11,000 prisoners, 7,500 died that day. 1,400 bodies have been swept ashore.

For six years, Paul had patiently waited for his freedom. On the day British troops arrived to liberate him, he met his destiny.

This is all I know at the moment—we still do not have all the details of the catastrophe. There are other things about which I cannot write-perhaps I can talk about them some day. We cannot permit ourselves to stir up our deepest anguish— there are too many tasks ahead of us for which our comrades died.

Most people who have lost the person they loved most, can go to the cemetery to visit his grave, and pour forth their grief in tears. We, however, know no definite place where we can find our dead. Because of that, they are everywhere, but not really gone. Their bodies have disappeared, but their spirit continues to live with us, as an inspiration to accomplish that for which they cannot continue to work themselves."

There was little I could say to Professor Rossert when I had finished reading. He was waiting to show me other letters from his daughter-in-law. One contained a poem Paul had written in 1938. Ilse had reconstructed it from memory:

> *Bleiche Gebeine toter Soldaten klagen Euch an:*
> *Unser Vermächtnis war: Friede uns allen,*
> *Ihr rüstet zum Krieg.*
> *Trostlose Augen hungernder Mütter klagen Euch an:*
> *Zum Leben in Freiheit und Glück gabaren wir*
> *unsere Kinder,*
>
> *Ihr lehret sie Knecht sein und Mörder*
> *Arbeiter und Bauern, die Ernährer der Menschheit.*
> *klagen Euch an:*
> *Wir schaffen in friedlicher Hoffnung fürs*
> *tägliche Brot,*
> *Ihr nähret die Feinde der Menscheit.*

I later tried to translate it:

> *Bleached bones of dead soldiers accuse you:*
> *Our last will was: Peace for mankind!*
> *You rearm for war.*
>
> *Sorrowful eyes for fear-ridden mothers accuse you:*
> *Children for freedom and peace we brought to the world:*
> *You teach them bondage and murder.*
>
> *Workers and peasants: Humanity's stewards accuse you:*
> *In peaceful endeavor we labor for God's daily bread;*
> *You nurture the foes of mankind.*

I asked Professor Rossert whether he had some of Paul's prison letters.

"No," he replied, "they were burnt when our house was bombed. They were wonderful letters—so full of faith in seeing us again soon."

I wondered how his house of all houses in Eberbach, and Eberbach of all towns in the Neckar valley, had attracted the bombers' attention.

"It was quite a ridiculous business," Mrs. Rossert said. "It happened a week before the Americans arrived. Six German army trucks were standing on the little dirt road out here, when your fighter bombers came over. They dropped five bombs. One fell in our house, the other four into the field across the street. You can still see the craters. Then the trucks drove away. It was early morning, and we had just risen when the bomb came. It crashed right through our bedroom. We missed being in there by a few minutes. It took us nearly an hour to extinguish the flames, and the house seemed to be nothing but ruins."

"That wasn't all," Professor Rossert said. "A few days later a bunch of kids came up in SS uniforms. They were going to defend the Neckar valley, 16 and 17 year olds. They had carbines and machine guns. They picked our house as their post, dug holes and a few trenches, and brought their machine guns in position. I asked them what they were going to do with their machine guns against American tanks, and they just laughed. An SS colonel was in charge, and he ordered us out of the house. We protested, but he said he'd evict us by force if we didn't follow his orders. So we went. When we came back after the Americans had breezed through, there was no trace of the SS boys, or of a fight. I don't know what happened."

After that, the Rosserts lived for about two months in a tent in the woods. At first they could not bear the sight of their house in ruins. For a few days they thought suicide would be the only right way out—they had had all the good things in life, and could expect only misery, starvation and cold from now on. Then they looked at their house again, and decided part of it could be salvaged after all. They scrounged the necessary building materials. All summer the professor and his wife rebuilt their house with practically no outside help. By now they had four livable rooms again, and had given two to a family of city evacuees.

"But come back to Paul's letters," Professor Rossert said. "They were actually a source of solace to us. To us, mind you, who were free. Paul's wife later said this was true. She had never lost faith while she was in prison, and she was sure Paul felt the same way. Germany would be beaten, and they would be free."

"You can imagine how my husband suffered through these war years," Mrs. Rossert said. "While he was painting, he often said he could not look out of the window, because there was the sun. And Paul was behind bars in a dark cell somewhere and could not see it. When he ate, he often nearly broke down, because Paul needed the food."

As long as Paul was in prison, no food parcels were allowed. After his transfer to Neuengamme concentration camp in September 1944, however, food parcels were suddenly invited. In his letters, Paul asked to send as much food as often as possible. However, the parcels could not contain a list of the contents, and the prisoners were forbidden to acknowledge any of the food received. Only once, after Mrs. Rossert had sent Paul some hard-boiled Easter eggs, Paul wrote back that he preferred his eggs soft. However, this may just as likely have been an SS guard's wish, dictated to Paul to blackmail the family for more. The professor and his wife went hungry from September 1944 on to send as much food as they could to Paul—actually, without any doubt, to feed the SS. They realized this of course, but hoped that Paul would get some scraps of it, at least, to keep him alive.

I asked Professor Rossert what Ilse was doing now.

"She is active in the reorganization of the Communist party in Hamburg," he replied. "As her special field is education, she is slated to take an important position in the city's school system. Here are some more of her letters. I still don't agree with her politics, but I can't help admiring her determination."

Her letters, occasionally peppered with a Lenin or Stalin quotation, showed how active she and her party were. "Theory doesn't get us very far right now," she wrote, "we must work." Elsewhere she stated the aims of her party:

"We are working for a united Germany closely allied to the anti-fascist forces of the world."

That this may make an attractive slogan in many German ears today, there can be little doubt. Many Germans have little faith in a united Germany under quadripartite control. They disbelieve official announcements that this is the common plan. So far, they argue, zone rule, which is generally admitted to be unworkable, is the only arrangement produced by the Big Three. A united Germany under western control appears to them unlikely, because the Russians would not give up their share of control. There remains a united Germany under Russian protection. This seems to them to be more within the realm of practical possibility.

Adopting "German unity" as their platform, the Communists may well attract many Germans to whom national unity is a first consideration. Communism on a nationalist platform may be a paradox, but the Communists have not been known to be too choosy or too consistent in their calculated propagandistic methods. Nor have Germans as whole a reputation for logical scrutiny of political slogans. The two may match.

In that case, developments depend on the extent of the sales resistance to practical communism built up among Germans by Goebbels, first-hand accounts of returned German soldiers and eastern refugees, and the reputation of the Red Army in recent months. This resistance at present is immense.

But some Germans of Dr. Erding's and Professor Rossert's type had the desperate hope that it would be bolstered by a positive, constructive program for Europe, championed by the United States and Great Britain.

While I was looking over the letters, the expected guests for the afternoon, a local lawyer and his wife, arrived. Professor Rossert, after introductions, insisted on reading one more passage from one of Ilse's letters:

> "... I have been working on a pamphlet about concentration camps, the methods used and the numbers of prisoners killed and tortured. It is a horrible job. I looked at some photographs from the various camps: I thought these were reproductions from medieval pictorial representations of hell. It is simply incomprehensible for a normal human being that such beasts could exist in human shape, and that such an infernal terror regime was able to maintain itself in power for 12 long years, without the people rising to sweep it from the face of the earth. This is a matter of shame for all of us, all Germans, and perhaps even for all of humanity. Now we must tackle the heritage. ..."

The quotation prompted the lawyer to launch into a political discussion. He said that of all the people he knew, Ilse Rossert was the one who had the right to indict the German people for its inaction against Nazis. But in spite of her sorrow and suffering, she was now at work rehabilitating the same people. Could not the western Allies, who, on the whole, had suffered less, adopt an equally charitable course?

Although Professor Rossert too appeared eager to discuss present-day political affairs, I had to decline the challenge. It had become late, and I had to return to Frankfurt. Almost as a parting remark Professor Rossert summed up what he had wanted to explain in detail:

"Your American policy is making reactionaries out of us, not democrats."

Dr. Erding had thought we were making Communists out of Germans. Whatever their differences, the two men were agreed that we were not producing democrats.

"Franz Kirchner assimilated himself well to the class structure which he entered late. He was adaptable. He was the picture of a physically healthy boy who slept well, without being 'sicklied o'er with the pale cast of thought.' Never endeavoring to appear more than he was, he became well liked, although mentally he did not come up to the relatively high standard of most of his fellow students. In contrast to some primadonnas in his class, he was not sensitive or easily hurt, nor was he indifferent or indolent. He listened with a smile to class room debates which often reached a remarkable intellectual level, neither taking part, nor demonstrating boredom or cynical disdain over so much mental effort. Thus, his school days passed so uneventfully that his principal never once had an opportunity to meet his parents.

It is not to be expected that Kirchner's ambitions will outrun his capabilities. Instead, he is more likely to find satisfaction and happiness within his limitations, led by his secure and healthy instinct."

Erding

If Franz Kirchner's name had not been on the list I obtained from the school, I would never have remembered him. My amnesia lasted until I had talked to him for some time. Then the sound of his voice, rather than his appearance, made me recall, at last, that I had been to school with him. But nothing beyond that. His was not a very obtrusive personality.

Obrecht's brief report on Kirchner read: "Married in Heuersbach. Was an officer in the war. Was shot through both legs in 1944. One leg stiff. Returned from a prisoner of war camp in August."

Heuersbach is a minuscule village east of Frankfurt which hardly managed to get on the map. I was supposed to find Kirchner at a mill there.

A village boy in rough wooden shoes directed me. As I drove into the yard, three women were loading sacks of flour on a horse-drawn cart from a ramp. The yard was complete with chicken, a barking, chained dog, a manure pile, geese, and a lone, well-fed turkey. One of the women went inside to call Franz Kirchner.

A nearly bald man in a flour-dust-covered work suit limped out of the humming mill to the ramp on a crutch. His left leg was in a plaster cast. He took some time to remember me. For a few seconds, as we went through an almost formal introduction ceremony, I thought I had perhaps found the wrong man. But then names, years, teachers' names, made contact between our memories. "You sat next to Weller, didn't you?" "Sure, and you were next to the wall with König, right?" "Right".

The entrance next to the ramp led to the "Stube",—the room literally, THE room actually. Kirchner showed the way. It was furnished in good bourgeois style. Kirchner introduced his mother-in-law, a typical middle-aged peasant woman, who proceeded to light a wood fire in the iron stove.

With the jeep as evidence in the yard, word spread of the American visitor. One after another, members of Franz's family appeared. There were about five girls of various ages, and every time one came in, I thought it was his wife. She was last in the procession, about as plain as the rest of them, but slightly better dressed.

"I'm glad you came out to see us," she said. "I'll go make some coffee."

We sat near the stove, and Franz's wife placed his crutch neatly in a corner as she left the room.

"How long have you been married?" I asked him.

"Eight years."

"Do you have children?"

"Thank God, no. This is no time for children."

One side of the room was almost completely taken up by a large book case, full of tomes which did not seem to be there for decorative purposes only. At one end of the top shelf, the Weimar Constitution was most prominently displayed. But Franz said that was an accident. Most of the books were his library, brought to the country when the war broke out. His Frankfurt home was bombed out later, and he was very proud of his foresight.

Kirchner seemed to be very tired. His eyes were red, and he sat slumped in his chair as though he wanted to go to sleep.

"I've worked all night," he said. "We haven't any fuel for the diesel engine, and with the rains of the last few days the brook has enough water to turn the wheel. Got to exploit the opportunity."

Franz explained the he was the only man in the house to carry on. His father-in-law was dead, and the help from the village were not willing to work at night.

"A little strenuous on my legs, but in a few days I can take a rest again," he said.

Of the whole group of former city dwellers I had looked up, whom the war had scattered over the country-side, Franz, seemed to be the one who was working most productively.

"Did you work at the mill all the time?" I asked.

"Oh no," he said. "I'm a lawyer. But there seems to be a greater need for bread now than for law suits."

His wife returned to the room and set the table. While she brought out some lovely, thin china and silver knives, forks and spoons from a bottom drawer, she said she hoped Franz would soon return to his law work. "Life in the city is so much more fun."

She heaped the table with dark peasant bread, marmalade, a huge plate of butter, sugar, and hot coffee. This was country life.

The coffee, however, was a disappointment. Germans would have called it the shotgun brand, because it seemed to be made by firing a coffee bean through a pot of hot water. But everything else was genuine, and Mrs. Kirchner encouraged us to eat heartily.

"Wonderful coffee," Kirchner said, "just what I needed to stay awake." He winked at me. His wife looked at him devotedly and thanked him for the compliment. "Coffee is so rare these days," she said, "you might as well make a few good cups when you do get some."

I asked Kirchner about his injuries.

"I wake up mornings," he said, "and still can't believe that I got home."

He was wounded on the Italian front in October 1944. For a while, apparently, it was touch and go whether he would live.

"I was a company commander. Infantry outfit. We had English and Polish troops against us, and they made it hot for us. One fine day my wireless operator was killed, and they sent me a replacement. A kid 18 years old. Damn fool thought his business was to operate a transmitter. All he did was to test his equipment, he said later. Well, the English direction finders spotted my command post immediately, and we got artillery. A fragment went through my legs."

There was no plasma, Kirchner said, and by all the rules of medicine he should have bled to death.

"Then that transport to the rear. I was unconscious most of the time. That was good. Our roads were a mess. Your fighters made holes in them like a sieve. Bridges were out. Nearest rail head was 200 kilometers to the rear. I still don't know how many days it took."

He was taken to a Wehrmacht hospital in the Palatinate, and was still there when our troops overran the area in March. At first it was decided that he was well enough to leave the hospital, but after a week in an overcrowded prisoner of war cage, the American camp doctor sent him back to a hospital.

"That was the life," he said, "I gained 30 pounds in two months. That's about what I had lost in Russia. Oranges and canned pine-apple and meat and all the things I hadn't seen since I went to war."

The hospital was run by German doctors and nurses under American supervision, and Kirchner said he improved rapidly. In August he was discharged and returned home.

'I've been milling flour since. Would be easier if I could get around a little better. If it's nice out, I take off to join your boys by the brook, fishing. Those Americans know how to fish. I like to talk to them. They come around to borrow fishing tackle. I'm glad to give it to them. Easier on my brook than the hand grenades they used to use. The woods around here are full of hand grenades. Two village children blew themselves to heaven a few days ago."

It appeared that German troops in flight in April had dropped much equipment in the forest. Rifle ammunition, even some rifles, were still lying around, and also a few Panzerfaust anti-tank grenades. It was difficult to keep the children away from there.

"I'm really fond of your boys," Franz said. "There's something about them our soldiers never had. They brought an officer out the other day to fish, and he was just one of them. Gay, friendly, kameradschaftlich,—could never have happened in the German army. They caught some good-sized trout and brought them in to fry. They stood around the stove and showed me how big trout are in the United States. I guess fishermen are all alike. You must have gigantic trout."

Kirchner had a very frank and unassuming, natural way about him. With the possible exception of Ingelmann, he of all my school mates made me least conscious of the fact that I was facing a former enemy soldier. I remembered the international camaraderie among veterans and their organizations after the last war in the heyday of pacifism, which the Nazis so cleverly exploited later, and I recognized some of the psychological origins. To keep the proper perspective, I had to rehearse the basic facts of the case. He had fought everything we stood for; he was an enemy officer; he had fought the Nazis' war, no matter what he thought of them. Had I forgotten this, he simply would have impressed me as a man who had gone through a lot, managed to survive, and was to be congratulated on his spunk and sense of humor through it all.

My questions began to fill in the past 15 years. After graduation, Kirchner had studied law. Political life left him untouched. Inter-party strife disgusted him. But when after 1933 it became a matter of either becoming a member of the National-Socialist party, or giving up his law studies and the career he had planned for himself, he chose to pay his monthly membership fee, and be done with it.

I asked him whether party membership was really that definitely a professional requirement.

"That depended on your university," he said. "It wasn't always officially required. But you may, for instance, have needed certain credits, say in athletics. To get the credits, you had to join the athletics club. To join the club, you had to be a member of the party, or perhaps of the SA. Or else, you'd be caught when you were ready for admission to the bar. To be admitted, you had to be a member of the Nazi lawyers organization, the NS Rechtswahrerbund. Anyone who tried to complete his studies and enter his profession without joining the party, or at least one of its sub-organizations, was simply stopped at every turn. Some students may have been able to escape it,—for instance if they had military training between 1935 and 1937. At that time party membership wasn't required, or rested, for members of the armed forces. But otherwise? Not a chance. I realize that you want to throw the Nazis out, and I agree with you—it would be a good thing. But I'm afraid you're using a wrong yardstick. There are too many people now favored because due to some accident they didn't become party members, and vice versa."

Most Germans, when discussing de-nazification, get somewhat excited about it, no matter from which angle they criticize it. Kirchner was very dispassionate in talking about the technicalities which, in his opinion, made our policies of categories and membership dates an unjust instrument which would earn us no credit among Germans. He did not, however, go beyond the technicalities. He did not answer the more fundamental question of what made a law-abiding citizen willing to throw his principles to the winds, and join the gangster organization with a mere gesture of cynicism.

Kirchner said he had just completed his studies, and taken the exams for the civil services, when he was called to the colors.

"In the middle of August, 1939, the mail came around with that famous slip which said I should report for extended military maneuvers."

He was assigned to the anti-tank company of an infantry regiment. His division "held" the west wall during the Polish campaign, took part in the Belgian and French campaign the following spring, and was assigned to occupation duty in a small town in central France.

"I had a wonderful time," he said. "We liked the people, and they liked us."

I have had occasion to speak to quite a few former German soldiers who were on occupation duty in France. Not one of them had anything but praise for the French, cheerful memories of cordial relations with them, and wonderment or smiles at our notions that the French hated occupation troops. It is clear that they had contact only with that sector of the French people who did not hate them. But still these memories of Franz and his comrades provided food for thought on our relationship to the Germans.

But Franz, just the same, had few illusions about the nature of the occupation. He had his commanding officer's example before him. This gentleman helped himself to everything of value in the town that appealed to him, and paid with IOU's redeemable at the end of the war. The mails to Germany were heavy with "legal" loot.

The French idyll lasted until March 1941. Then Kirchner's division was alerted and shipped east over a roundabout route. When it arrived in Cracow in German-held Poland, a station official told Franz that a troop train was arriving every ten minutes.

Kirchner had meanwhile been advanced to the equivalent of staff sergeant, and his men looked to him for political guidance.

"I told them war against Russia was impossible," he said. "We were probably concentrating at the border to fool the British into thinking we were about to attack Russia, and then in reality we'd cross the channel."

But more and more troops and materiel arrived, and Franz's unit was assigned a position along the border. His commanding officer one day appeared in the uniform of a customs official, and then went forward to reconnoiter Russian border positions.

"Then," Franz said, "they told us that zero hour would be 0315 hours on June 22, 1941. I'll never forget it. Until three in the morning my boys and I thought it may turn out to be a diplomatic maneuver after all. But at five minutes past three the Stukas roared overhead into Russian territory. Then we had another ten minutes of silence. The last silence. At three fifteen, artillery shells screamed through the sky and crashed beyond. Hell was loose. Two of my boys began to cry. This wouldn't be like France. We all knew that."

The first ten kilometers were easy going. It was a Sunday morning, and the Russian soldiers were asleep in their bunkers, usually with their women.

"After a few days," Franz continued, "we thought the whole Red Army was in flight. We were motorized, but still weren't fast enough to keep up with the Russians. We didn't really fight till fall. We left immense distances behind us. But, you know, we had a pretty good geography course at school. I never forgot that Russia was big. And another thing I couldn't forget was a painting we had hanging at home. . . . French soldiers in retreat in 1812. . . . in bloody rags, frozen and starved. I kept seeing that picture before me till I saw it repeated in reality. Our Russian campaign was no picnic."

The stream of Russian prisoners was endless, and their treatment, Franz knew, was terrible. He said that Russian revenge on Germany was no matter of surprise to him. Nobody had made preparations to receive these masses of prisoners. There was no food for them, nor transportation to the rear. They were crammed standing up into boxcars, and a load of corpses arrived after the three or five-day trip. They had no shelter in their cages: "I saw thousands of them," he said, "in the early winter of 1941 crammed behind barbed wire. Their good overcoats had been taken from them, and they were digging with cups in the frozen ground to get some shelter from the icy wind at least for their heads."

However, Franz did not think that it was a Wehrmacht policy to have these people die. He had heard of the cold-blooded shootings of prisoners by SS units, but even this, he thought, had been due to the inability of feeding them, or of transporting them to the rear. These conditions, he thought, were caused by neglect, not by intention: "No human being," he said, "could have devised such horrors as policies."

"Well, you had better watch for the evidence at the trial in Nuremberg," I said.

"I will," he said. "The trial interests me immensely. Throughout all these years at the front I've been entirely ignorant of what went on. Whatever the truth is, I want to hear it."

This remark made Kirchner one of the very few people in Germany to whom I have spoken who did not, in a psychological defense of their moral existence, shut their eyes to the evidence of Nazi horrors.

He continued his story. Winter came. Franz was promoted to the rank of lieutenant and given command of an anti-tank platoon.

I'm afraid I cannot adequately report Franz's account of his two winters in Russia. He used a soldier jargon which defies translation, or even repetition in the original. It was a Wehrmachtsbericht (official communique) in reverse. When he said that his unit disengaged itself from the enemy according to plan, I saw the white, cold wastes before me through which these frozen men attempted to withdraw out of reach of the murderous mortar and artillery fire. When he said that the enemy was pinned down by friendly artillery, I realized that swarms of Red Army infantrymen were pushing through the thin line of Nazis, and that German artillery ammunition supplies had bogged down in the rear. When he said the situation was nice, or lovely, or very pretty, these terms indicated progressive degrees of horrors. He was not consciously sarcastic. He never cracked a smile. For him, these words and phrases simply had the meaning he implied.

As an officer, Kirchner was held responsible by his superiors for the health of his men. They were not prepared to spend the winter in Russia. Instead, Franz said, they were given directives:

> They were to live on the land. That meant digging sugar beets from under meters of snow and ice, and boiling them down to a spoonful of horrible brew per man.
>
> They were to learn how to protect themselves against the cold with newspapers. No comment from Kirchner.
>
> They were to force the local population to make straw overshoes for them. There was no straw; the local population had either taken off, or did not know how to make straw shoes.

During the winter 1941/42, Franz's whole unit was moved south to another sector of the front. It had received a few replacements—city boys who had no idea how to protect themselves from the cold, and had no resistance to it. It was 20 degrees below zero Fahrenheit when they started.

"We had orders to stop all vehicles every two kilometers," Franz said. "Everybody had to get out and run twice around the truck. Our new boys soon couldn't run. They couldn't walk either. Their feet were frozen and when we reached our destination I sent them to a hospital. They had to have their feet amputated. I was court-martialed, but they couldn't prove neglect on my part."

By this time, "fortunately," as he put it, Franz had contracted dysentery. He was returned to Germany. Only about one third of his unit was then still in the line. The rest were casualties, not of the fighting for the most part, but of the winter.

Franz had the good luck to be sent to a hospital near his home. His wife came to visit him often. Although he improved only slowly, he was considered well enough again by fall, and returned to the Russian front for his second winter.

Franz Kirchner seemed much less tired as he recalled his war experiences. He even turned down a second cup of coffee his wife offered him. Instead, he asked her to bring him a small envelope with pictures from the book shelf. He looked through it and handed me a small photograph of a heavy tank.

"This is a T 34," he said, "in case you haven't seen one yet. The Russians sent it to us as a Christmas gift in 1942. It turned up everywhere all of a sudden. See these treads? Wide enough to run on snow. Our tanks got stuck, of course. We and our Heeresanklopfgerät were supposed to stop it."

The "Heeresanklopfgerät" was the 37mm anti-tank gun with which Franz's unit was equipped. A GI translation would make it the "knock-knock-who's-there gun."

Soon after, Franz said, his unit was equipped with a new infantry anti-tank weapon, the hollow-charge grenade. It had to be thrown at the tank like a hand grenade from a short distance. It would stick to the hull of the tank by magnetism, and blow it open. To use the weapon against the monsters which could cover all approaches by machine gun fire, took great personal daring. But Franz and his men were glad to take their chances. To do or die was the lesser evil than sticking it out in the Russian winter.

"They gave us a splendid incentive," Franz said. "Every man who had finished a tank was given a furlough at home. My company commander was the first to show how it was done. He was the boss, of course, so he could choose a good opportunity. One day a T 34 came up. It got stuck in a snow drift. After a few bursts, its machine guns were silent. Out of ammunition apparently. Our commanding officer crawled to it, threw his grenade, and finished the tank. Then he went home on leave, and left me in charge of the company. My boys went out and got themselves killed trying to get their furloughs. Not all: T-34s were stuck in the snow and out of ammunition."

By February of 1943, Franz's division was reduced to about one tenth of its former strength. With a few supporting units, he said, it had to hold a sector of 24 kilometers, two and half times as long a frontage as the German book of strategy allowed as the unstretchable maximum for a full-strength division.

"I think we held out only because we knew our only chance to live would be to stay in our holes. Going back would have meant death as much as going ahead. If the Russians had attacked seriously, they would have sliced through us as a knife through melted artificial margarine."

Finally, the remnants of Franz's division were pulled out for reactivation. He was sent to the great training center at Döberitz near Berlin and retrained in the use of the new German 75 mm anti-tank gun. Then the division was filled up with fresh recruits and sent to the Italian front. Franz looked forward to sunny Italy.

His regiment was sent into the line to relieve a paratrooper unit which bore the proud name of "Hermann Goering." Rumor had it that the cocky elite troops were going to the eastern front. Franz thought they would soon lose their arrogance.

"We loved them especially for pushing our vehicles into the ditch as they pulled out over the crammed roads at top speed." Franz remarked.

Franz spent about a year in Italy before being wounded. Compared to Russia, he thought, it was a recreation trip.

"Just the same,—I was so fed up with war, tanks, anti-tank guns, hollow-charge grenades, dead men and wounded men and ruined towns and air strafings,—believe me I would have deserted. The only thing that stopped me was the thought of my wife. The Nazis would have taken revenge on her. The clearer it became that the war was lost, the more Himmler foamed at the mouth. If a man was suspected of having deserted, his whole family was threatened with concentration camp or death."

For a German officer, thoughts of desertion were an unusual thing to admit. But Franz was not a professional soldier, and his attitude altogether, the complete lack of braggadocio, his comparative open-mindedness, his sarcasm, and the energy he had left over in spite of it all, reminded me more of the average German worker than of the intellectual. As the German worker, he had not sufficient courage to fight the Nazi regime in peace, or to refuse to fight for it in war. Somehow, the Nazi terror machine had him isolated as an individual, and he considered himself powerless.

I said something to the effect that Germans had no one but themselves to blame for the consequences of the war, even if, as Franz, they hadn't liked to fight in it.

He answered with a desperate shrug of the shoulder: "Ja, was konnten wir den tun?" — What was there we could have done?

This "was konnten wir den tun?" with very few variations has become the standard apology of probably most non-Nazi Germans for their political lethargy. It is usually implemented by some inconsequential story of how the terrible Gestapo had nearly arrested them and put them in a concentration camp, although they had done nothing, absolutely nothing at all, to offend the Nazi regime. Franz, I was glad to see, at least did not attempt to add such proof of his political impotence.

But Franz Kirchner's thoughts were dominated by his experiences in six years of war, rather than by the crucial period which preceded it. His attitude to the causes of the suffering he had undergone, and the suffering he knew the world had undergone, was not the fatalistic apathy so common in Germany today.

"I think we have a job," he said. "The next generation of Germans must be vaccinated against militarism. We soldiers who were cheated out of our youth and health are the ones to teach them. I've seen the destruction in Russia and in Italy, and I understand why Germany is destroyed. The people at home don't know that. My own family didn't know it. We have to tell them."

We turned to current questions—the most burning one: Were the US and Britain about to go to war against Russia? After hearing the question from nearly every German whose confidence one gains, it becomes somewhat monotonous. But the rumors on which the questions rest usually differ from town to town and from week to week.

This week's rumors were the following: Somebody coming back from the Russian zone had seen tanks deployed along the border between the occupation zones. Somebody coming from Bremen had said that Russian planes had flown over the town, and had been shot down. Also, the continued difficulties in US and British foreign relations with Soviet Russia were the reason why we were not releasing SS troops from captivity and were holding on to the German General Staff. The SS were being retrained with the latest American weapons, and the General Staff was planning our strategy for the impending campaign.

I felt that Kirchner received my efforts to ridicule all this nonsense with gratitude and relief. Just how long my influence with him would last, however, against the feverish rumor mongering which in Germany has taken the place of the truth disseminated by a free press, was hard to say.

Kirchner picked up his crutch in the corner and limped out with me to the jeep. I wanted to leave some cigarettes with him, but he did not want to accept them unless I took some farm products along. His wife asked me what I would like most.

Christmas was around the corner, and I pointed at the turkey.

"B ... but that's our <u>only</u> one," she exclaimed. She had taken me quite seriously, and the phrase sounded as though she had had occasion to use it before—to plead with retreating Nazi troops, marauding displaced persons, foraging city dwellers, official German agricultural agencies, refugees from the east, and whoever else was roaming the countryside in search of food.

Conclusion

When I first set out to visit my former school mates, I had not expected to trace as many as eleven out of the twelve who had remained in Germany. This was the score: I had found six alive, two dead, three missing.

Of the twelfth, Erhard Billing, no trace could be found from 1933 on. He was a dentistry student and moved with his whole family to Breslau in Silesia in that year. Breslau lies behind the "iron curtain" of the new Polish Oder-Neisse border, and there was no chance of finding him. His story would have been interesting. He belonged to the clique of class bullies, – a cynic distrustful and disdainful of all those who placed rational thought above muscle power in their scale of values. His intention in 1931, I believe, was to become an officer in the German army.

My search for the men with whom I had gone to school in pre-Hitler Germany has thus ended. The fate of the remaining eight who had left Germany interested me less. They belong to the Jewish faith or "race", and they never had the chance to compromise their ideals and beliefs. Their course was clear, and their conscience remained untested. These eight knew the enemy and his character from the beginning. Inside Germany, they would have faced slavery or death. They needed courage to leave their homes – and often their loved ones – in Germany, and some needed courage again to fight Germany. Most of them, I believe, had that.

Even this small group failed to maintain contact, and I have only vague information about them. First mention belongs to the outstanding intellect of our class. His nickname, appropriately, was The Philosopher. When he was 15, he wrote a paper on a subject of medieval philosophy which was accepted as a doctor's thesis by the University of Munich. He left Germany for the United States, and became a chemist of some distinction. Nobody has been able to find out from him just what he was working on during the war years, which led me to the conclusion that he may have been concerned with atomic research.

One of the hardest working, if slightly less talented members of our class became a certified public accountant in San Francisco. The army refused him on physical grounds.

Next to him at the Ebert Schule sat a man whose life was determined by his political and religious ideals. He was a Zionist. The creation of a Jewish National Home in Palestine to him was worthy of any sacrifice. To those of us who did not share his ideals or his Jewish racial and religious consciousness, he held up a highly realistic appreciation of the Hitlerite danger in Germany as early as the twenties. The only chance for Jewish survival was in Palestine, he said, where the Jews would form a nation as every other nation on earth.

Because I preferred to hope for fewer nations, nationalists, and nationalism in our shrinking world, I disagreed with him. He often told me: "The world is not ready for effective international and supra-national cooperation. As an individual, you must belong somewhere. You must identify yourself with your group and work for its collective aims, even if you don't agree with all of them. Otherwise you'll be walking a tight-rope all your life."

One day in 1935, I visited my friend in Palestine. I found him driving a tractor near a newly established agricultural colony, his bronzed back exposed to the scorching sun. With pioneer pride, he told me of the growth of his village – the start with a stockade; the building of the large, square, white building where the children were housed; the drying of the swamps; the first crop; the defensive preparations against Arab attack. One year after my visit the tragic news reached me that he had died of malaria.

Recently a friend wrote to me about another class mate who had migrated to the United States in 1934. He had become a prosperous broker on Wall Street. In 1940 he joined the Army. As a Master Sergeant, he went through a long string of Pacific campaigns, and has recently returned home with a chest full of ribbons and decorations.

Through a newspaper announcement in a community paper in New York, I learnt that another man was married to an Argentine girl in Buenos Aires. His fate appears to be to witness the birth of fascism for a second time.

Of the remaining two I only know that they took part in the invasion of the Continent, one through Normandy, the other through Southern France, as soldiers in the US Army. If they visited the ruins of Frankfurt, they did so without contacting any of their former teachers and class mates. They have probably since returned to their homes in the United States.

The visits to my former class mates or their relatives described in this book were not a matter of sentimental reminiscence, but the attempt to answer a rather vital question. My German author friend in the United States who had not seen Germany since he was forced to leave in 1933 had raised it: Would the people of other nations, if they were placed in the same position as the German during the Hitler regime, behave in the same manner?

As we gain perspective on the horrible conflict which lies behind us, and realize that victory has not solved all international problems, it is this question which gains in importance over the one of German guilt.

The formal guilt of the German State, as represented by its former government, general staff, party organizations etc., was established at the unprecedented Nuremberg trial, where great and constructive principles of international law were applied for the first time in history. However, the trial stopped short of the human foundations of this infernal regime. It did not answer what Ilse Rossert demanded to know after spending six agonizing years in a Nazi prison: "What was it for 12 long years that kept the German people from sweeping the Nazi government from the face of the earth?"

My eleven class mates were not a complete cross-section of Germans on whose motives of action or inaction a sound judgment may be based. But perhaps they provided a clue. My visits to them, and my conversations with other Germans have led me to believe that the majority had become a victim of two things: The secondary effect of the Nazi terror, and their readiness to be cowed by it. These are the conclusions at which I arrived after a year in post-Hitler Germany:

Himmler's terror could not have held millions of active opponents in check. But the number of anti-Nazi fighters inside Germany remained small, – too small. The world knew, the Germans knew, that concentration camps existed. Subconsciously or consciously the German masses grasped that Nazi denials of "atrocity stories" were fabricated in bad faith, and meant to deceive them. As a result, the denials served as confirmation of the original stories.

Not the present claim that Germans were ignorant of concentration camp gas chambers, Gestapo cellars and slave labor camps caused their apathy, but the fact that they vaguely knew. Coupled with the Nazis' internal intelligence system, which the Germans believed to be omniscient, this knowledge had the effect of causing deathly fear of the party's ever-threatening terror. The Nazis could not have used their methods on a determined majority of Germans. Not the terror itself, but the fear they spread, the mixture of known facts, official denials, and rumors, achieved the desired political paralysis.

This is one part of the explanation. It is complemented by the individual comfort and standard of living German workers had largely achieved, and the middle-class saw slipping away during the twenties and early thirties. The average German meant to maintain his material standards at all costs. As long as he could hold on to his possessions and savings, the other fellow was not a matter of his concern. Common action was indicated only if it appeared to promise to further individual interests. The Nazis promised the workers better wages and the end of unemployment, the farmers higher prices, the middle-class a reestablished position in the economy, the industrialists nice profits, and all of them a share in Jewish wealth. It worked. Human, moral, and ethical principles were tossed overboard. Not necessarily because the promises were implicitly believed, but because they were thought to contain at least enough truth to prevent a further slipping of the standards to which Germans were accustomed. To sacrifice a job, or an income or a raise, or perhaps a planned career in order to live up to one's normal human principles, was considered silly. To risk one's life, possibly endangering the lives of one's family in order to oppose the regime actively, seemed utter unrealistic lunacy. For those who disagreed with Nazi ideas, the obvious course was to make themselves realize that all opposition was futile, that the terror was overwhelming, that events had to run their course unchecked. The average German's sole aim in life became to keep out of trouble.

"Was konnten wir denn tun? – What was there we could have done?"

In German, all this could have been summed up in a few words: Too many Germans were afflicted with Gleichgültigkeit, Gesinnungslumperei or Mangel an Zivilcourage, or a combination of them. The first word means indifference – 'Am I my brother's keeper?' The other terms defy adequate translation – a most hopeful sign that English-speaking nations have found no need to boil their distasteful meaning down into single words.

Gesinnungslumperei is characteristic of persons who will suit their convictions to their material advantage – as frequently as this should become necessary.

The term "Mangel an Zivilcourage" describes the often-criticized failure of the German to stand up for his and his neighbor's rights in the face of authority – especially uniformed authority.

During the past year, I have had occasion to discuss the problem of German guilt with a great number of Germans of all ages and political backgrounds, confirmed Nazis included. Because of its immense implications for Germany's future, the guilt problem has become the focal point of all political discussion. I have had a remarkable experience: nearly all agreed that 'Gleichgültigkeit, Gesinnungslumperei, Mangel an Zivilcourage', demonstrated in varying degrees by the mass of the people, were at the root of their national misery. Often, they had this to add: "We are not improving. What is to become of our political future?"

There was no easy answer to this question. The verdict at Nuremberg and the denazification process will not by themselves affect German political immaturity and its roots, as some members of the newspaper profession seem to expect. 'Gleichgültigkeit, Gesinnungslumperei, Mangel an Zivilcourage', rather than profound democratic convictions, have furnished the occupation authorities with many a willing collaborator. And the selfishness which is blind to the common fate was intensified among Germans rather than reduced under the impact of war, defeat and ruins. This, at least is my impression after 14 years' absence.

The flaw in this view lies in its broad generalization. There appear in this book, and I have known everywhere in Germany, personalities whose integrity has been and remains above criticism, men and women who deserve the world's admiration as well as a hearing. The very decay of public ethics among the German masses has brought the intellectual stature of this minority into bold relief. It has also served to isolate them from their people. To restore a measure of ethics to German public life involves a sermon on the past which the masses do not care to hear. Instead, they prefer to point at the "post-war crimes," the expulsion of Germans from the lands east of Oder and Neisse and from Czechoslovakia, to prove that, even after the victory of democracy and the four freedoms, other nations commit inhumanities of the same type and on a scale to those for which Germany was humiliated. The voice of the minority who recognize the disastrous fallacy of such continued escape from ethics is not heard in this spiritual desert. German intellectuals whose integrity is unquestionable, may slowly be gaining a hearing abroad. But inside Germany, they are talking to themselves. Whatever conclusions this somber impression may warrant, it is a measure of the obstacles faced by those Allied educators who believe democracy can be spoon-fed from without.

There is a significant passage in Dr. Netzer's memorandum: "The western powers ... are able in a relatively short time to repair the immense war damages in Central Europe at least to such an extent that for the German masses, life would again be worth living."

The debasement of German morals is directly connected with the deterioration of the country's living standards from the peaks achieved before the first World War. Conversely, if I interpret Dr. Netzer's ideas accurately, there may be hope, though not assurance, that Germany would recover the ethical foundations for her national life, if her living standards rose again to former levels. There is no prospect of such an economic development. The hope that Germany may substitute ethics for boundless selfishness as a primary motive force in her national and international life is therefore slim. This implies foreign control of German affairs for an indefinite period.

To many Germans, this is not unwelcome. There has been dissatisfaction and grumbling about one phase or another of the occupation, but I have not heard of any outspoken demand for an end to it. Germans are incessantly comparing conditions in the four occupation zones – good rations, the behavior of Allied soldiers, the effectiveness of military government. They habitually try to play one occupation power against another. But even their wildest rumor-dreams about the future only concern a possible change in the occupation power, never national freedom. Perhaps they do not expect to resume control of their country. Some go further. When they say to the victors: "You have to own the war, – go ahead, do as you please," they imply: "Thank God we're no longer responsible for our own affairs."

A few days ago, a middle-aged German woman who takes care of our requisitioned billet, came to me with a request. She had a son of 17, she said, who had been sitting at home doing nothing for four months. He could find no suitable work. According to a new regulation, he could not obtain his food ration card, unless he was employed. Could I not find a job for him "with the Americans?"

I asked her a few questions about her son, his health, his training. She replied that he was a strong boy, but had had no training in any occupation. He wanted to become a radio mechanic, but there were at present no opportunities to learn this trade.

"Why doesn't your son enter the building trades?" I asked. "There is a tremendous demand for young people who are strong and interested enough to become masons and carpenters, plumbers and roofers. In a job with the Americans he'd only waste his time."

"Well," she said, "you know how young people are these days. They don't want to dirty their hands."

I gave her a lengthy and, I thought, pretty effective talk on the destruction of Germany, the ruins of Frankfurt, which no one would rebuild if not her son and his generation. She listened with great attention, and then she said:

"Na ja, unser Haus steht ja noch. – After all, our house is still standing."

If other nations were subjected to a regime like Hitler's, would they react as the Germans did?

My author friend who asked this question will, I hope, read these pages. As soon as I return home from duty in Germany, I intend to visit him. Early in the morning I shall go with him to a public school in the vicinity and we shall listen to the children reaffirm their allegiance to the flag and to the principles of liberty and justice for all. That will be my answer.

Walter Jessel –
A Chronology

BORN APRIL 1, 1913, FRANKFURT AM MAIN, GERMANY

Education:

Abitur, Musterschule, Frankfurt am Main, 1931

One Semester: Dolmetscher (Interpreters) Institut, Mannheim. French, summer 1931

BA Trinity College, Hartford, CT, 1942. Major in modern languages.

One Semester: Hartford Seminary Foundation. Classical Arabic, Spanish, fall 1942.

One Semester: Columbia University, winter 1943. Intensive course in Egyptian Colloquial Arabic

Dec. 1931 – Oct. 1933

Radio business advertising in Germany and France.
Employers: Ideal Werke A.G., Berlin and Point Bleu S.A., Paris

EMIGRATED TO PALESTINE IN OCT. 1933.

Nov. 1933 – Feb. 34

Tried to start small electric installation business, and failed.

Feb. 34 – Dec. 37

The Palestine Post, Jerusalem. Asst. advertising manager, then Tel Aviv Branch business manager and learned English. Naturalized Palestinian (British Mandate) citizen in July 1936. Obtained U.S. immigration visa, 1937.

Jan. – Feb. 24, 1938

Month-long trip through Egypt, then Switzerland and home to Frankfurt to pack up for emigration to US. Arrived in New York on February 24, 1938.

Apr. – May 38

Operated an adding machine and ran errands for a textile importer for two months.

June 1938 – Feb. 1940

TIME Magazine, New York. Office boy and foreign news research asst. Screened foreign language publications for information related to current *TIME* stories.

Feb. 40 – June 40

The *Newsdaily*, Hartford, Conn., an experimental offset-printed tabloid. Picture Editor. Paper folded June 14, 1940, the day Paris fell.

Aug 40 – Jan 43

The Hartford Courant, Conn. Staff photographer. Left to study Arabic at Columbia U. in New York.

May 43 – June 44

US Army; reported to Ft. Devens, Mass; by rail to Keesler Field, Miss. Basic Training. Naturalized U.S. citizen 18 Sep 43.

Army Specialized Training Program (ASTP) at U of Miss at Oxford then U of Indiana, Bloomington. ASTP was disbanded in May 44.

Ninth Tank Division at Camp Polk then being formed.

Assigned to Signal Corps. Request for transfer to Military Intelligence Okd.

June 44 – Sept 44

Assigned to Camp Ritchie, MD for PW Interrogation and Military Intelligence training. Commissioned 2d Lt. AUS

Nov 44 -Sep. 45

USS Marine Wolf to England: Published the *Wolf Call*.
Assigned to Mobile Field Interrogation Unit.
> Strategic interrogations during hostilities, then specialized in interrogations of German intelligence officers.

Sept. 45 – Jan. 46

Economic Branch, FIAT (6800th Field Information Agency, Technical)
> Reporting and interrogation of high-level German economic officials. Translations and summaries. Liaison with other agencies.

Feb. 46 – Feb. 49.

Strategic Services Unit, War Dpt. (Post-OSS, pre-CIA intelligence organization).
> Reports Officer. Promoted to Captain, MI, and separated in Aug. 46. Continued as civilian War Dept. employee.

Aug. 47 – Aug. 63,

Central Intelligence Agency, Germany and Washington, D.C., Clandestine Services Division.
> Chief, Austrian desk;
> Chief, Foreign Intelligence staff;
> Chief, Information Systems design group.

Sept. 63 – Feb. 79.

IBM Corporation, White Plains NY and Boulder, CO.
> Senior Planner, large storage systems; text handling systems; publishing systems. Retired March 1, 1979.
> Environmental volunteer since moving to Boulder, CO in Sept. 1966:
> Colorado Mountain Club, State president 1976.
> Colorado Open Space Council, Board member
> Published COSC Corner, a bi-monthly column for newsletters of member organizations 1979-1982.
> Secretary/editor/co-chair of Political Action for Conservation, a Colorado political action committee 1982-1991.

Environmental Caucus (on Two Forks Dam Project), member and chair, 1987-1991.

Source: Walter Jessel, A Travelogue Through a Twentieth Century Life, Appendix A (1996)

Lightning Source UK Ltd.
Milton Keynes UK
UKHW020632170621
385672UK00004B/360